W9-DDS-725

Register of

St. Philip's Parish

1720–1758

REGISTER

OF

ST. PHILIP'S PARISH,

CHARLES TOWN, SOUTH CAROLINA,

1720-1758.

EDITED BY

A. S. SALLEY, JR.

University of South Carolina Press
Columbia, South Carolina

Geneal.
*
929.3
S168

Copyright © University of South Carolina Press 1971

First Edition printed for A. S. Salley, Jr., by the
Walker, Evans & Cogswell Co., Charleston, S. C., 1904

This edition published in Columbia, S. C., by the
University of South Carolina Press, 1971

International Standard Book Number: 0-87249-216-8
Library of Congress Catalog Card Number: 77-153483

Library of Congress classification of 1904 edition
furnished by
McKissick Memorial Library of the University of South Carolina:

F
279
.C4
C468

Manufactured in the United States of America by
Benson Printing Company

Direct SEP 20 '71 1795

FOREWORD

On November 30, 1706, the Assembly of South Carolina passed an act to establish the Church of England in the province. By this act each parish was to provide "a fit person for a register" who was to "make true entry of all vestry proceedings, and of all births, christenings, marriages and burials, (negroes, mollatoes and Indian slaves excepted,) that is to say, the christian and sir-name with the day and month and year of every such births, christenings, marriages and burials. . . ." The churchwardens of each parish were to "provide good and substantial writing books, well bound, sufficient for registering such proceedings" and making such entries. Thus each parish was to keep two sets of records: the minutes of the vestry and the register of births, christenings, marriages, and burials.

The originals of these records for the parish of St. Philip's, which have recently been laminated and rebound, are preserved in the office of the church in Charleston. The vestry minutes which are still extant begin in 1732. The eighteenth-century records of vital statistics were printed in two volumes: in 1904 A. S. Salley, Jr., edited the *Register of St. Philip's Parish, Charles Town, South Carolina, 1720–1758,* which was printed by Walker, Evans & Cogswell Co. of Charleston; in 1927 D. E. Huger Smith and A. S. Salley, Jr., edited the *Register of St. Philip's Parish, Charles Town, or Charleston, S. C. 1754–1810,* which was published by the South Carolina Society, Colonial Dames of America, and printed in Charleston. The vestry of St. Philip's Church has now made arrangements with the University of South Carolina Press to republish these two volumes, which have long been out of print, as a contribution to the South Carolina Tricentennial celebration. This is a wise decision for these volumes are valuable to both the genealogist and the historian.

There are similar records for the nine other Anglican parishes established in 1706 and for the eighteenth-century dissenting congregations, but, although some are older, none are more important than these since the parish of St. Philip's included the entire town of Charleston until the town was divided in 1751 by the creation of the parish of St. Michael's. St. Michael's, however, did not function as a parish until February 1, 1761, when Robert Cooper, the first rector of the parish, held divine service in the new building for the first time. Therefore, these are the vital statistics for the most important center in the early history of South Carolina.

It would be difficult to estimate the number of persons who are descended from those whose births, baptisms, marriages, and burials are recorded in these records, but they are legion and are spread over the United States today. These volumes should, therefore, be in every library in the United States that has a genealogical section.

Historians have continually used these records to solve a number of historical problems. The date of marriage may provide the earliest evidence of the presence of an individual in the province. The record of children born over a period of years to a couple can be used as evidence that that couple was continuously resident in the province during that span of years. The only official record of the presence of a Jamaican visitor to the province is the entry in these records of a burial notice.

The demographers, a new breed of historians, will find partial answers to many questions among these statistics. At what average age did men and women marry and die in South Carolina? Were there any seasonal variations in births and deaths? Perhaps the reprinting of these volumes will provide the occasion for some eager young historian to attempt to answer these and other questions in the field of demography. Already a great deal of work has been done by analyzing the church records of New England.

In 1897 Edward McCrady, then senior warden of the parish, wrote a short history of the church which was published under the title: *An Historic Church. The Westminster Abbey of South Carolina. A Sketch of St. Philip's Church, Charleston, S. C., From the Establishment of the Church of England under the Royal Charter of 1665 to the Present Time (July, 1897).* A new history is now needed to place beside the volume of George W. Williams on St. Michael's Church. The reprinting of these records should be prelude to a thorough study of both the history and the architecture of what McCrady called "the old church."

Salley faithfully followed the form of the original register. A spot check confirms the accuracy of the transcription. The user of this volume should be cautioned that there are two indexes and two sets of pagination. The manuscript index is printed at the beginning of this volume and the numbers there refer to the manuscript page numbers which Salley placed in brackets in the printed text. Salley's index is at the rear, and the page numbers there refer to the pagination of the printed volume.

One further explanation may help the user. The original registrar had divided his large bound volume into four equal portions for the recording of births, baptisms, marriages, and burials. But when the section set aside for the recording of burials had been filled, the registrar entered the later burials in the section of the volume reserved for marriages. When the section for marriages had also been filled, the registrar used the remaining portion of the section reserved for baptisms. Thus in the original and in this volume the burials for 1744–1753 precede those for 1720–1743; also the marriages for 1753–1755 precede those for 1720–1753. The user of the volume will, therefore, find in succession the record of births from 1718 to 1758, of christenings from 1720 to 1758, of marriages from 1753 to 1755 followed by those from 1720 to 1753, and of burials from 1744 to 1753 followed by those from 1720 to 1743.

George C. Rogers, Jr.
June 1971

PREFACE.

In 1719 the General Assembly of South Carolina directed that a parish register be kept in each parish in the Province. The register of St. Philip's Parish starts with the year 1720, but a few records of earlier dates were entered subsequently. St. Philip's Parish dates from 1682, but it is not now known whether any sort of register was kept prior to 1720.

This copy of the register of St. Philip's Parish was made by me from the original. The letters and figures in brackets indented into the printing show the pagination of the original. The index to the original is arranged in double column, but here the large letters represent the beginning of each page and the small letters the beginning of the second column of each page.

A. S. S., Jr.

Register of

St. Philip's Parish

1720–1758

[1] Top half of this page has only one column; the bottom half two.

[1] William in record.

* Elizabeth Wilson in the Record on p. 170.

[1] Should have been 269.

do. Hartman Wm to Ruth Scanlen 182.
do Humpress Thos. to A Armstrong 182.
do. Hutchins Joseph to C Cuttice .... do
do Harris Geo to Lance Rachell 183.
do. Heathly Thos. to Sus Monro 183
do Hall Thos: to Deb Hancock 183.
do Hurst Samll to Henderson M 183.
do Harremond Henry to Eliz Moncrief 183
do Honyhorn Thos: to Woodbery Sarah .... 184.
do. Hext Alexr: to Weaver Jane 185.
do Hopton Wm. to Sar Clapp 186.
do Hall Thos. to Eliz Hale .... 187.
do. Herbert Wm. to Oram Eliz 186.
do. Harvey John to C Croft .... 187.
do. Hains Mark to Eliz Porter 187.
do. Hawkins Jas. to Tipper Reb 187.
do. Herry Robt. to Pope Margt 187.
do.. Hamilton Robt to Mary Derber 188
do Hoyland Thos to A: M. Linth-waite .... 188.
do Hill Chas. to Sar Smith .... 188.
do Hunter James to Fayssoux Frances 190
do Hegerman Jasper to Froney Craven 190
do. Hart Wm: to M. Coursey 191
do. Heap Benjn: to Wood My. 191.
do. Harvey Robt. to Eliz. Mongin 192.
do Hall Wm .to Sus Tresvant 195.
do Henderson Samll to Jane Mattrass .... 195.
do. Harvey Benjn to M. Mortimore 196.
do. Harris John to Elnr Watson 196.
do Hildyard Wm.. to Han Wills 198.
[IJ] B & C Izard Charlotte .... 1&81
Johnson Thomas .... 1&81
Izard Anne .... 2&82
M Jouneau James & Magdalen Beauchamp 165
Jerman Ralph & Margaret Graham 165
Bu: Jones 251
Johnson Peter 251
Izard Anne 254
B Johnston Priscilla 2.

---

[1] This entry is in a handwriting different from that in the rest of this index. The writing is very much like that of Chief-Justice Charles Pinckney.

B C Richard Mary Delvincourt 9 91
B C Read James 10 92
B C Randal Catherine 11 93
B C Read 12 94
M Read Charles & Debora Honor Petty 172
[r] M Robinson David & Eliza Bruer 173
do Ropper Will: & Mary Wilson 174
do Rose Thomas & Beuller Elliott 174
do Rawling Robt: & Eliza Cole 175
do Roche Jordan & Rebecca Brewton 175
do Risby William & Mary Sams 175
do Robertson Joseph & Ann Neves 175
do Richards John & Mary Tomlinson 176
Bur Robertson William 262
do Ramsey Ann 263
do Robyns Frances 263
do Rice John 264
do Rogers Ann 264
do Rove Richard 265
do Rays David 265
do Robyns Thomas. 265
do Ransford George 265
do Roule Mary 265
do Read James 266
do Richard Edward 266
do Read Mary 266
do Rillam Lemon 267
do Rolfe George 267
do Randell John 268
do Ramsey William 269
do Randall Catherina 269
do Rolfe John 270
do Read James 271
do Roberts Saml: Nathaniel 273
do Read Deborah 273
do Read Elizabeth 274
do Roberts Joseph 275
do Ryall Catherina 277
do Raynolds John 277
M. John Roche to Jane Romage 178
do Abijah Russ to Moore Rachll. 179.
do Row Michl Chrisr to Hesy Margt 179
do Rivers John to Tathom Hannah 179
do Roberts Benjamn- to Holton Mary 179
do Reid Charles & Cannon Mary 179
do Rodda Ralph To Evans Doroy. 180
do Rattray Alexr to Hannah Shell 180

Bu	Sharp John		260
Bu	Splat Richard		260
Bu	Smith Elizabeth*		260
Bu	Stanford Timothy		261
Bu	Smith John		261
Bu	Stollard John		261
Bu	Satur Thomas		261
Bu	Sullivan William		261
Bu	Simmons Jacob		261
Bu	Stevenson Stephen		262
Bu	Stanaway James		262
M	Scott John & Hanah Fogarty		171
M	Summers Joseph & Elizabeth Rol		171
M	Stone John & Susanna Marshal		171
M	Squire Thomas & Mary Saunders		171
M	Savy John & Elizabeth Green		171
Bu	Smith Mary		262
Bu	Sinclair George		262
[S] B & C	Stevenson James	10	91
B C	Smith Mary	10	92
B C	Smith Rebecah	10	92
B C	Shesheunt Mary Ann	11	93
B C	Staynford Ann	11	93
B C	Sarazin Edward	12	94
B C	Sutherland Ann	12	94
B C	Savey Daniel	12	94
B C	Sharp Robert	12	94
B C	Sharp Martha	13	95
B C	Sarazin Moreau	13	94
B	Stephens Ann	13	
B C	Stricker Moses	13	95
B C	Sutherland John	13	96
B	Scott John	13	
B	Sharp Martha	14	
C	Stevenson Stephens		92
Ma	Scott John & Hannah Fogarthie		171
Md:	Summey Joseph & Eliza. Roll		171
do	Stone John & Susannah Martha		171
do	Squire Thos: & Mary Sanders		171
do	Stanhover John & Deborah Sharp		172
do	Surreau Francis & Mary McKpherson		172
do	Stocks Thomas & Rachael Howman		172
do	Snow Thomas & Eliza Cartwright.		172
do	Sullivant John & Ester Nelson		172
do	Shaw Robert & Eleonor Mills		173
do	Spencer John & Dory McKgregory		173

*Margaret on page 260.

1. The top half of the page has only one column; the bottom half two.

*929.3 S16

do Shubrick Rd to E Vicaridge .... do
do. Sym Wm: to Jane Negus........ do
do Smith Saml1 Jur to Dill Elizth. 183
do Stone S. M. to C Cayer........ Do.
do Stoutenburgh Luke to Mcken zie Sarah .... 183.
do. Saxby Geo to Eliz Seabrook 183.
do St Martin Henry to Henning Philippine .... 183.
do. Saxby Wm to Sar Hales 184.
d. Smith Anty to Middleton Ann 184
do Solom Cornelius to Barns Ann .... 184.
do Smith Thomas to Chick M 185.
do Swann Edwd to Rach Robin son .... 185.

[s2] Steadman Charles to Simpson Ann .... 185.
Stewart Robt to Eliza: Clifford........ 185
Sanders Peter To Fishbourn Eliz 185.
Smith Wm: to Dennistone M 185.
Stoutenburgh Luke to Sus Mcken zie .... 187.
Summers James to M. Lang........ 187.
Singletary Joseph to Han Dunham 187.
Summersett Edmd to Shrewsbury Cath 188.
Shubrick Thos. to Sar Motte........ 188.
Spencer George to Rowland Cath 189.
Scott John to Darkis Heskett........ 190
Smith Thos. Senior to Oliver Ann 191.
Smart Samuel to Cathne.. Johnson 191.
Shaick Van Levinas to Elizabeth Clarke .... 191.
Suthey John to M. Grant........ 194.
Spencer Frans to M Richards .... 194.
Smith Thomas to Mary Daniell.. .... 194.
Stevenson Chas: to M: Benoist 195.
Screven Wm: to Sar Stoll........ 195.
Shevie Lawrce to Sar Dellgrass .... 195.
Stead Benjamin to M. Johnson 196
Savage John to Ann Allen........ 197.
Sinclair John to Sarah Cartwright 198.
Schermerhoorn Arnout to Eddy. Hildreth .... 198.

[T] M Tough Robert & Hannah Bennet 165
Toomer Henry & Mary West 166
Thomas James, & Mary Waters........ 166

[Unmarked page facing 1] Births
Anno
1713/4
March 15 John The Son of Daniel Fidling and Elizabeth his Wife was Born, between 9 and 10 a Clock in the Morning.—
1717
Septemb. 30 Jacob the Son of Daniel Fidling and Elizabeth his Wife was Born about Ten a Clock in the Morning.—

1719
Decemb: 17 Robert the Son of Rebert Brewton & Millecent his Wife was Born—
1720
June 29 Joseph the Son of Joseph Palmer & Patience his Wife was Born.
1723
January 15 Samuel the Son of Joseph Palmer & Patience his Wife was Born
June 14 Anthony the Son of Anthony Mathews & his Wife was Born—
John Williams was Born the 16h Septr. 1715.

Births [1]

1718
Novr. 10 John, Son of Joseph Wragg & Judith his Wife was Born—.[1]
1719/20
Janry-: 16 Mary daughter of John Smith, and Mary his Wife was born—
1720
May 28th. Richard, Son of Richard Rowe, and Martha his Wife, was born—
Charles, son of Samuel West, and Sarah his Wife, was born—
Augt: 24th Joseph, Son of Joseph Wragg, & Judith his Wife, was born—
1719 Isaac, the Son of John Barksdale Esqr: & Sarah his Wife, was
27th Jany-: born—
Sepbr: 14th Joseph, Son of John Hutchinson, and Anne his Wife, was born—
4 Mary, daughter of Wm-: Loughton & Mary his Wife was born—
24 Mary, daughter of Jonathan Skrine & Eliza: his Wife, was born—
30 Charlotte. daughter of Ralph Izard Esq:, & Magdalen—Elizabeth, his Wife, was born—
1720
Novbr-: 8 William, Son of James Benbury and Judith his Wife, was born—
Elizabeth, daughter of Nehemiah Partridge & Anne his Wife, was born—
Sarah, daughter of Do: Do: was born.
Anne, daughter of Thomas Dymes & Mary his Wife, was born—
Thomas, Son of Thomas Loyd & Mary his Wife, was born—
Mary Anne, daughter of Benjamin Godin & Mary Anne, his Wife, was born—

---

[1] This entry was evidently made after the book had been started.

1720
April 16 Alice, daughter of John Smith & Mary his Wife, was born—
24 Joseph, Son of Joseph Holbich & Mary his Wife, was born—
July 24 Hillersdon, Son of Richard Wigg, and Sarah his Wife, was born—
26 Elizabeth, daughter of Thomas Gadsden & Elizabeth his Wife, was born—
Mary, daughter of Morrice Harvey, and Mary his Wife, was born—
William, Son of Benjamin Berry & Isabella his Wife, was born—
1720
Jan^ry-: 24 Mary, daughter of Alexander Clench & Mary his Wife, was born.—
Anne, Daughter of Benjamin Clifford & Sarah his Wife, was born.—
Nov^r: 3 Mary, daughter of Robert Brewton, & Millecent his Wife, was born.—
1720
Jan: 24 Rebekah, daughter of Nathaniel Partridge & Anne his Wife, was born.—
1722
Nov^r: 13th Thomas, Son of John Hutchinson & Anne his Wife, was born.—
Thomas, son of Robert Johnson Esq: & Margaret his Wife, was born.—
1721
Octob: 8 Samuel, son of Joseph Wragg, & Judith his Wife, was born.—
[2] Anne, daughter of Richard Rowe, and Martha his Wife, was born.—
Jane, daughter of William Weatherly & his Wife, was born.—
Mary, daughter of Thomas Capers & Mary his Wife, was born.—
1722
May 18th: Elizabeth, daughter of James M^c:Cune & Mary his Wife, was born—
Mary, daughter of Benjamin Godin & Mary Anne his Wife, was born.—
Ap^ll: 10th: Anne, daughter of Ralph Izard Esqr: & Magdalen Elizabeth his Wife, was born.—
July 22^d: Sarah, daughter of Elias Ball & Mary his Wife, was born.—
April 30 Mary, daughter of Hill Crofft & Prissilla his Wife, was born.—
Deborah, daughter of Elias Hencock & his Wife, was born.—
Anne, daughter of Thomas Hepworth Esqr: & Anne his Wife, was born.—
July 16th Peter, Son of James Benbury & Judith his Wife, was born.—

1721
Janry: 11th Martha, daughter of Francis Croxson & Elizabeth his Wife, was born.—
1722
Octob: 16th Richard, son of William Hale & Elizabeth his Wife, was born.—
Novb: 9th: Elizabeth, Daughter of John Stollard & Penelope his Wife, was born.
1720
May 5th: Mary, Daughter of Willm: Watis & Dorothy his Wife, was born.
1722
Novb: 22 Joshuah, Son of Willm: Lancaster & Mary his Wife, was born.
14 Sedgwick, the Son of Isaac Lewis & Sarah his Wife, was born.
Xbr: 26 Anness daughter of Willm: Tattle & Bershaba his Wife was born.
1722
July 17 Mary, daughter of John Stevenson & Mary his Wife was born.
Novbr: 6 Thos:, son of Danl: Green & Elizabeth his Wife, was born.
1722
Janry-: 2d. Thomas, Son of Thomas Dymes & Mary his Wife, was born.
Anne, daughter of John Oldham & Priscilla his Wife, was born.
1720
Febry-: 7th Thomas, Son of Thomas Lockyer & Elizabeth his Wife, was born.
1722
Febry..: 7th George, Son of George Lee & Lydia his Wife ,was born.
Xbr:.. 29 William, Son of Adam Sturde and Mehittabele his Wife was born.
Sepbr: 1s Anne, Daughter of John Smith & Mary his Wife, was born.
1722/3
Febry-: 14th Anne, Daughter of Nathl: Marriner and Ann his Wife, was born—
1723
Novemr: 18 Sarah Lee, the Daughter of John Lee and Mary his Wife was Born.—
1723
April 16 Edward, Son of Edward Croft and Elizabeth his Wife, was Born—
3 Jacob, Son of Paul Viart and Lydia his Wife, was Born.—
May 7 John the Son of John Fenwick and Elizabeth his Wife was Born—

1719
Augu^t: 22 Priscilla, the Daughter of Robert Johnston & Mary his Wife was born

1722/3
Jany. 15 Lidia, Daughter of Robert Johnston & Mary his Wife was Born

Febr^y. 13 Deborah, Daughter of Thomas Hancock & Elizabeth his Wife was Born

1721 [3]
August 23 Francis the Son of Richard Splatt and Ann his Wife was Born—

1722
January 20 John the Son of Richard Splatt and Anne his Wife was Born—

1723
June 4 Thomas the Son of the Reverend M^r. Thomas Morritt & Margaret his Wife was Born—

1722
Novem^r: 20 Sarah the Daughter of Samuel Woodberry and Penelope his Wife was Born—

Octob: 17 Margret the Daughter of Robert Johnson & Margret his Wife was Born.

Febru^y. 28 Leonard the Son of Thomas Burton & Elizabeth his Wife was Born.

1723
AugusT 5 George the Son of George Martin and Catherine his Wife was Born.

11 John the Son of John Hogg and Hannah his Wife was Born.

17 Sarah the Daughter of Thomas LLoyd and Sarah his Wife was Born.

Septem^r: 13 Mary the Daughter of James Thompson & Mary his Wife was Born.

16 Ann the Daughter of William Blakewey & Sarah his Wife was Born.

Octob^r. 12 William the Son of Roger Moore & Catherine his Wife was Born.

Septem^r D^o. Lidia the Daughter of Capt. David Abbot and Catherine his Wife was Born.

October 14 John the Son of Hill Croft and Priscilla his Wife was Born—.

Novemb. 13 Sarah the Daughter of Joseph Monk and Sarah his Wife was Born.

Decemb. 9 Thomas the Son of Thomas Fairchild and Elizabeth his Wife was Born.

Janu^ry. 21 Jonathan the Son of Jonathan Collins & Sarah his Wife was Born.

27 Sarah the Daughter of Thomas Lockyer and Elizabeth his Wife was Born.

Februy. 16 Christopher the Son of Thomas Gadsden and Elizabeth his Wife was Born

24 Henry the Son of Henry Laurens and Hester his Wife was Born—

21 Catherine the Daughter of Richard Wigg and Sarah his Wife was Born

March 13 Lidia the Daughter of Samuel Grasset and Jane his Wife was Born.

21 Morrice the Son of Morrice Harvey and Mary his Wife was Born.

1724 26 Elizabeth the Daughter of Robert Brewton & Millecent his wife was Born at 1 a Clock in the afternoon—

June 22 Susanna the Daughter of Edmund Croft and Elizabeth his Wife was Born

July 3 Elias the Son of Elias Hancock and his Wife was Born

Octobr: 12 Isaac the Son of Daniel Fidling & Elizabeth his Wife was Born about 1 a Clock in the morning—

17 John the Son of John Up John and Mary his Wife was Born—

8 William the Son of William Blakewey & Sarah his Wife was Born—

Novembr: 9 Edmund the Son of Edmund Robinson and Ann his Wife was Born

[4] Births continued

1723

October 31 William the Son of William Dick and Rebecca his Wife was Born.

1724

July 8 John, the Son of John Stevenson & Mary his Wife was Born.

Do- 19 Edward, the Son of John Smith & Mary his Wife was Born.

1722

October 16 Josiah the Son of John Pandarvis & Hanna his Wife was Born.

1721

Janury: 9 Phillippa, the Supposed Daughter of John Ellis & Ann his Wife was Born, and left to the Parish Charge.

1723

Septemr: 4 Mary the Daughter of Job Rothmahler and Anne his Wife was Born at Woodford in Essex in Great Britain.

March 17 Nathaniel, Son of Daniel Green Esqr. & Margaret his Wife was Born.

1724

May 27 Mary the Daughter of Robert Johnson Esqr. & Margaret his Wife was Born.

Septem^r. 10 Gabriel, the Son of Henry Gignilliat & Esther his Wife was Born.

Decem^r. 4 Anne the Daughter of Col: John Fenwick & Elizabeth his Wife was Born.

19 Elizabeth, the Daughter of Vincent Pain & Elizabeth his Wife was Born.

28 Charlotte, the Daughter of Charles Lewis & Elizabeth his Wife was Born.

Janu^ry: 3 Jacob, the Son of Benj^a: Godin & Mary Ann his Wife was Born.

6 Judith the Daughter of Joseph Wragg Esqr. & Judith his Wife was Born.

9 Job the Son of Job Rothmahler & Anne his Wife was Born.

Febru^ry 14 David the Son of Robert Johnston & Mary his Wife was Born.

1725

April 5 James the Son of James Thompson & Mary his Wife was Born.

May 25 Richard the Son of William Lancaster & Mary his Wife was Born.

Ditto 25 John the Son of Thomas Burton & Elizabeth his Wife was Born.

31 Rebeka, the Daughter of Richard Day & Mary his Wife was Born.

June 8 Sarah the Daughter of John Delabere & Jane his Wife was Born.

13 Sophia the Daughter of Thomas Lockyer & Elizabeth his Wife was born.

July 29 Sarah the Daughter of John LLoyd & Sarah his Wife was Born.

Septem^r. 7 Francis the Son of Ferdinando Geÿer & Angelica his Wife was Born.

11 Samuel William, the Son of Samuel Grasset & Jane his Wife was Born.

Novem^r 6. Hanah the Daughter of Othniel Beale & Catherine his Wife was Born.

28 Sarah the Daughter of William Rhett & Mary his Wife was Born.

28 Elizabeth the Daughter of James Banbury & Judith his Wife was born.

Decem^r 21 Elias the Son of George Lea & Lydia his Wife was Born.

29 Sarah the Daughter of Jonathan Collings & Sarah his Wife was Born.

January 1 Alexander the Son of William Mackenzie & Sarah his Wife was Born.

20 Benjamin the Son of Morrice Harvey & Mary his Wife was Born.

Februry: 26 Sarah the Daughter of William Blakewey Esqr. & Sarah his Wife was Born.

Mar 14 1724. Ailce, Daughtr of Thomas Morritt & Margaret his Wife was Born.

Births continued— [5]

1725/6

January 25 William the Son of William Byrem & Mary his Wife was Born.

Februry: 3 James the Son of James Rows & Sabina his Wife was Born.

1724/5

Ditto 3 Benjamin the Son of Benjamin Clifford & Sarah his Wife was Born

Februry: 28 John the Son of Francis Wood & Sarah his Wife was Born.

1725/6

March 31 Elizabeth the Daughter of Edward Crofts & Elizabeth his Wife was Born.

1726

June 3 Mary Magdalen the Daughter of Henry Gignilliat and Esther his Wife was Born—

Ditto 28 Sarah the Daughter of Joseph Warmingham & Sarh his Wife was Born

July 4 John the Son of John Moore & Rachel his Wife was Born—

Ditto 4 John the Son of Edmond Robinson & Anne his Wife was Born.

Ditto 8 George the Son of Philip Delagal & Eleanor his Wife was Born.

Septr: 4 George the Son of Elias Hancock & Mary his Wife was Born.

Octob. 2 Lydia the Daughter of John Laurens & Esther his Wife was Born.

Septr. 30 Jane the Daughter of William Warden and Margaret his Wife was Born.

Augt: 20 William the Son of James Wilkie and Loveridge his Wife was Born—

Octob. 29 Elizabeth the Daughter of Joseph Morgan and Anne his Wife was Born

1725

Janury. 9 1725, Samuel the Son of John Wood and Prudence his Wife was Born

Do- 11 Elizabeth the Daughter of Dr. John Hutchinson and Charlotte his Wife was Born in the year 1725—

1726

Octob: 20 1726. Martha the Daughter of the Reverend Mr. Alexander Garden and Martha his Wife was Born.

Sept. 19 1726 Elizabeth the Daughter of Samuel Prioleau & Mary his Wife was Born

May * 1726 Eleana the Daughter of Mr. John Wright and Jane his Wife was Born

Do * 1726 Sarah the Daughter of Robert Hawkes and Mariann his Wife was born

April * 1723 Margaret the Daughter of Henry Parsons and Martha his Wife was Born

June * 1726 Sarah the Daughter of Col John Fenwicke and Elizabeth his Wife was Born

Decemr. * 1726 Jacob the Son of Samuel Pickering and Martha his Wife was Born

Janury: * 1726/7 Mary the Daughter of William Pinckney and Ruth his Wife was Born—

[6] Day Year Births continued—

January: 11 1726/7 Mary the Daughter of Thomas LLoyd and Sarah his Wife was Born

Decemr 26 1726 Martin the Son of Jacob Motte and Elizabeth his Wife was Born

Do. 27 1726/7 Ann the Daughter of Mr. Richard Splatt and Ann his Wife was Born

Februy. 18 1726/7 John the Son of Henry Parsons & Martha his Wife was Born—

Do. 24 1726/7 Joseph the Son of Mr. William Yeomans and Mary his Wife was Born—

Hanah the Daughter of William Wattson and Mary his Wife was Born

April 3 1727 Anne the Daughter of Thomas Weslyd and Margaret his Wife was Born—

Febry 3 1724 Benjamin the Son of Benjamin Clifford and Sarah his Wife was Born—

do. 3 1724 James the Son of James Rous and Sabina his Wife was Born

June 29 1720 Joseph the Son of Joseph Palmer & Patience his Wife was Born

July 15 1723 Samuel the Son of Joseph Palmer & Patience his Wife was Born

Februy 1726/7 Hanah the Daughter of William Wattson and Mary his Wife was Born—

July 12 1727 Esther the Daughter of Samuel Grassett and his Wife was Born—

Augt: 13 1727 John the Son of John Conyers and Hanah his Wife was Born—

---

* Date of month destroyed.

Aug[t]. 24 1726 Susanna the Daughter of M[r]. Benjamin Godin Mercht. & Mary Ann his Wife was Born.

Anne the Daughter of the said M[r]. Benjamin Godin & Mary Anne his Wife was Born.

Sept[r]. 28 1727 Robert the Son of James Thompson & Mary his Wife was Born.

d[o] 28 1727 Charles the Son of Jonathan Collings & Sarah his Wife was Born

Aug[t]. 23 1727 Thomas the Son of William M[c]:kenzie and Sarah his Wife was Born

Nov[r]. 15 1726 Joseph the Son of D[r]. John Hutchinson & Charlotte his Wife was Born—

Octob 12 1726 Lydia the Daughter of John Lawrence & Esther his wife was Born[1]—

[7]

June 7 1725 Paul the Son of M[r]. Paul Douxsaint and Jane his Wife was Born—

Jan[ry]: 20 1721/2 John the Son of John Shelf Planter at Ox Creek & Hanah his Wife was Born

Jan[ry] 2 1720 Gregory Moore the Son of Gregory Haines & Alice his Wife was Born—

April 22 1727 Katherine y[e] Daughter of Childermas Croft & Katherine his wife was born.

Octob. 14 1727 James the Son of James Loydell and Anne his Wife was Born—

D[o]. 31 1727 John the Son of John Neufville and Elizabeth his Wife was Born

Nov[r] 4 1727 Benjamin the Son of Christopher Smith and Susanna his (supposed) Wife was Born

Dec[r]. 3 1727 William the Son of William Rhett Esq[r]. & Mary his Wife was Born

Feb[r]. 12 1727/8 John the Son of John Wright Esq[r]. & Jane his Wife & Thomas the Son of the said John Wright Esq[r]. and Jane his Wife, Twins were Born—

d[o]. 12 1727/8 William the Son of Ebenezer Wyatt & Mary his Wife was Born—

John the Son of Henry Gignilliat & Esther his Wife was Born.

Jan[ry]: 5 1727/8 Mary the Daughter of James Talbert & Mary his Wife was Born.

d[o]. 11 1727/8 Richard the Son of Thomas Wigg & Mary his Wife was Born

Dec[r]. 25 1727 Sarah the Daughter of John Sharp and   his Wife was Born—

Aug[t]. 2 1727 Jane the Daughter of Thomas Weaver & Ruth his Wife was Baptized by the Rev[d]. M[r]. Garden) See Fol 89

---

[1] A repetition, Oct. 2d. is given on p. 5 of register.

July 21 1728 Elizabeth the Daughter of Capt. Willm. Warden and Margaret his Wife was Born— ....

Sept 30 1728 William John the Son of William Linthwait and Eleana his Wife was Born

Oct. 14 1728 George the Son of George Bampfield and Elizabeth his Wife was Born—

Novr 10 1728 Robert the Son of Thomas Fairchild and Elizabeth his Wife was Born—

D^{o}. 11 1728 Thomas the Son of William Lancaster & Elizabeth his Wife was Born.

[8] Day Year Births continued

Month

Novr. 11 1728 Francis the Son of John Hope & Susanna his Wife was Born—

Jan^{ry}. 1 1728/9 John the Son of Maurice Harvey and Mary his Wife was Born

Jan^{ry}: 18 1728/9 John the son of Dr John Moultrie and Lucrecia his Wife was Born—

22 1728/9 Susanna Mary the Daughter of Stephen Duvall & Esther his Wife was Born—

25 1728/9 Elizabeth the Daughter of Willm. Osborne and Helena his Wife was Born—

Oct. 28 1728 Gibbon the Daughter of Robert Wright and Gibbon his Wife was Born—

16 1728 George ye son of George Bamfield and Elizabeth his Wife born

Novr 10 1728 Robert the Son of Thomas Fairchild & Eliz^{a}. his wife born.—

October 27 1728 Mary Esther the Daughter of Paul Douxsaint & Jane his wife born—

Decem^{r} 21 1728 Susan Mary the Daughter of Steven Duval & Esther his wife was born.

March 5 1727 Elizabeth the Daughter of Isaac Lewis & Sarah his wife was born—

Jan^{ry} 1 1728/9 John the Son of Maurice Harvey & Mary his wife Was born—

Jan^{ry} 20 1728/9 Anne Clemens the Daughter of William Watson & Mary his wife, born—

January 13 1728/9 Mary Jane the Daughter of William Rhett & Mary his wife was born—

January Charlotte the Daughter of John Hutchinson & Charlotte his wife was born.

Mary the Daughter of Thomas Weaver and Ruth his wife was born.

Novem^{r} 10 1728 Hannah the Daughter of Richard Miller & Judith his wife was born

David the Son of John Davis & Anne his wife was born

April 1 Mary the daughter of Elias Hancock & Mary his wife was born

15 1728 Abraham ye son of Wm Yeamans & Mary his wife was born

August 9 1729 Edward the Son of Edward Croft and Elizabeth his wife was born.

December 4 1724 Robert the Son of Robert Hume & Sophia his wife was born—

Septemr 15 1722 Susanna the Daughter of Sd Robert Hume & Sophia his wife was born

Septemr: 24 1729 Alexander the Son of Sd Robert Hume & Sophia his wife was born.—

Novemr. 25 1727 William the Son of James Kilpatrick & Elizabeth his wife was born.

Janry: 5 1729 Anne the daughter of sd James Kilpatrick & Elizabeth his wife was born—

Janry 29 1729 Wm Jefferys Son of Charles Hill & his wife was born

Decemr 29 1729 John the Son of Isaac Holmes, & Susanna his wife was born

August 28 1729 Mehetable the daughter of Thos: Cooper mercht & Margaret his wife—

Novemr: 21 1729 Rebeka the daughter of Benja: Clifford & Sarah his wife born—

April 3 1730 Anne the daughter of Moses Wilson & Margaret his wife was born

August 6 1728 Thomas Son of William Pinckney & Ruth his wife was born

Febry- 3 1729 Elizabeth daughter of William Pinckney & Ruth his wife born

Month day Year Births continued [9]

Septemr.. 11,, 1728. Elizabeth the daughter of Edmond Holland & Henrietta his wife born

January 13,, 1728,, Anne Daughter of Thomas Tucker, & Catherine his wife was born.—

March 23,, 1729 Maria Delvincourt daughter of Edward Richart & Ann his wife was born

March 1,, 1729,, Susanna daughter of Thos: Townsend and Abigail his wife was born—

March,, 22,, 1729,, John the Son of John Bounetheau & frances his wife was born

Janry,, 4,, 1729,, Hannah Catherin the daughter of Willm. Warden & Mary his wife was born

March,, 29,, 1729,, Anne the daughter of Matthew Glasebrook & Ruth his wife born

April 6,, 1730,, Mary the daughter of Edmond Holland & Henrietta his wife was born

April,, 15,, 1730,, Elizabeth daughter of Willm. Byrum & Mary his wife born—

June,, 17,, 1730,, Charles the Son of James Crokat & Esther his wife born.

July,, 28,, 1730,, James the Son of James Banbury & Judith his wife born

August,, 27,, 1730,, John the Son of Edward Croft & Elizabeth his wife born

August 25,, 1730,, Prudence Mary daughter of Jno. Bonine & Mary Magdalen his wife born

October,, 1,, 1730,, Breton Son of Thomas Cooper Mercht. & Margaret his wife born

Septemr: 30,, 1730,, Mary Daughter of Richard Bodycott, & Ann his wife born

Octor=,, 21,, 1730,, Marian daughter of George Bampfield & Elizabeth his wife born

October,, 30,, 1730,, Robert Son of Thomas Weaver & Ruth his wife born.

October,, 25,, 1730,, Stephen Son of Stephen Duval & Hester his wife born—

Janry- 21,, 1728,, Susan & Mary daughter of Stephen Duval & his wife Esther was born

Augt.,, 10,, 1730,, David Son of Peter Hoppe, & Mary Magdalen his wife was born

Augt.,, 28,, 1729,, Susanna daughter of William Mckenzie & Sarah his wife born

March,, 18,, 1730,, Hannah daughter of James Tomson & Mary his wife born.—

Novemr,. 8,, 1729,, Edward Son of John Neufville & Elizabeth his wife born.

Novemr,, 20,, 1730,, John Son of William Gibbes & Alice his wife born—

January 22,, 1730,, Samuel Son of Maurice Harvey & Mary his wife was born

Septemr: 30,, 1711,, Thomas Son of Stephen Bedon & Mary his wife was born.

April 28,, 1714,, John Son of Stephen Bedon & Mary his wife was born.

June 30,, 1718,, Stephen Son of Stephen Bedon & Mary his wife was born.

Novemr: 24,, 1725,, Sarah daughter of Stephen Bedon & Mary his wife was born.

April 21,, 1728,, Benjamin Son of Stephen Bedon & Mary his wife was born.

April 14., 1730,, Rebecca daughter of Stephen Bedon & Mary his wife was born.

Janry.,, 18,, 1729,, John Son of John Moultrie & Lucretia his wife was born.

Novemr,, 23,, 1730,, William Son of John Moultrie & Lucretia his wife was born

August 10,, 1730,, David Son of Peter Hoppe & Mary Magdalen his wife was born

July 23,, 1731,, Thomas Son of Samuel Puckham & Ann his wife was born

May,, 6,, 1731,, Sarah & Ann 2 daughters of Stephen Proctor & Ann his wife was born

July,, 16,, 1731,, Elizabeth Daughter of Paul Douxsaint & Jane his wife was born

July 26 1731,, Lydia daughter of George Lee & Lydia his wife was born

[10] Births Continued

August 8th 1729,, Mary the Daughter of Joseph Wragg & Judith his wife was born

May,, 10,, 1731,, Anne Daughter of sd Joseph Wragg & Judith his wife was born

Janry,, 5,, 1730,, Sarah Daughter of William Yeomans & Mary his wife was born

Septemr,, 4,, 1731,, Caroline Daughter of Captn. Thomas Arnold & Eliza. his wife was born

Novemr,, 23,, 1730,, Samuel Son of Maurice Harvey & Mary his wife was born

Novemr 7,, 1730,, Thomas Son of Thomas Hargrave & Mary Hargrave his Wife was born

Septemr 17,, 1730,, James Son of John Stevenson & Mary his wife was born—

August 30,, 1730,, James Son to James Withers & Mary his wife was born

Janry 22,, 1730,, Elizabeth daughter of Jacob Motte & Elizabeth his wife was born.

April 11,, 1731 Edmund Son——of John & Hannah Scott was born—

May 7,, 1731,, Thomas Linthwaite Son of William & Eleanor Linthwaite was Born

february 28 1730,, Elizabeth daughter of Archbald Young & Martha his wife was born.

Novemr 12 1730 John Francis Son of John Fountain & Lucia his wife was born.

April,,20,, 1731 Jane Daughter of James Dothan— & Katherine his wife was born

April 10,, 1730 Jonathan Son of John Turner & Mary his wife was born

May 2,, 1731,,Daws Son of John Vicaridge & Elizabeth his wife was born

October 28,, 1730 Sarah Daughter of Childermas Croft & Katherine his wife was born.

June 5,, 1731 Benjamin Son of Thomas Blundell & Sarah his wife was born—

Septem^r 15,, 1722 Susanna the Daughter of Robert Hume & Sophia his wife born

Decem^r. 4,, 1724,, Robert the Son of Robert Hume & Sophia his wife was born died Infant 1731

August 14,, 1731 James the Son of James Lechantre & Marian his wife was born

August 28,, 1731,, Marian daughter of Henry Gignilliat & Hester his wife was born

Novem^r 5,, 1731,, Mary daughter of the Rev^d. Alexander Garden & Martha his wife born

October 10,, 1731 Peter the Son of Gabriel Manigault & Anne his wife was born

January 7th 1731,, William the Son of George Bampfield & Elizabeth his wife was born

Decem^r,, 27,, 1731,, James the Son of John Greenland & Elizabeth his wife was born

January,, 29,, 1731,, Miles the Son of Robert Brewton & Mary his wife was born.

Decem^r,, 26,, 1731,, Anne the daughter of John Eves & Hannah his wife was born

March 8,, 1731 James the Son of Charles and Deborah Read was born

February,, 9,, 1731,, Margaret the Daughter of Isaac Holmes & Susanna his wife was born

Septem^r,, 11,, 1731 Jane the Daughter of John Owen & Marian his wife, born

Decem^r * 1724 Mary the daughter of William Smith & Elizabeth his wife born

Novem^r,, 11,, 1731,, Rebekah the daughter of William Smith & Elizabeth his wife born

July 27,, 1731 Jane the daughter of Samuel Grassett & Jane his wife was born

April 29 1729 Mary the daughter of Samuel Grasset & Jane his wife was born

Births Continued [11]

Septem^r 24,, 1729 Anne the daughter of the Rever^d. Alexander Garden & Martha his wife born

Septem^r,, 2,, 1729 Anne the daughter of Willm- Yeomans & Mary his wife was born

Novem^r,, 9,, 1729 George the Son of James Dickson & Elizabeth his wife was born

---

* Date undecipherable.

August 27,, 1729 Margaret the daughter of John Hext & Mary his wife was born

Novemr.,, 24,, 1730 Mary the daughter of Wm. Watson & Mary his wife was born

January 19,, 1731,, Margaret daughter of Moses Wilson & Margaret his wife was born

febry— 9,, 1731 Margaret daughter of Isaac Holmes & Susanna his wife was born

Janury 16 1731,, Thomas Son of John Collins & Hannah his wife was born

June 6 1732,, Trevor Son of Thomas LLoyd, & Sarah his wife was born

July,, 23,, 1732 Martha daughter of Jacob Motte & Elizabeth his wife was born

August,, 12,, 1732,, Richard Son of Richard Bodicote & Anne his wife was born

May,, 6,, 1732,, Dorothy daughter of James Tomson & Mary his wife was born

March 9th,, 1731 Charles Son of Willm: Pinckney & Ruth his wife was born

August 10,, 1732,, Catherine daughter of Stephen Randall & Elizabeth his wife was born

August 10,, 1732,, David John Son of Lewis & Mary Tuber was born

August 19,, 1732,, Mary Anne daughter of Philip Shesheun & Jane his wife was born

October 14 1730,, Richard Son of Richard Miller & Judith his wife was born

Septemr,, 2,, 1732,, Childermus Son of Abraham* Croft & Anne Maria* his wife was born

Decmr.,, 14,, 1731,, Mary daughter of John Edmonson & Mary his wife—was born

August,, 27,, 1732,, Mary daughter of Samuel Bullock & Elizabeth his wife was born

1732,, John Son of Thomas Weaver & Ruth his wife was born—

October * 1732,, Anne Daughter of Childermus Croft & Catherine his wife was born

October 19,, 1732,, Richard Son of Charles Codner & Anne his wife was born

October 14,, 1732,, Anne Daughter of John Staynford & Mary his wife born

October 2,, 1732,, John Son of Joseph Miller & Mary his wife was born

---

*First names blurred so as to make it uncertain.

*Date of month undecipherable.

Novem^r 21 1732 Joseph Son of John Lea & Susanna his wife was born

October 12 1732 Mighells the Son of Capt: John Gascoign Comandr: of His Majesties Ship The Alborough By his wife Mary Anne Eldest daughter of the Honor:able James Mighells Esqr: Comptroller of His Majestys Navy was born 12th. Octor: 1732 and Dyed the said day in the afternoon, being first christned.—

Decemr. 3,, 1732,, Stephen Son of capn: Stephen Proctor & Hannah his wife was born

febry— 1,, 1732 Mary Daughter of John Hext & Hannah Hext his wife was born

[12] Births Continued.

June 3 1732 Meler the Daughter of David Hext and Anne his wife was born

March 5 1732 John the Son of Stephen Graves and Mary his wife was born

January 4 1732 John the Son of John Bruce & Jeane his wife was born

february 8 1732 James the Son of John Owen and Miriam his wife was born

March 9 1732 the Daughter of John and Elener his wife was born

January 14 1732 Benjamin the Son of Archibald Young & Martha his wife was born

January 28 1732 Edward the Son of Moreau Sarazin & Elizabeth his wife was born

April 9 1733 Sarah the daughter of William Mc:kenzie & Sarah his wife was born

March 25 1733 Mary the Daughter of James Crokatt & Hester his wife was born

January 17 1732 Elizabeth Daughter of John Vicaridge & Elizabeth his wife was born

March 26 1733,, Mary the Daughter of Edward Croft and Elizabeth his wife was born

March 15 1732,, Catharine Daughter of Maurice Harvey & Mary his wife was born

June 6 1732,, Trevor Son of Thomas LLoyd & Sarah his wife was born.|

february 15,, 1731 Sarah Daughter of Andrew Hellerd & Hannah his wife was born

febry— 3 1732 Jerrom, of Andrew Hellerd & Hannah his wife was born

May 18,, 1733,, Anne Daughter of James Sotherland & Mary his wife was born

June 11,, 1733,, Frances daughter of Robert Brewton & Mary his wife was born

January 16,, 1732,, Thomas Son of John Collins & Hannah his wife was born

July 19 1733,, Thomas Son of Thomas Brown & Hester his wife was born

May 2,, 1733,, Thomas Son of Thomas Blundel & Martha his wife was born

August 14,, 1733,, Rachel daughter of John Fairchild & Rachel his wife was born

Septem[r],, 27 1733,, daughter of Charles Read & Daphne his wife was born

Septem[r],, 1 1733,, Anne daughter of Thomas Henning & Anne his wife was born

August 13,, 1733,, Daniel Son of John Savy & Elizabeth his wife was born

July 9 1733,, Charlotte daughter of Joseph Wragg & Judith his wife was born

Novem[r],, 2 1733,, Elizabeth Millitts daughter of francis LeBrasseur & Ann his wife was born

Novem[r],, 7,, 1733,, Mary daughter of W[m]— Pinckney & Ruth his wife was born

Aug[t]. 25 1732 Richard Withers Son of James Withers & Mary his wife was born

Sep[r]. 25 1733 Robert Son of Alen Sharp & Sarah his wife was born

Novem[r]. 14,, 1733,, James Batterson Son of John Batchelor & Eliz[a]. his wife was born

Jan[ry],, 4,, 1733 Richard Son of Richard Brickles & Sarah his wife was born

Novem[r],, 28 1733 Alberick Son of Alberick Brown & Mary his wife was born
Sho[d] be Almerick

Decem[r],, 13 1733,, John Son of Joseph Wilson & Mary his wife was born

March 29th 1734,, Catharine daughter of Jacob Woolford & Eliz[a]. his wife was born

March 12 1733/4,, Elizabeth daughter of Peter Jeyer & Mary his wife was born

March 28 1734,, William Son of William Kerr & Elizabeth his wife was born

March 11 1733 Peter the Son of Joseph Prew & Charity his wife was born—

Births Continued. [13]

1734

Octoebr 3 1734 David Brown & Henrietta his wife was born

July 9,, 1734 Anne Daughter of John & Deborah Colcock was born

April 15,, 1734,, Margaret Daughter of Thomas Cooper & Margaret his wife was born

October 8,, 1734,, Martha Daughter of Thomas Sharp & Sarah his wife was born

Novem^{r},, 3,, 1734,, Gilson Son of Gilson Clapp & Sarah his wife was born

febry.- 8,, 1734,, Frances daughter of Robert & Anne Miller was born

October,, 8,, 1734 Mary Daughter of John & Theodora Davis was born

March 31,, 1734,, Peter Son of Joseph Pearce & Charity his wife was born

Septem^{r} 1,, 1734 Son of Thomas Gooder & Francis his wife was born

Novem^{r},, 3,, 1734 James Son of Doc^{r}. John Moultrie & Lucretia his wife was born

June 8 1734,, James Son of Archbald Yonge & Martha his wife was born

Jan^{ry}-,, 8,, 1734 Moreau Son of Moreau Sarazin & Elizabeth his wife was born

May 26,, 1734,, Anne Daughter of Edward & Catharine Stephens was born

Decem^{r} 30 1734 Francis Son of Francis LeBrasseur & Anne his Wife was born

July 19th 1734 Mary Setrudes of the Trinity de Castro born—

Nov^{r}:- 16th 1734 Sarah Daughter of William Pinckney & Ruth his Wife was born

Dec^{r}:- 18 1734 Robert Son of Robt: Poling & Elizabeth his Wife was born—

Dec^{r}: 23 1734 Catherine Daughter of Edwd. Croft & Elizabeth his Wife born—

Octob^{r} 8th 1734 Mary Daughter of John Davies & Theodora his Wife was born—

April 14 1735 Martha Daughter of Martin Kean & Martha his Wife was born—

July 6 1735 William Son of Wm Perryman & Rebekah his Wife was born

Septr. 15 1734 William Son of James Withers & Mary his Wife was born

Augst:- 3^{d} 1735 Susannah Daughter of Joseph Prew & Charity his Wife was born

June 11th 1735 Moses Son of John George Stricker & Ann Barbara was born

June 12 173* Mary Daughter of William Yeomans & Mary his Wife born

Sept^{r}: 1st 1735 Ester Daughter of Antonio Pereira & Ann his Wife was born

---

*Last figure obliterated.

Septr: 12th 1735 John Son of James Sutherland & Mary his Wife was born

Septr 17th 1735 Peter Son of Peter Dalles & Rachel his Wife was born

Septr 22d 1735 John Son of John Scott & Mary his wife was born

Octor: 2d 1735 Elizabeth Daughter of Robert Colles & Elizabh: his Wife was born

April 5th 1735 Ann Daughter of Thomas Blundel & Martha his Wife was born

Octor: 24 1735 Sarah Daughter of John Hearn & Elizth: his Wife born

Octor: 29 1735 Elizabeth Daughter of John Bassnett & Elizath his Wife was born

[14] Births Continued

Novr: 20th 1735 Ann Isabella Daughter of John Cleland & Mary his Wife was born

Octor 28th 1735 Jonah the Son of Michael Millure & Mary his Wife was born

Novr 6th 1735 James Son of James Crokatt & Hester his Wife born—

Novr 10th 1735 Sarah Daughter of Richard Wright & Mary his Wife was born

Novr 27 1735 Catharine Daughter of Benja: Godin & Mary Ann his Wife born

Octor: 1st 1735 Martha Daughter of Collins Sharp & Sarah his Wife was born

Decr: 1st 1735 Charles Hill Son of John Guerard & Elizabeth his Wife was born

Augst. 14 1735 Eleonor Daughter of William Yeomans & Mary his Wife was born

Septr:- 13 1735 John Abraham Son of Jacob Motte & Elizabeth his Wife was born

Decr. 29th 1735 Peter Son of Robert Godfrey & Margaret his Wife was born

Febry 29th 1735 Robert Son of John Bezwicke & Silence his Wife was born

Mar: 2d 1735 Lucy Daughter of Giles Holliday & Elizabeth his Wife was born

March 3d 1735 Henry Son of Henry Haramond & Mary his Wife was born

June 11th 1728 Sarah Daughter of Jacob Motte & Elizabeth his Wife was born

Octobr: 15 1729 Jacob Son of Jacob Motte & Elizabeth his Wife was born

April 3d 1734 Anne Daughter of Jacob Motte & Elizabeth his Wife was born

Augst.- 17 1736 George Son of George Higgins & Anne his Wife was born

July 5 1736 Anne Daughter of William Pinckney & Ruth his Wife was born

ffebry: 11. 1736 Barnabe Son of John Owen & Mariam his Wife was born

June 21st 1736 John Milner Son of John Colcock & Deborah his Wife was born

July 21st 1736 Sarah Daughter of Richard Wigg & Anne his Wife was born

July 3 1736 Joel Son of Isaac Holms & Susannah his Wife was born

April 26 1726 Thomas son of Benjamin Pool & Sarah his Wife was born in Boston

Octobr 24 1736 George Son of James Tompson & Mary his Wife was born

April 27 1736 Charlotte Daughter of Francis LeBrasseur & Charlotte his Wife born

Septr: 26 1736 William Son of Mary Adams Illegitimatte was born

Novr: 25 1735 Margareth Daughter of George Beard & Elizabeth his Wife was born

Augst:- 9th 1736 Elizabeth Daughter of Joseph Wragg & Judith his Wife was born

Decr:- 16th. 1736 Thomas Son of Lawrence Ryall & Sarah his Wife was born

Novr- 24 1736 Hannah Daughter of Jacob Motte & Elizabeth his Wife was born

Decr:- 5 1736 Hannah Daughter of Henry Cassells & Margaret his Wife was born

July 31 1736 Martha Daughter of Archibal Yong & Martha his Wife was born

Births Continued [15]

Octobr: 1st 1736 Elizabeth Daughter of John Green & Phebe his Wife was born

Novr: 21st 1736 Peter John Son of Andrew Darbalestier Monclar & Amey his Wife born

Octor: 13th 1736 James Son of James Howell and Elizabeth his Wife was born

Novr: 6 1736 Elizabeth Daughter of Mary Robinson Illegitimate was born

Decr:- 19 1736 John .... } Twins of Lawrence Coulliette & Mary
Elizabeth } his Wife were born

Septr: 23d 1736 Andrew Son of Peter Olivier and Margaret his Wife was born

Jany 6th 1736/7 Patrick Son of Henry Duffey and Deborah his Wife was born

May 1st 1736 Mary Daughter of Thomas Harris & Elizabeth his Wife was born

Septr: 24th 1736 John Son of John & Katherine Dunn was born—
March 18th 1736 Rebeca Daughter of Thomas Brown & Ester his Wife was born.

May 13 1737 Robert Son of Robert Pringle & Jeane his Wife was born

June 30th 1734 James Son of James Osmond & Mary his Wife was born

January 24th 1736/5* Thomas Son of James Osmond & Mary his Wife was born

March 23d: 1736/7 Martha Daughter of James Osmond & Mary his wife was born

May 12 1737 John Son of George Vane & Sarah his Wife was born
Jany 20th 1736/7 Mary Ann Daughter of John Scott & Mary his Wife born

Mar 13 1736/7 John Son of Peter Laroche & Rose his Wife—born—
Mar 2d do John Son of Richard Lampart & Mary his Wife born
May 23 do Mary Daughter of Thomas Dale & Mary his wife born
May 12th do: William Son of Edward Simpson & Sarah his Wife born

Decr: 29 1733 Marianne Prioleau Daughter of Samuel & Mary Prioleau born

Novr: 9th 1732 Mary Daughter of Peter Benoist & Abigal his Wife born

May 29th 1737 Elizabeth Daughter of Jacobus Kipp & Elizabeth his Wife born

June 1737 Jacob Son of Benja: Godin & Marianne his Wife born
June 3d 1736 Mary Daughter of Henry Kelly & Elizabeth his Wife born.

Mar: 9th 1735 Anne Daughter of James Witthers & Mary his Wife born.

Decr: 23d 1736 Benjamin Son of the Revd: Alexr Garden & Martha his Wife.—

July 2d 1735 Elizabeth Daughter of William Pool & Lucretia his Wife born

April 11th 1735 Anne Daughter of Edward Orom & Elizabeth his wife

Mar 22d 1736 Edward Son of................................& Margaret Lightwood— —

Janry 3d 1736 George Son of Paul and Elizabeth Jenys was born

[10] Birth Continued

Novr: 2d 1733 John Son of the Revd Mr Alexr. Garden & Martha his Wife was born

June 16th 1737 Jane Daughter of Thomas Aurrt & Eleanora his Wife born

* Should have been 1735/6.

Mar: 30th 1737 Robert Son of Robert Colles & Elizabeth his Wife — — do

Novr: 24th 1735 Mary Daughter of George Butterworth & Mary Anne his Wife

Mar 26th 1736 Elizabeth Daughter of Mary Middleton Illegitimate—

July 5th 1737 John Son of John Owen & Meriam his Wife——born

June 15th 1737 Rebecca Daughter of Robert Brewton & Mary his Wife Born

Decr: 25th 1735 Alexander Son of John Monroe & Susannah his Wife.—Born

July 25 1737 Mary Daughter of Edward Stephens & Cathrina his Wife Born

June 20th 1737 Catherina Daughter of Moreau Sarrazin & Elizabeth his Wife

Augst: 17th 1737 John Son of Giles Holliday & Elizabeth his Wife—

Augst: 18th 1737 Mary Daughter of Jordan Roche & Rebecca his Wife—

May 25th 1737 Anne Daughter of Robert Whittford & Mary his Wife—

Octobr 16th 1737 James Son of Thomas Weaver & Ruth his Wife—

Augst: 17th 1737 John Son of Daniel Pepper & Mary his Wife

Augst: 8th 1737 Magdalena Daughter of Magdalena Peraud Illegitimate

Octor: 10th 1737 Lewis Son of Charles Shepherd & Anne his Wife— —

Novr: 2d: 1737 Sarah Daughter of Hugh Evans & Mary his Wife—

Augst 12th 1736 Elizabeth Daughter of Griffith Bullard & Hephzibah his Wife

Mar: 27th 1737 Mary Daughter of Daniel Green & Sarah his Wife

May 9th 1737 John Son of John Guerarard & Elizabeth his Wife—·

Octor: 10th 1737 Mary Daughter of Henry Harramond & Mary his Wife

Novr: 7th 1737 Anne Daughter of Rice Price & Jane his Wife.—

Novr: 7th 1737 Andrew Son of George Higgins & Anne his Wife

July 14th 1737 Sarah Daughter of John Davies & Theodora his Wife.

Novr: 10th 1737 Elizabeth Daugher of William Roper & Mary his Wife

Decr: 1st: 1737 Rachel Daughter of Xtopher Smith & Susannah his Wife

Decr: 6th 1737 Lewis Son of Lewis Thimoty & Elizabeth his Wife.

June 2d 1737 Elizabeth Daughter of William Day & Anne his Wife

ffebry 16th 1737 Francis Bathurst Daughter of Francis Piercy & Mary his Wife.

May 26th 1737 Thomas Son of William Yeomans & Mary his Wife.

August 25th 1737 Henry Son of Henry & Sarah Christie was Born

Birth Continued [17]

Jany 19th 1737 John Son of John Cleland & Mary his Wife
Septr 29th 1737 John Son of Henry Fletcher & Mary his Wife
Septr 18th 1737 Thomas Son of Thomas Hollins & Hannah his Wife
ffebry: 22d 1737 Anne Daughter of William Stone & Anne his Wife
Octor: 15th 1737 Anne Daughter of John Beswicke & Silence his Wife
Jany 24th 1737 Sarah Daughter of George Dela Pierre & Elizabeth his Wife
Jany 21st 1737 William Son of Elizabeth Lindsey Illegitimate—
Augst: 28th 1737 Anne Daughter of Xtopher Hopkins & Anne his Wife
Septr 14th 1729 Mary Daughter of Thomas Honaham & Rose his Wife
Mar: 17th 1737 Francis Daughter of John Miller & Julia his Wife
Mar 30th 1737 John Son of William Mckenzie & Sarah his Wife
Decr: 17th: 1736 William Son of Duncan Campbel & Hannah his Wife
April 2d 1738 Susannah Daughter of George Tabart & Rebecca his Wife
May 3d 1738 Peter Son of Thomas Goodman & Barbara his Wife
Septr 18th 1717 William Son of William Harvey & Sarah—his Wife born
May 30th 1722 Benjamin Son of William Harvey & Sarah his Wife do
April 14th 1724 John Son of William Harvey & Sarah his Wife do
Mar 25th 1726 Sarah Daughter of William Harvey & Sarah his Wife do
Jany 16th 1728 Arnall Son of William Harvey & Sarah his Wife do
Septr 7th 1732 Anne Daughter of William Harvey & Sarah his Wife do
Mar: 1st 1733 Charlotte Daughter of William Harvey & Sarah his Wife do
Jany: 21st 1737 Mary Daughter of William Harvey & Sarah his Wife do
ffebry 19th 1737 Mary Hester Daughter of Archibal Yong & Martha his Wife
April 29th 1738 William Son of John Dunn & Katherina his Wife
Decr: 20th 1737 Joseph Son of Joseph Griffith and Mary his Wife
October 11th 1737 Thomas Son Thomas Gadsden & Alice his Wife
June 29th 1738 John Son of Charles Fanshawe (of his Majestys Ship the Fenix) and Elizabeth his Wife, born—
July 24th 1738 Thomas Son of Tho* *ggles and *y his Wife—

[18] Birth Continued

† † 1737 Rachel Daughter of Daniel Bourget & Susannah his Wife

* Parts of names destroyed. † Month and day destroyed.

‡ ‡ 1730 Daniel Son of Daniel Bourget & Susannah his Wife
§ 3d 1738 Ann Daughter of Charles Shephard & Anne his Wife
§ 1st 1738 Anne Daughter of Jordan Roche & Rebecah his Wife
§ 21st 1738 Thomas Son of James Reid & Dorothy his Wife
§ 4th 1738 Mary Daughter of George Cockel & Elenor his Wife
§ 27th 1738 John Son of John Brathwaite Esqr & Silvia his Wife
§ 3d 1738 Elizabeth Daughter of John Owen & Mariam his Wife
§ 1st 1738 Sarah Daughter of John Lewis Poyas & Susannah his Wife
§ 13th 1738 Priscilla Daughter of Samuel Glaser & Sarah Lewisa his Wife
§ 13th 1738 William Son of Richard Masson and Margaret his Wife—
§ 3d. 1738 Thomas Son of Thomas Cooper & Margaret Magdelaine his Wife—
§ 3d 1738 John son of the Honble Capt Henry Scott & Eliza his wife was Born
§ 4th 1738 Henry Son of John Scott and Mary his Wife.
§ 30th 1738 Mary Daughter of James Osmond & Mary his Wife
§ 7th 1738 Martha Daughter of James Mechie & Martha his Wife
§ 10th 1738 Eyda Daughter of John Beekman & Ruth his Wife
Octor: 22d 1738 Sarah Daughter of Thomas Sharpe & Sarah his Wife
Decr: 8th 1738 Isaac Son of Jacob Motte & Elizabeth his Wife
Decr: 10th 1738 James Son of John Watsone & Abigal his Wife
Novr: 18th 1738 Eleonor Daughter of George Austin & Anne his Wife
April 1st 1739 John Brand Son of Peter Jeyes & Mary his Wife.
April 2d 1739 Thomas Son of Henry Harramon & Mary his Wife
April 12th 1739 William Son of William Woodrope & Elizabeth his Wife
May 12th 1739 Richard Son of Richard Lampart & Mary his Wife
May 24th 1739 William Son of William Dean & Anne his Wife
May 26th 1739 Anne Daughter of David Malice by Ann Harris—
June 6 1739 Anne Daughter of George Vane & Sarah his Wife
Septemb. 2 1738 Elizabeth Ann, Daughter of Maurice Lewis and Jean his Wife
* * * * Sharlot, * * of Rebeka Tattle
† † † † † †
October 10 1739 Rice Price, the Son of Rice Price and Jane [19] his Wife
Septemr 13 1739 Joseph Taylor, Son of William Williamson & Sophia Christiana his Wife

---

‡ Month and day destroyed. § Month destroyed.

* Parts of record destroyed. † Whole entry so much mutilated as to make it undecipherable.

Sept^r: 10 1739 Charles the Son of Charles Patchelbel and Hannah his Wife

July 29 1739 John, the Son of John Hollybush and Sarah his Wife

Septr. 23 1739 Daughter of Peter Horry and Martha his Wife

Novem^r 18 1739 Robert, the Son of John Remington and Margaret his Wife

Septr. 15 1739 Mary, Daughter of William Stone and Anne his Wife

June 11 1739 William, Son of William Pinckney and Ruth his Wife

April 13 1739 Peter, Son of Robert John's and Anne his Wife

Janu^ry. 18 1739/40 Mary the Daughter of Jacob Motte Esqr. & Elizabeth his Wife

Februy 1 1739 Josias, the Son of Thomas Tatnell and Elizabeth his Wife

9 1739 John, the Son of Archibald Young & Martha his Wife

16 1739 Walay Edmond, Son of Charles Sheppard and Anne his Wife

14 1739 John the Son of James Howell and Elizabeth his Wife

Decem^r 16 1739 Mary Ann the daughter of Martin Coleman & Mary Ann his Wife

Febru^ry. 3 1739 Mary the Daughter of Daniel Wood & Mary his Wife was Born

April 2 1740 Martha the Daughter of James Osmond & Mary his Wife was Born

Febr^y. 27 1739 David the Son of John Mackall & Martha his Wife was Born.

Febru^y. 18. 1739 William Son of William Yeomans & Mary his Wife was Born

Sept^r: 30 1739 Sarah Hilliard Daughter of Moses Hilliard & Mary his Wife was Born.

July 20 1739 Ann, Daughter of Thos: & Bulah Rose was Born—

Augu^t 17 1740 Ann, Daughter of Samuel Prioleau & Providence his Wife was Born

Septr. 23 1740 James Watsone Son of John Watsone & Abigail his Wife was Born

d^o d^o Ann Wren Daughter of Cornelius Rand & Hester his Wife was born

15 d^o Sarah, Daughter of Samuel Leger & Mary his Wife was Born

June 11 1740 Abraham, Son of Peter Shaw & Martha his Wife was Born

Augu^t.. 17 1740 William Son of John Miller & Julia his Wife was Born

August 11 1740 Sarah, Daughter of Capt. John Colcock & Deborah his Wife was Born

Octobr. 24 1740 Thomas, Son of Dr. John Moultrie & Lucretia his Wife was Born

Novr. 8. 1740 Joanna Dewick Daughter of Henry Dewicke and Anne his Wife was Born

Dcemr. 8 1739 Mary, Daughter of William Comer and Mary his Wife was Born

July 13 1740 Christian, Daughter of John Robertson & Margaret his Wife was Born

Octobr. 6 1740 Joseph, the Son of John Scott and Mary his Wife was Born

Febry. 6 1740 John the Supposed Son of Francis Thompson by Mary Slater was Born—

[20] August 17 1740 Teresa Elizabeth Trueman the Daughter of William Trueman, and Elizabeth his Wife was Born—

*mber 8 1740 Rebecca, the Daughter of Jordan Roche & Rebecca his Wife was Born

Ditto 2 1740 Robert, the Son of Robert Harvey and Mary his Wife was Born

Ditto 24 1740 William Crosthwaite Son of Thomas Crosthwaite & Mary his Wife was Born

*uary 25 1739 Elizabeth, Daughter of James Withers & Mary his Wife was born

July 15 1735 Rebecca, the Daughter of William Ridgill & Rebecca his Wife was Born

Octob: 31 1740 Anne, the Daughter of James Michie & Martha his Wife was born

August 4 1736 Joseph, the Son of Antonio Perare & Hanah his Wife was Born—

*emb. 1 1740 Elizabeth, the Daughter of Capt. James Sutherland & Mary his Wife; was Born

*cembr. 5 1740 Hanah, the Daughter of William Passwater & Hanah his Wife, was Born

July 17 1740 Richard, the son of Richard Howard and Sarah his Wife was Born

Februry: 6. 1740 John the Supposed Son of Francis Thompson & Mary Slater was Born

February 22 1740 William, Son of William Farrow & Rachel his Wife was Born

1741

April 3 1741 Cornelia Amorentia Daughter of Daniel Welchuyson & Cathr his Wife was Born

May 1 1738 Jane Carolina, Daughter of John Wathen & Jane his Wife was Born

Novem. 8 1739 John the Son of Peter Oliver & Margret his Wife was Born.

---

* Part of month destroyed.

Octob 20 1740 Susannah, Daughter of Thomas Lea & Mary his Wife was Born

March 20 1740 Mary, Daughter of Zech: Brazier & Mary his Wife was Born

June 6 1741 William, Son of William Stone & Anne his Wife was Born

Augut. 4 1741 John, the Son of John Thompson & Anne his Wife was Born

Septr 15 1741 Richard the Son of Richard Shubrick & Elizabeth his Wife was Born

Novemr. 24 1741 Sarah the Daughter of Docr: J Lining & Sarah his wife was Born

Do. 27 1741 Sarah, Daughter of Wm. Mc.Carty & Maryanne his Wife was Born

Decemb. 13 1741 Mary Elizabeth, Daughter of Alexr. Dingwall & Mary his Wife was Born

Do. 14 1741 Hanah the Daughter of Jeremiah Leaycroft & Mary his Wife was Born

Februy. 13 1741 Joseph, Son of Dr. Henry Dewicke & Anne his Wife was Born

March 4 1741 William George, Son of George Avery & Mary his Wife was Born

April 9 1742 Mary the Daughter of Robert Harvey & Mary his Wife was Born

Februy. 2 1741 John the supposed Son of Thomas Buckle by Kathrine Bird was Born

Septemr. 28 1741 Mary the Daughter of George Vane & Sarah his Wife was born

May 1 1738 Jane Carolina the Daughter of John Wathen & Ann his Wife was Born

23 1738 Ann the Daughter of John Nightingale & Ann his Wife was Born

August 4 1741 John The Son of John Thompson & Ann his Wife, was Born

Decemr. 4 1741 Benjamin the Son of Benja. Burnhame & Ann his Wife was Born

January 20 1741 Thomas, Son of Thomas & Sibell Charnock was Born

Births continued— [21]

I John Remington, Register, at request of Mr Rice Price Do Enter That on........

Decr: 1st- 1741 Samuel Price Son of Rice Price & Jane his Wife was born 45 m. past 12. a night

Februry 10 1741 Benjamin the Son of William Hare & his Wife was Born

Februry[ry] 23 1741 Elizabeth, Daughter of William & Martha Wright was Born

March 20 1741 John the Son of John Mc. Call & Martha his Wife was Born

April 11 1742 Jane, the Daughter of John Townsend & Hannah his wife, was Born.

16, 1742 William the Son of John Scott & Mary his Wife was Born

May 25 1742 William, the Son of William Farrow & Rachael his Wife was Born

June 23 1742 Ann the Daughter of Richard Powers & Esther his Wife was Born

July 2 1742 Alexander, the Son of Dr. John Moultrie & Lucrece his Wife was Born

Septr. 6 1742 Cooper Dicker ye Son of Benjan Whitaker Esqr & Sarah his Wife was Born

March 6 1741-2 Grace the Daughter of Charles Codner & Ann his Wife, was Born—

July 27 1742 Elizabeth, the Daughter of Willm: Smith & Ann his Wife was Born

July 1 1742 Thomas, the Son of Thomas Honyhorn & Sarah his Wife was Born—

July 14 1742 William Brounchurst, the Son of Hillman Hutchins & Sarah his Wife was Born—

January 30 1741-2 Edward the Son of Griffith Bullard & Hephzi-bah his Wife was Born—

July 15 1742 Sarah the Daughter of Dr. John Rutledge & Sarah his Wife was Born

Augut. 8 1742 Martha the Daughter of Jacob Motte & Elizabeth his Wife was Born

Augut 25 1742 Samuel the Son of Samuel Prioleau and Providence his Wife was Born at 11 a Clock in the morning.

Novemr. 6. 1742 Mary the Daughter of William Smith & Elizabeth his Wife, was Born—

Novemb. 16 1740 Joseph the Son of Joseph Norton & Mary his Wife was Born

May 13 1740 Margret the Daughter of John Barksdale & Ann his Wife was Born

Augt: 29 1742 Samuel the Son of William Smith & Elizabeth his Wife was Born

October 14 1742 Elizabeth the Daughter of Henry St: Martin & Philipine his Wife, was Born

Decemr: 5 1742 Martha Isabell the Daughter of James Wright & Sarah his Wife was Born

———— 18 1742 Thomas the Son of Jordan Roche & Rebecca his Wife was Born

August 30th: 1742 Mary the Daughter of Joseph Hutchins & Catherine his Wife was Born
Janury 10 1742 William the Son of Richard Lampert & Mary his Wife was Born.
January 15 1742 Esther the Daughter of William Boon and Jane his Wife was Born at Two of the Clock in the morning.
Decemb: 7 1742 Peter the Son of John Bounetheau & Mary his Wife was Born, at 6 Clock in ye Morning.
January 17 1741 Sarah the Daughter of John Smith and Sarah his Wife was Born—
March 8. 1742 Hanah the Daughter of Joseph Norton & Mary his Wife was Born at 3 aClock in the Afternoon
January 15 1742 Mary the Daughter of Dr. John Lining & Sarah his Wife was Born.
August 11. 1742 Thomas the Son of James Howell & Elizabeth his Wife was Born—
February 17 1742 John the Son of John Francis & Anne his Wife was Born.
March 10 1742 Ellinor the Daughter of William Watkins & Rachel his Wife was Born
Sepr: 8 1742 Sarah, Daughter of Henry & Sarah Christie was Born—

[22] Births continued—

Month Days Years
Novembr: 3d. 1742 Margaret, the Daughter of John Remington and Margaret his Wife was Born—
Februy 16 1742-3 Elizabeth, the Daughter of William Comer & Mary his Wife was Born
Septemr. 22 1742 Peter, the son of Peter Shaw and Martha his Wife was Born.
Novemr. 11 1742 Joseph, the Son of Thomas Lee and Mary his Wife, was Born.
May 15 1741 William the Supposed Son of William Laws by Mary Howard was Born.
Septemr. 20 1742 Anne the Supposed Daughter of John Swain by Mary was Born
May 20 1743 Anne the Daughter of John Craston & Julia his Wife was Born
April 28 1743 Elizabeth the Daughter of Peter Laurens & Lydia his Wife was Born—
Februy. 4th. 1742-3 Thomas the Son of Benja: Burnham & Anne his Wife was Born—
Novemb. 26 1742 John the Son of Jacob Fidling & Rebecca his Wife was Born
May the 29 1743 Charles Thomas the Son of John Beckman & Ruth his Wife was Born—

June 1. 1743 Elizabeth Esther Bellinger, the Daughter of John Watsone & Abigail his Wife, was Born—

July 9 1743 Samuel Roger and Hannah } Two Twins of Dr Henry Dewicke and Anne his Wife was Born—

Novemr. 25 1741 Joseph, Son of Cornelius Rand and Esther his Wife was Born

Janury: 3d: 1742 Charles, the Son of Charles Peele and Jane his Wife was Born

March 29 1743 John the Son of Robert Harvey and Mary his Wife was Born—

Augut 16 1743 Catherine Keith the Daughter of Hugh Anderson and Elizabeth his Wife was Born

July 31 1743 William the Son of Edward & Elizabeth Richardson was Born

Augut 26 1743 Joseph the Son of George and Mary Avery was Born

February 1 1741 Evelin the Daughter of Daniel and Mary Pepper was Born

Augut. 19 1743 Robert the Son of Richard and Sarah Howard was Born

Do. 21 1743 Adam the Son of Henrick and Margaret Metz was Born

Decembr 8 1743 William the Son of John Bee and Martha his Wife was Born

ditto 10 1743 Elizabeth the Daughter of William & Rachael Farrow was Born

ditto 27 1743 John the son of Benjamin and Anne Smith was Born

ditto 28 1743 Anne the Daughter of Robert & Mary Wright was Born

Februy: 5 1743 Mary the Daughter of William and Anne Stone was Born

ditto 11 1743 Elizabeth the Daughter of John and Mary Lancaster was Born

Janury. 14 1743 Amey the Daughter of Jacob & Elizabeth Motte was Born

ditto 21 1743 John the son of Henry and Mary Middleton was Born

ditto 29 1743 Elizabeth the Daughter of James & Sarah Lesesne was Born

ditto 30 1743 Mary the Daughter of John & Mary Houghton was Born

March 1 1743 Richard the Son of John Guerard &   his Wife was Born

ditto 12 1743 Thomas the son of John & Lucy Hanson was Born

Augt 3 1743 Mary the Daughter of Heny & Eliza Harramond was Born

Months days Years
March 3 1743 George Son of William & Mary Yeomans was born
Mar 16 1743 Ann the Daughter of James & Eliza Smith was Born
Feby. 3 1743 Jane Margaret the Daughter of Peter & Margaret Oliver was Born
Octor 26 1743 William Ward ye Son of Thomas and Mary Croswait was Born
May 26 1744 Mary ye Daughter of Thomas & Mary Smith was Born
ditto 9 1744 Mary ye Daughter of Thomas & Mary Ryebout was Born
April 23 1744 Susanah the Daughter Elisha & Catherine Poinset was Born
Febry 11th 1742 Ann, Daughter of Thomas & Sibell Charnock was Born
ditto 25 1744 There Was Born Henry ye son of Thomas & Sarah Frankland
July 6 1744 Sarah the Daughter of James & Sarah Wright was Born
Jany 13 1743-4 Sarah the Daughter of George & Sarah Vane was Born
Augt 6 1744 Samuel Jeremiah Son of Michall Cristopoth & Margeret Row was Born.
July 8 1744 Elizabeth Daughter of Benjamin & Anne Burnham was Born
June 6 1744 John the Son of John & Deborah Colcock was Born
5 1744 John the Son of William & Anne Moat was Born
Septr 23 1744 Mary Anne the Daughter of Michael & Barbarah South was Born
July 31 1744 Sarah the Daughter of John & Martha McCall was Born
14 1744 Anne the Daughter of William & Elizabeth Smith was Born
Septr 30 1744 Moses Heasel Son of Jos: & Anjulinah semor was Born
Mar 10 1743-4 Rebeccah Daughter of Thomas & Mary Lee was Born
June 1 1742 Rebeccah Daughter of William & Mary Gay was Born
July 20 1744 Elizabeth Han'y Daughter of Francis & Mary Bremar was Born
June 13 1744 Thomas Son of Jacob & Rebeckah Fiddling was Born
James the Son of
Decr 8 1744 Sarah the Daughter of Jeremiah & Anne Lecrafts was Born
Novr 20 1744 Daniel the Son of John & Susanah Crocket was Born
Septr 15 1744 William the Son of John & Margaret Remington was Born
Jany 4 1744 Isabella the Daughter of John & Susannah Hume was Born

14 1744 Mary Magdalen Daughter of Samuel & Providence Prioleau was Born
Feby 11 1743-4 John the Son of George & Mary Avery was Born
Augt 7 1744 Matha the Daughter of Richard & Mary Ackerman was Born
Feby 13 1744-5 John the Son of Samuel & Mary Leger was Born
Jany 5 1744-5 Samuel the Son of Samuel & Jane Lacey was Born
Octor 3 1743 John the ye Son of James & Sarah Atkins was Born
Augt 1 1742 Francis the Son of James & Mary Withers was Born
Octor 19 1744 Sarah the Daughter of James & Mary Withers was Born

30 1744 Mary the Daughter of William & Marth Edwards was Born
May 6 1742 Mary the Daughter of George & Hannah Newcomb was Born
April 12 1745 Charlotte the Daughter of Jacob & Elizabeth Motte was Born—
Novr. 22 1744 Mary the Daughter of James & Martha Michie was Born
June 8 1745 William the Son of Richard & Hester Powers was Born
[24] Months days Years Births continued
Febry:—17th 1744 William the Son of William & Elizabeth Woodhouse was born—
March 16th 1744 Ann the Daughter of John & Martha Coleman was Born—
Augt..... 4th 1745 Rodger the son of Thomas & Sarah Smith was Born—
June.. 26th: 1745 Ann, the Daughter of William & Rachel Farrowe was Born—
Febry:.. 16th 1744 John Houghton, the Son of Charles & Ann Sheppard was Born—
Augt:.. 2d 1741 Charles, the son of Charles & Ann Sheppard was Born—
Augt... 9th 1745 Mary Christiana, the Daughter of Wm: & Sarah Hopton was Born—
Septry... 16th 1736 Martha, the Daughter of William & Mary Coomer was Born—
Janry.. 6th. 1744 Sarah, the Daughter of William & Mary Coomer was Born—
Febry: 5th. 1743 Mary, the Daughter of William & Ann Stone was Born—
Septr... 22d 1745 Christian, the Daughter of William & Ann Stone was Born—
Novemr 15. 1745 Thomas, the son of Thomas & Mary Doughty was Born——

Decem^r 28^h. 1745 John, the son of Philip Jacob & Mary Elizabeth Ernst was Born—

Decem 26. 1745 Mary Elizabeth, the Daughter of Mark & Rachel Smith was Born

Februry: 14th 1744 Henrietta, the Daughter of Henry & Elizabeth Harramond was Born

Augt. 31st. 1745 Catharine, the Daughter of John & Deborah Colcock was Born.

Decr: 23d 1745 Sophia Maria Henrietta, the Daughter of John & Susannah Crokatt was Born.——————

March 1st. 1745 Sarah, the Daughter of William & Marian. Kirk was Born ....

Febry.. 15. 1745-6 Sarah the Daughter of Hilman & Sarah Hutchins was Born

Decem 21 1745 Childermas, the Son of John & Catherine Harvey, was Born

Febry. 16 1745 Henry, the Son of Peter & Lydia Laurens was Born.—————

April 18th 1745 Anne, the Daughter of Benjamin & Anne Smith was Born

Novr 29h 1745 Timothy, the Son of Timothy & Mary Briton was Born

Febry.. 14th 1745 Charles Cotesworth, the Son of Charles & Elizabeth Pinckney was Born—————

April 15th 1746 James, the Son of James & Sarah Lessene was Born...............

June 23. 1746 Mary the Daughter of Meller & Mary St. John was Born

May. 24 1746 Mary the Daughter of Peter & Elizabeth Sanders was Born

Febry. 2d. 1745 Isaac Walker, son of Isaac & Elizabeth Lesene was Born

June.. 29 1746 Nathaniel, Son of Henry & Charlotte Izard was Born

Febry: . 6 1745 Gabriel, son of John & Mary Bounetheau was Born

March 29 1745 Susannah, Daughter of Edward & Elizabeth Richardson was Born

March 17 1745 Catherine, Daughter of John & Ruth Beekman was Born

May 27 1746 Robert, the Son of James Wright Esqr; & Sarah his Wife was Born

Janry 10 1745 James, Son of Francis & Mary Clarke was Born——

Births Continued [25]

June 21st 1746 Mary, Daughter of Benjamin & Anne Smith was Born

Daniell's 3 Children — At the desire of Mr John Daniell of Charles Town Shipwright it is Registred, That Adam and John being Twins & Sons of the said John Daniell by Mary his Wife, were both Born the Eight Day of April One thousand seven Hundred and thirty four; And Also Mary their Daughter was Born the thirtyeth day of November One thousand seven Hundred and thirty six———John Remington Regr

Heskett's 5 Children — At the Desire of Mr George Heskett of Charles Town Shipwright It is Registred, That Joseph, Son of the said George Heskett by Mary his Wife was Born, the first day of February One thousd: seven Hundred & Eighteen, Darkes, Daughter of the said George & Mary was Born the twenty fifth day of March One thousd: seven Hundred & twenty, Sarah, Daughter of the said George and Mary was Born the tenth day of November One thousd: seven Hundred & twenty seven, George, Son of the said George & Mary was Born the fifteenth day of January One thousand seven Hundred & twenty Nine, & John, son of the said George & Mary was Born the twenty fourth day of September One thousand seven hundred & thirty three——Remington Regr.

June 29t. 1745 Martha, Daughter of James & Elizabeth Smith was Born

July 25 1746 Richard, Son of Richard & Esther Powers, was Born—

March 14th 1741 William, Son of William & Ann Glen, was Born—

July 26 1744 John, Son of William & Ann Glen was Born—

May 14 1746 Elizabeth, Daughter of William & Margaret Shepard was Born

Septr 10 1746 Isaac, Son of John & Marian Guerard was Born—

June 28 1746 David Thomas, Son of William & Grace Roper was Born

Octr. 6th 1746 William Son of William George Freeman & Jane his Wife was Born

Octr 24 1746 Samuel Son of Samuel & Elizabeth Carne was Born

Septr. 18 1746 James, Son of John & Martha McCall was Born

Janry- 4th 1724/5 aune heure du Matin Est né Estienne Mounier fils D'Estienne et De Marie Mounier——————

Janry 19h 1726/7 A Minuit, Est né Jean Glaude, fils, D'Estienne Est de Marie Mounier——

Novem^r 3^d 1746 Margaret, Daughter of Kenneth Michie & Mary his Wife was Born.——

Decem^r 17th 1746 Morreau, Son of Morreau Sarracen & Elizabeth his Wife was Born.——

Jan^ry.. 9th 1746 Martha, Daughter of Thomas & Martha Weaver was Born

Dec^r: 4th: 1745 Joseph, Son of William & Mary Harvey was Born—

Dec^r: 21 1746 Elizabeth Ann, Daughter of Peter & Ann Timothy was Born

Jan^ry 26 1746 Mary, Daughter of Maurice & Mary Keating was Born ——

July.. 1st. 1737 James, Son of Colen & Sarah Sharpe was Born——

Augt. 9 1739 John, Son of Colen & Sarah Sharpe was Born——

Jan^ry 1st 1742 Daniel, Son of Colen & Sarah Sharpe was Born——

Mar 3^d 1744 Alexander Son of Colen & Sarah Sharpe was Born——

Jan^ry 16 1745 Ann, Daughter of Colen & Sarah Sharpe was Born——

Augt. 26 1746 George, Son of George & Mary Avery was Born——

Feb^ry- 26 1744 William, Son of William & Alice Lupton was Born——

Octr 12^h 1746 Ashby, Son of Thomas & Ann Easton was Born——

Feb^ry. 15 1746 Elizabeth, Daughter of Frederick & Elizabeth Strubel was born——

Novr 3^d 1746 Margaret, Daughter of Thomas & Joan Tew was Born.——

Marc 16: 1746 James, Son of John and Susannah Hume was Born

Feb^ry: 19 1746 James, Son of John & Sarah Lining was Born——

Decem 26 1746 Charlotte, Daughter of Thomas & Mary Roybould was Born——

Marc 6 1746 Providence, Daughter of John Paul Grimke & Ann his Wife was Born——

Jan^ry 3^d 1746 Elizabeth, Daughter of Robt. & Mary Harvey was Born

Novr 8 1746 Elizabeth Ann, Daug^r: of Thomas & Ann Greene was Born

March 24 1746 William, Son of John Watson & Abigail his Wife was Born

Mar 1. 1746 Elizabeth, Daughter of Samuel & Mary Leger was Born

Feb^y.. 18 1746 William, Son of William & Marian Kirk was Born

Augt. 6^h 1746 Hepsibah, Daughter of Thomas & Bulah Rose was Born

April 8 1747 Richard Son of Richard & Mary Peak was Born—

March 19 1746/7 William, Son of Thomas & Mary Doughty was Born—

June 8h: 1747 Roger....... & Rebeccah } Twins, Son and Daughter of John and Sarah Champneys was born—

Mar 11h 1746 Elizabeth, Daughter of Edward & Martha Fenwicke was Born

April 18 1746 Jane, Daughter of Hugh & Ann Anderson was Born

June 14h 1747 George Lucas, Son of Charles & Elizabeth Pinckney was Born

March 17h 1746/7 Jane Daughtr. of Roger & Jane Saunders was Born

March 7th 1746/7 Mary Daughter of Benja: & Ann Burnham was Born

Births Continued [27]

1747 May 18th: Sarah, Daughtr. of Samuel & Hannah Lacey was born

1747 May 27th: Margaret Daughtr. of Willm: & Jane Duthy was born

1744 Septr: 22 John, Son of William & Sarah Webb was born

1745 Novr 20 William, Son of William & Sarah Webb was born

1746/7 Mar 6 Elizabeth, Daughtr. of Henry & Elizabeth Harramond was born—

1747 Augt. 15 Sarah, Daughth. of William and Sarah Webb was born

1746/7 Janry 19 Martha, Daughter of Vincent & Elizabeth Leacraft was born

1742 Octobr 29 Catherine, Daughtr. of Thomas & Elinor Legeré was born

1744/5 Febry 10th. Samuel, Son of Thomas & Elinor Legeré was born

1746/7 Febry 9th. Amey, Daughter of Thomas & Elinor Legeré was born

1732 Octor: 28 Isabella Shute
1735 Novr: 12 Elizabeth Shute
1739 April 18 John Shute
1743 July 31 Mary Shute
} The Children of Joseph & Anna Shute were Born.—

1746 July 9th Mark Anthony Besselleu son of Mark Anthony & Martha Besselleu was Born.

1747 June 8h. James, Son of Alexander & Catherine Livie was Born.

1747 May 8h. Ebenezer, Son of Francis & Anne Roche was Born.

1745/6 Marc 14 Susannah Elizabeth Daughter of George and Sarah Vane was Born.

1747 Augt. 27 Charlotte, Daughter, of Daniel & Catherine Welshuyson was Born.

1740 July 24 John Bocquet
1741/2 Marc 5 Ann Bocquet
1744 Octor: 6th. Peter Bocquet
1746 Septr. 6th: James Bocquet
} The Children of Peter Boquet & Barbary his Wife were Born.

1742 Octr.. 31 John Peter Chopard 1744. Decr. 16 Susannah Chopard 1746 April 14 Ann Chopard 1747 Augt. 27h. Daniel Chopard	The Children of Daniel & Maria Clef, Chopard, were Born.

1746 Novr: 7th: Daniel, son of Samuel & Katherine Stevens was born

1746 Decem 9th: Hannah, Daughter of Abraham & Sarah Snelling was born

1744 Septr 29 Sarah, Daughter of James & Penelope Edes was born—

1739 June 1st. Charles, Son of Henry & Elizabeth Beekman was Born

1743 April 10th: Mary, Daughr: of Henry & Elizabeth Beekman was Born

1734 Octr... 30th: Nathaniel, Son of Lawrence & Elizabeth Withers was Born

1746 Novr 12 William, Son of Justinus & Mary Stoll was Born—

1747 Augt. 15 Charlotte, Daughter of Henry & Charlotte Izard was Born

1746 Decr 4 Anne Daughter of Morgan & Mary Esther Sabb was Born

1747 Octr. 6th: Catherine Daughter of James & Mary Kirkwood was born

[28] Births Continued

June.. 3d. 1747 Rebecca Daughr. of Jacob & Elizabeth Motte was born

June.. 14h 1747 James Samuel, Son of Peter & Margaret Oliver was born

Septr.. 17th 1747. Elizabeth, Daughr. of Elias & Mary Snell was born

Novem 12th 1747 Sophia, Daughter of John & Sophia Snow was born

Novem 2d: 1747 Catherine, Daughter of William & Margaret Shepard was born

Octr.. 30h 1747 George Hall, Son of Hall & Mary Richardson was born

April 18 1741.. Anne, Daughter of Francis & Elizabeth Holmes was born

July.. 14h 1744 Elizabeth, Daughr. of Francis & Elizabeth Holmes was born

Septr... 1st 1747 Richard, son of Richard & Susannah Butler, was born

August 27th 1747 Tucker, son of William & Sarah Harris was born—

June 8h 1747 Thomas, son of William & Rachel Farroe was born

Novr:. 11th. 1747 Ruth, Daughr. of Alexander & Jane Hext was born

Nov[r]: 20 1747 James, Son of James Wright Esq[r]: by Sarah his Wife was born

Sept[r]... 16th 1747 Thomas, Son of John & Susannah Crokatt was born

Jan[ry] 1st. 1747 Mary Ann, Daughter of Thomas & Sarah Newton was born

June 21 1747 William ,son of Thomas & Mary Lee was Born

Novem 6 1747 Elizabeth Daughter of Frederick & Rose Holzendorf was born

Oct[r]... 19 1747 William, Son of Peter & Mary Edwards was Born

Sept[r].. 5 1747 Jane, Daughter of George & Hannah Duckett was born

March 8 1742/3 Elizabeth Daughter of Jeremiah & Elizabeth Theus was born

January 31 1744/5 John, Son of Jeremiah & Elizabeth Theus was born

Decem[r] 20[h]. 1747 William, Son of Peter & Mary Cattel was born

January 3[d]: 1747. David, Son of David and Katherine Caw was born

July... 7th. 1740 Thomas, Son of Thomas Lamboll & Margaret his Wife was Born—

August 25th: 1745 Mary, Daughter of Thomas Lamboll & Elizabeth his Wife was Born.—

April 20th 1747 Benjamin, Son of Thomas Lamboll & Elizabeth his Wife was Born—

June- 5th: 1741 Elizabeth, Daughter of William & Elizabeth Smyth was born.————

Novem[r] 21st Amee, Daughter of Thomas & Ann Easton was born

Septem[r]. 1st:. 1747 Esther Daughter of Richard & Esther Powers was born

February 20 1744 Ann Bellamy, Daughter of Mathew & Ann Roche was born

March 30 1739 William
October 31 1741 John,
January 23[d] 1746 Samuel } Sons of William & Anne Nelme were Born.

October 23 1744 Jorden, Son of Jorden & Rebecca Roche was born

Year day Month Births Continued [29]

1747 2[d] Septem Luke, Son of Luke & Sarah Stoutenburgh was Born

1747 16th Novem: Edward, Son of John & Grace Fitzgerald was Born——

1747 19[h] February Martha, Daughter of Samuel & Providence Prioleau was born.—

William, Son of Robert & Elizabeth Collis was Born

1746 1st. February John, Son of Samuel & Sarah Perkins was Born Ent[d]. below

1747 3d: Februyt— Jane McLaughlan, Daughter of Daniel & Catherine Roulain was Born ———

1747 22d Novemr Stephen, Son of Stephen & Ann Cater was Born ———

1746 18h July... William, Son of Thomas & Frances Hamett was Born

1747.. 24. Novem Charles Son of George & Mary Avery was Born...

1747 6h. Febry... Anthony, Son of Levinus & Elizabeth Van Schaick was Born

1747. 28 February Elizabeth Daughter of John & Sarah Nelson was Born

1747 15 March Mary Daughter of Frederick & Francis Grienzeig was born

1747 23 Novem Martha Daughter of Lionel & Martha Chalmers was born

1746 22d February Elizabeth, Daughter of Thomas & Elizabeth Poole was born

1746 23d Novemr Ann, Daughter of John & Catherine Harvey was Born

1747 14th May Mary Ann, Daughter Supposed of Thomas White by Sarah Lowe was Born. ———

1746 1st. Februry John Son of Samuel & Sarah Perkins was Born

1748 21st May Thomas, Son of Thomas & Mary LLoyd was Born

1748 5 July Thomas, Son of Thomas & Sarah Smith was Born

1748 18 July Sarah Daughtr. of John & Sarah Wheeler was born

1748 30 July Susannah Daugr: Charles Jacob & Susannah Pischard was Born

1746 28 Augt. Samuel Son of Wm: & Sarah Hopton was Born

1748 10th Septr: Jacob, Son of John & Margaret Remington was Born

1747 6th Febry: William, Son of William & Ann Cattell was Born

1748 13th August Robert, Son of Richard & Susannah Muncreef was Born

1748 19th June Robert, Son of John & Judith Vaun was Born

1747/8 8th Janry: Marian Cook Daughter of Joseph & Hannah Cook was born ———

do-... 23d March James, Son of William & Martha Tyre was born Polley Hill Daughter of Wm: Geo: Freeman & Jane his Wife was Born—

[30] Births

1743	Decr. 31t	Ann	Children of Alexander & Judeth Chisolme, of Charles Town were Born & by me John Remington Registr- Entred at the request of the parents the 24h Octr: 1748.—
1745	Novr 21t	Christina	
1747	May 30h	Alexander	
1748	June 14	Judeth	

1748 Septr 10 Francis, Son of Francis & Ann Roche was born
1748 ..Octr... 17th John, Son of John & Susannah Crokatt was born
1748 Septr 9h Mary, Daughter of Elisha & Catherine Poinsett was born

1747 April 10 Jane, Daughter } of Thomas Shubrick of Charles Town Merchant & Sarah his Wife
1748 June 23d Thomas, Son .. }

1748 Octr- 25 Robert, Son of Robert & Ann Waller was Born——
1747 Decr: 20th Jane Daughter of Hugh and Ann Anderson was Born
1748 Janry 19 Henrietta, Daughter of Charles & Easter Carroll was Born
1748 Febry 3 Charlotte Daughter of William & Ann Glen was Born
1749 July 28th Mary, Daughter of Thomas & Mary Doughty was Born
1749 Octr... 29 Mary Daughter of James & Penelope Edes was Born
1749 Augt 23 Mary Daughter of John & Mary Corbett was Born
1749 July 9th Rachel Daughter of Hugh & Ann Anderson was Born

Ann Stewart On the 11th: day of November 1749 was Born Ann Daughter of Col. William Stewart & Ann his Wife

Corbet Freeman On the 21st. day of February 1749/50 was Born, Corbett Freeman Son of William George Freeman & Jane his Wife ——

Willm. Air On the twelfth day of April 1749. was Born William the son of William Air and Ann his Wife

Mary Air On the 31st. March 1750 was Born Mary the Daughter of William & Ann Air. ——

John Bryan On the 16th. day of September 1749 was Born John the son of John & Sarah Marguerita Bryan.

George Vane On the 15thday of October 1749 was Born George the Son of George and Sarah Vane.

Susn Snell Colleton On the Seventh day of December 1750, was Born Susannah Snell Daughter being a posthumous Child of the Honble. John Colleton Esqr. & Susannah his Wife.

Births [31]

1748 Jany 20th Thomas, Son of Dr. David Caw by Catherine his Wife was Born } Thomas & John Caw
1750 Janry 5 John, Son of Dr. David Caw by Catherine his Wife was Born .... }

1749 Dec[r]... 21 Ann, Daughter of John & Ann McQueen was Born	Ann McQueen
1749 Nov[r]: 24 Saxby, Son of George & Abigail Dymond was Born	Saxby Dymond
1750 Octob[r]. 1 Elizabeth Daughter of Michael & Dorothy Pomer was Born	Elizabeth Pomer
1750 May 14 Elizabeth Daughter of John and Mary Churchwell was Born	Elizabeth Churchwell
1750 June 9 Thomas, Son of William & Susannah Hall was Born	Thomas Hall
1750 Sept[r]. 8 David, Son of David Oliphant and Hannah his Wife was Born	David Oliphant
1750 May 23 Edmund Son of Alexander and Elizab[h]: Petrie was Born	Edmund Petrie
1750 Sept[r]. 13 Hannah Daughter of Solomon and Mary Milner was Born	Hannah Milner
1749 Nov[r]. 10 Thomas, Son of Thomas & Joan Tew was Born	Thomas Tew
1750 Dec[r]. 13 Charles, Son of Thomas & Mary Doughty was Born	Charles Doughty
1750 March 2[d] John, Son of Catherine McAulit a Spurious Child Father unknown was Born	John McAulit
1750 April 16 Ann Daughter of John & Margaret Harman was Born	Ann Harman
1750 January 3 William son of William & Mary Searug was Born	William Searug
1751 Sept[r]... 9th Charles Son of John & Susannah Hume was born	Charles Hume

1750 Decr: 11th Benjamin Son of Thomas & Sarah Tucker was born	Benjamin Tucker
1750 Octr. 22d Edward son of Samuel & Mary Leger was Born..	Edward Leger
1751 May 7th... Martha Daughter of William and Ann Glen was born	Martha Glen
1750 Novr: 1st: Robert Son of Alexander & Katherine Livie was Born. (baptized by Mr Chas Lorimore)	Robert Livie
1747 Decr: 29- Elizabeth. 1749 Decr... 6- James.. 1750 Octr. 17- William.. Daughter & Sons of James Irving & Elizabeth his Wife were Born	Elizabeth James and Wm Irving
1751 Decr: 12th Robert Son of Robert & Isabella Rutherford was Born	Robert Rutherford
1751 Nov 13 Elizabeth Daughter of John & Margaret Remington was Born.	Elizabeth Remington
1751 Nov 8th Mary Daughter of David & Mary Deas was born—	Mary Deas
1749 Febry 20 William Son of William and Mary Coomer was born—	William Coomer
1750 May 2.. Sarah, Daughter of John & Sarah Sinclair was Born —	Sarah Sinclair
1750 April 16 William Raper an Adult Mulatto was publickly baptized in St. Philips Church by the Revd. Mr Alexr Garden	Wm Raper
1752 Febry: 16 James Son of William & Anne Air was Born —	James Air
1735. Octr 29 Alexander 1737. Octr 27 James..	Sons of James & Rebecca Elsinore were Born
1751. Novr Joel Son of Elisha & Catherine Poinsett was born	Joel Poinsett

1751 Oct^r^- 16 Daniel Son of Esaie Brunett and Susannah his Wife was Born —	Daniel Brunett
1750/1 Jan^ry^ 22^d^ Mary Daughter of William & Mary Campbell was born ————	Mary Campbell

Births [33]

1751 Nov^r^: 29 William son of David & Hannah Oliphant was Born ————	W^m^: Oliphant
1751 Novr. 29 Philip, Son of Sampson & Martha Neyle was born——	Philip Neyle
1748 Jan^ry^ 11th Charlotte Mary........ 1749 May. 18 Margaret Catherine Mary 1750 Nov^r^: 30 Frances Anne.......... Daughters of Peter & Anne Timothy were Born.	Charlotte Mary Marg^t^ Cath^e^: Mary Francis Anne Timothy
1751 Nov^r^: 14 Amelia Daughter of James Irving & Elizabeth his Wife was born . . .	Amelia Irving
1752 July.. 7th. Mary Daughter of John Cooper & Mary his Wife was born	Mary Cooper
1748 Feb^ry^: 9 Peter Son of Charles being Ash wednesday Stevenson & Mary his Wife was Born	Peter Stevenson
1752 Sept^r^: 14th Mary Daughter of N. S. Charles Stevenson & Mary his Wife was Born........................	Mary Stevenson
1752 Octob 14 John, Son of Thomas Doughty & Mary his Wife was Born........................	John Doughty
1753 June 11th: John of John Howell & Elizabeth his Wife was Born	John Howell

1753 March 7th Martha Daughter of William & Mary Coomer was Born....	Martha Coomer
1752 Octr: 9 Ann Daughter of John & Mary Corbett was Born	Ann Corbett
1753 Septr.. 6 Catherine Daugh- N. S. ter of David Deas & Mary his Wife was Born..	Catherine Deas
1753 July.. 24 Ann Daughter of John Remington & Margaret his Wife was Born	Ann Remington
1753 Novem 25 James Son of being Sunday Thomas & Mary Doughty was Born	James Doughty
1753 October 10th Mary Daughter of Joseph & Ann Pickering was Born	Mary Pickering

[34] Births

1753 Novr 22d Coll MacDonald Son of Coll MacDonald & Ann Elizabeth his Wife was born

1753. Octr. 4th Ann Daughter of Thomas & Mary Burnham was born

1754 March 20 John Christian Henning son of Philip & Catherine Henning was born

1753 March 25th Henry, Son of Henry Laurens & Eleanor his Wife was Born

1754 March 7th Ann, Daughter of William & Ann Air was born

1751|2 Janry 4th. Ann, Daughter
1754 Mar 16th William, Son } of William & Elizabeth Gibbes were born

1753 Augt. 22 Sarah, Daughter of Thomas & Sarah Smith was born

1729 April 14 O. Stile Thomas Cole a Mulatto, Son of Jonathan Cole of Wadmalaw was born

1754 May 25th: Paul, Son of Michael & Elizabeth Kolien was born

1747 Sepr:18th.. O: S. Elizabeth, Daughter of Christopher & Jane Gadsden was Born——

1750 Sepr: 5th O S. Christopher, Son of Christopher & Jane Gadsden was Born ——

1754 Decr. 21st N S. Harriot Daughter of Thomas Clarkson & Elizabeth his Wife was Born

1754 Nov 5h: N S Jane Daughter of David Oliphant & Hannah his Wife was Born

1755 Feby 8th Mary Daughter of William Burrows Attorney at Law & Mary his Wife was Born

1751 Novr 30h O S Frances Claudia Daugr. 1755 May 17th N S Lewis William. Son	of Peter & Ann Timothy were born

1755 March 3d- N S Eleanor Daughter of Thomas & Ann Linthwaite was Born——

Births [35]

1754 May 15th Grissel, Daughter of Robert Wells & Mary his Wife was born in Charles Town 10. oClock A M on Wednesday the 15th May 1754——————

1755 Novemr 18h Louisa: Susanna, Daughter of Robert Wells and Mary his Wife was born in Charles Town on Saturday at 9 oClock A M 18 Novr. 1755——————

1752 October William, Son of William & Sarah Henderson was born.

1754 July... 1st: Othniel, Son of John & Jane Giles was Born

1752 July 2d- O S John Son of Robert & Mary Wells was Born

1754 Feby 1 Elizabeth Martha 1755 October 6 Charlotte .... 1758 Feby. 16 John	The Children of Theodore & Catherine Treasvant of Charles Town Taylor was born N: B: the above Children was Baptized ℘ Mr. Tetard and Mr. Suberly......................
1753 August 1 William Elfe 1756 May 1 Elizabeth Do 1758 January 30 Hannah Do,	The Children of Thomas and Rachel Elfe of Charles Town Cabinet Maker was born
1753 August 24 Mary Dewar 1755 December 21 Robert Do, 1757 December 5 Elizabeth Do	The Children of Charles and Elizabeth Dewar of Charles Town Merchant Was Born
1752 April 11 Peter Butler 1754 March 26 Graham Ditto 1756 April 17 John Ditto	The Children of Peter and Elizabeth Butler of Charles Town Perukemaker Was Born

<table>
<tr><td>1751 June 12 James Creighton</td><td rowspan="4">The Sons and Daughters of John Creighton Adjutant of the South Carolina Provincials and Barbary his wife Was Born
Recorded the 5th. Day December 1758 ꝑ Thos Linthwaite Register</td></tr>
<tr><td>1753 January 19 Ann Creighton</td></tr>
<tr><td>1755 February 17 George Creighton</td></tr>
<tr><td>1755* August 26 John Creighton</td></tr>
</table>

[36] Births

<table>
<tr><td>1755 August 6 Susannah</td><td rowspan="2">The Daughters of Daniel & Elizabeth Trezevant Silver smith was Born</td></tr>
<tr><td>1757 April 13 Martha</td></tr>
</table>

<table>
<tr><td>1755 March 9 Benjamin</td><td rowspan="3">The Sons & Daughter of Benjamin Godfry & Mary his Wife was Born</td></tr>
<tr><td>1756 November 3 Mary</td></tr>
<tr><td>1758 November 21 Robert Richd.</td></tr>
</table>

<table>
<tr><td>Jose ph Ash</td><td>At the Request of Mr. Richard Cockran Ash of Tooboodoo and Ann his Wife That Joseph his Son was born the 14th. November 1758 and was Baptized ꝑthe Revd, Mr. Morrison of the Scotch Meeting 22d of the Same Month</td></tr>
</table>

<table>
<tr><td>1753 July 22 John</td><td rowspan="3">The Sons & Daughter of Robert Pringle Esqr and his Wife was Born</td></tr>
<tr><td>1755 April 4 Robert</td></tr>
<tr><td>1757 March 29 Elizabeth</td></tr>
</table>

<table>
<tr><td>1753 January 7 Matthew</td><td rowspan="2">The Son and Daughter of John Quash and Sarah his Wife was Born</td></tr>
<tr><td>1756 Novembr 21 Rachel</td></tr>
</table>

1755 Novr. 19 Ann Simmons Daughter of Ebenezer & Jane Simmons was Born

<table>
<tr><td>1753 Sepr. 2 James McQueen</td><td rowspan="3">The Sons of John McQueen Esqr. and Ann his Wife was Born</td></tr>
<tr><td>1755 January 19 Alexander Ditto</td></tr>
<tr><td>1758 May 22 George Ditto</td></tr>
</table>

<table>
<tr><td>1753 September 4 William Brailsford</td><td rowspan="2">The Son & Daughter of Mr. Samuel Brailsford & Elizabeth his Wife was Born</td></tr>
<tr><td>1757 November 15 Elizabeth Brailsford</td></tr>
</table>

<table>
<tr><td>1754 July 29 Amerinthia</td><td rowspan="2">The Daughter & Son of Rawlins Lowndes Esqr. and Mary his Wife was Born</td></tr>
<tr><td>1757 Novr. 5 Rawlins</td></tr>
</table>

* Evidently a clerical error.

1749 April 2d Sarah 1751 May 10th Benjamin	The Daughter & Son of Thomas & Elianor Legaré was Born
1752 May 21 Susannah 1754 November 5 Grace 1757 April 6 William	The Daughters & Son William Hall and Susannah his Wife was Born
1749 February 5 Elizabeth O S 1751 September 27 Richard O S 1753 January 17 Sarah N S 1754 February 11 Mary 1756 December 27 Thomas 1757 July 2 Jacob	The Sons & Daughters of Thomas Shubrick Esqr and Sarah his Wife was Born
1753 Novr... 17 Sarah 1755 Septr... 13 William 1756 Novr... 13 Elizabeth 1758 Septr. 7 Henrietta	The Son & Daughters of William Lloyd and Martha his Wife was Born
1748 November 6 John 1749 January 4 Alicia 1752 July 28 Sarah	The Son & Daughters of Mr. William Hopton & Sarah his Wife was Born
1755 Novr. 11 Ann 1757 July 13 Margaret 1758 July 6 Elizabeth	The Daughters of Mr. Robert Williams and Elizabeth his Wife was Born N B Robt. Williams Junr Esqr Attorney at Law
1748 August 21 William O S 1750 August 29 Ann O S 1752 November 20 Martha N S	The Son and Daughters of Wm. Roper Esqr. and Grace his Wife was Born
Broughton Laurens	On the 27 Day of September 1753 N S Broughton Son of James Laurens and Mary his Wife was Born

1753 October 31 Hext 1755 September 1 Philip	The Sons of Samuel and Providence Prioleau was Born
Johan na Mackinzie	On the 9th. Day November 1753 Mary Daughter of Robert and Johanna Mackinzie was Born
1755 August 17 Dennis 1758 September 10 Catherine	The Son and Daughter of John Desmond and Martha his Wife was Born

1755 March 24 Sarah 1757 November 1 Ann	The Daughters of Thomas Hargrove and Elizabeth his Wife was Born
1755 February 22 Cathrina 1756 September 30 Edward Stephens	The Daughter and Son of Daniel Sinclair and Mary his Wife was Born
1749 May 29 William 1753 January 3 Thomas 1757 December 15 Elianor Sarah	The Sons and Daughter of Thomas and Anna Maria Hoyland was Born
1753 November 27 William 1755 September 3 Loveridge 1758 January 25 John	The Sons and Daughter of James & Mary Willkye was Born
Eliza Webb	On the 7 Day March 1757 Elizabeth Daughter of Wallace John Webb and Mary his Wife was Born
Elianor Pritchard	On the 14th June 1757 Ann Daughter of James and Elianor Pritchard was Born
1748 November 13 James 1754 April 3 John 1756 October 27 Thomas 1758 November 22 Ann	The Sons and Daughter of John and Jane Stevenson was Born
1751 October 13 Elizabeth 1755 August 10 Richard 1758 October 17 Susannah	The Son and Daughters of Richard and Susannah Muncrief was Born
Elizab eht Webb	Elizabeth 'Webb Daughter of Wallace John Webb and Mary his Wife was Born March ye 7th. 1757 and was Baptized ℘ the Revd Mr. Andrews May ye. 5th. 1757
Watson Charles	Charles Watson, Son of John & Abigail Watson was Born July 3d. 1749 ——
Cooper Ann	Ann Cooper daughter of John & Mary Cooper was born the 28h. day of August 1754. & was privately Baptized by the Revd. Mr. Alexr. Keith—assistant to St. Philips parish.

Christnings. [81*]

1719|20

John Smith

Febry: 16 Mary daughter of John Smith & Mary his Wife, was Baptized—

* Pages 39 to 80, inclusive, are blank.

1720
Rowe
May 31 Richard, Son of Richard Rowe & Martha his Wife, was Baptized
West
Do: Charles, Son of Samuel West & Sarah his Wife, was Baptized—
Wragg
SeptR: 1s: Joseph, Son of Joseph Wragg & Judith his Wife, was Baptized—
Barksdale 14 Isaac, Son of John Barksdale, Esqr:, & Sarah his Wife, was Baptized
Hutchson 16 Joseph, Son of John Hutchinson, & Ann his Wife, was Baptized—
My. Loughton 28 Mary, daughter of Wm— Loughton, & Mary his Wife, was Baptized—
My. Skrine Octbr-: 4 Mary, daughter of Jonathan Skrine & Eliza: his Wife, was Baptized—
Chartte Izard
Novbr—: 5 Charlotte, daughter of Ralph Izard Esqr-: & Magdalen Eliza: his Wife, was Baptized—
Wm. Benbury
Xbr: 14 William, Son of James Benbury & Judith his Wife, was Baptized—
Eliza Partridge
28 Elizabeth, daughter of Nehemiah Partridge & Anne his Wife, was Baptized—
Sarah Partridge
Do. Sarah, daughter of Do: Do, was Baptized——————
Anne Dymes
Febry—: 20 Anne, daughter of Thomas Dymes & Mary his Wife, was Baptized—
Thos Loyd
March: 10 Thomas, Son of Thomas Loyd, & Mary his Wife, was Baptized—
M A Godin
1721
May 31 Mary Anne, daughter of Benjamin Godin, & Mary Anne his Wife, was Baptzed.—
Joseph Holbitch
Do: Joseph, Son of Joseph Holbich & Mary his Wife, was Baptized—
Alice Smith
Sepbr: 3d: Alice, daughter of John Smith & Mary his Wife, was Baptized.—

Hillersdon Wigg
5 Hillersdon, Son of Richard Wigg, & Sarah his Wife, was Baptized—

Eliza. Gadsden
Do: Elizabeth, daughter of Thomas Gadsden & Elizabeth his Wife, was Baptized.—

Mary Harvey
Octobr: 6 Mary, daughter of Morrice Harvy & Mary his Wife, was Baptized.—

Willm Berry
Xbr: 3 William, Son of Benjamin Berry & Isabella his Wife, was Baptized.—

Mary Clench
Do: Mary, daughter of Alexander Clench & Mary his Wife, was Baptized. ℘ Dr: B*

Ann Clifford
14 Anne, daughter of Benjamin Clifford & Sarah his Wife, was Baptized—

Mary Brewton
15 Mary, daughter of Robert Brewton &   his Wife, was Baptized.—

Rebecca Partridge
18 Rebekah, daughter of Nathaniel Partridge & Anne his Wife, was Baptized.—

Thos: Hutchison
Janry:.. 3 Thomas, Son of John Hutchinson & Anne his Wife, was Baptized.—

Thos. Johnson
4 Thomas, Son of Robert Johnson Esqr: & Margaret his Wife, was Baptized.—

[82] 1721|2
Janry—: 26: Samuel, Son of Joseph Wragg, & Judith his Wife, was Baptized.—

March 14 Anne, daughter of Richard Rowe, and Martha his Wife, was Baptized.—

1722—
April 15 Jane, daughter of William Weatherly, &   his Wife, was Baptized.—

May 16 Mary, daughter of Thomas Capers, & Mary his Wife, was Baptized.—

June 13 Elizabeth, daughter of James Mc:Cune & Mary his Wife, was Baptized.—

July 4th: Mary, daughter of Benjamin Godin & Mary Anne his Wife, was Baptized.—

---

* Rest undecipherable.

Augt: 9th: Anne, daughter of Ralph Izard Esqr: & Magdalen Elizabeth his Wife, was Do..—

24 Sarah, daughter of Elias Ball & Mary his Wife, was Baptized.—

29 Mary, daughter of Hill Crofft & Prissilla his Wife, was Baptized.—

Sepbr: 21 Deborah, daughter of Elias Hencock & his Wife, was Baptized.—

Do: Anne, daughter of Thomas Hepworth & Elizabeth his Wife, was Baptized.—

Novembr: 9th: Peter, Son of James Benbury & Judith his Wife, was Baptized.—

Do: Martha, daughter of Francis Croxson & Elizabeth his Wife, was Baptized.—

23 Richard, Son of William Hale & Elizabeth his Wife, was Baptized.—

Novbr: 20th: Eliza:, Daughter of John Stollard & Penelope, his Wife, was Baptized.—

1722

Xbr.... 18 Mary, daughter of Wm: Waties & Dorothy his Wife, was Baptized.

23 Joshuah, Son of William Lancaster, & Mary his Wife, was Baptized.

Janry—: 4 Sedgwick, Son of Isaac Lewis and Sarah his Wife, was Baptized.

9th: Amess, daughter of William Tattle & Bershabah his Wife, was Baptized.

16 Mary, daughter of John Stevenson & Mary his Wife, was Baptized.

Thomas, Son of Daniel Green & Eliza: his Wife, was Baptized.

21 Thomas, Son of Thomas Dymes & Mary his Wife, was Baptized.

Febry—: 6 Anne, daughter of John Oldham & Priscilla his Wife, was Baptized.

13 Thomas, Son Thomas Lockyer, & Elizabeth his Wife, was Baptized.

22 George, the Son of George Lee & Lydia his Wife, was Baptized.

William, Son of Adam Sturde & Mahitabell his Wife, was Baptized.

1722|3

March 23 Anne, daughter of John Smith & Mary his Wife, was Baptized.

Febry: 17 Anne, daughter of Nathal: Marriner & Anne his Wife, was Baptized.

1723

April 22d. Edward, Son of Edward and Elizabeth Croft his Wife was Baptized.

May 13 John, the Son of John and Elizabeth Fenwick his Wife was Baptized.

15 Jacob, Son of Paul Viart and Lydia his Wife, was Baptized.

17 Edward, Son of Edward Newman and Elizabeth his Wife was Baptized.

Mary, Daughter of Robert Boyde and Hannah his Wife was Baptized.

June 2d Sarah, Daughter of John Lee and Mary his Wife was Baptized.

April 4 Margaret, Daughter of Mr. Robert Johnson & Margaret his wife, was Baptized.—

1723 [83]

May 31 Elizabeth, the Daughter of Smith & his Wife was Baptd. —

Septemr. 13 Sarah, Daughter of Thomas LLoyd & Sarah his Wife was Baptized

Augt. 21 Thomas, Son of the Reverend Mr. Thomas Morrit and Margaret his Wife, was Baptized

22 John, the Son of John Hogg and Hannah his Wife was Baptiz'd

Septr. 6 James, Son of Sharp, and his Wife was Baptized.

Octob: 18 Anne, the Daughter of Majr. William Blakewey and Sarah his Wife was Baptized

Novemr-. 15 William, Son of Roger Moore and Catherine his Wife, was Baptized

29 Francis, Son of Richard Splatt and Anne his Wife was Baptized.

29 John, Son of Richard Splatt and Anne his Wife was Baptized.

Decemb. 20 Sarah, Daughter of Joseph Monk and Sarah his Wife was Baptized

Octob: 27 Mary the Daughter of James Thompson & Mary his Wife was Baptize'd

Novemb: 3. George the Son of George Martin and Catherine his Wife was Baptized

Decemb: 28 Leonard the Son of Thomas Burton and Elizabeth his Wife was Baptized

Janury. 10 Thomas Fairchild Son of Thomas Fairchild and Elizabeth his Wife was Baptized by the Reverend Mr. Murritt

27 Martha the Daughter of Ralph Izard and Magdalene Elizabeth his Wife was Baptized by the Reverend Mr. Garden

Februy. 19 Jonathan the Son of Jonathan Collins and Sarah his Wife was Baptized—

28 Sarah the Daughter of Thomas Lockyer and Elizabeth his Wife, was Baptized

March 7 Christopher the Son of Thomas Gadsden and Elizabeth his Wife was Baptized

16 Henry the Son of John Larans and Hester his Wife was Baptized by the Reverend Mr. Murritt

25 Keinard Parrie De la Bere Son of John De La Bere and

1724 and Jane his Wife was Baptized

James Parris Son of Alexander Parris & his Wife was Baptized.

Do Frances, the Daughter of Benjamin Godin & Mary Ann his Wife was Baptized.

1723

Octob: 22 Sarah the Daughter of Samuel Woodbury & Penelope his Wife was Baptized—

[84] 1723

Octob. 1 Lidia the Daughter of Capt. David Abbot & Catherine his Wife, was Baptized.

April 6 John the Son of Hill Croft and Priscilla his Wife was

1724 Baptized by the Reverend Mr. Garden

do. Anne................the Wife of Captn. Robinson was Baptized

10 Susanah the Daughter of Peter Normand of Winyaw and Susanah his Wife, was Baptized—

15 Catherine the Daughter of Richard Wigg and Sarah his Wife was Baptized

17 Maurice the Son of Maurice Harvey and Mary his Wife was Baptized

May 8 Nathaniel the Son of Daniel Green and Elizabeth his Wife was Baptized—

June 3 Lidia the Daughter of Samuel Grassett and Jane his Wife was Baptized.

5 Bath-shebah the Daughter of William Tattle & Bath-Sheba— his Wife was Baptized—

July 17 Joseph Ellicot Son of Robert Ellicot and Mary his Wife was Baptized.

Septemr: 11 Lidia the Daughter of Robert Johnson & Mary his Wife was Baptized.

July 12 Susannah the Daughter of Edward Crofts and Elizabeth his Wife was Baptized—

Augut: 1 Elias the Son of Elias Hancock and his Wife was Baptized—

Octob: 30th. John the Son of Edward Up John and Mary his Wife was Baptized

Novemr. 6 William the Son of William Blakewey and Sarah his Wife was Baptized—

13 Isaac the Son of Daniel Fidleing and Elizabeth his Wife was Baptized—

April 24 Elizabeth the Daughter of Robert Brewton and Millecent his Wife, was Baptized—

Novr. 20 Mary, Daughter of Job Wiggins and Mary his Wife was Baptized by the Reverend Mr. Murritt

Decemb: 16 Edmund the Son of Edmund Robinson and Ann his Wife was Baptized by the Reverend Mr: Garden—

1724/5

January 1· William the Son of William Dick and Rebecca his Wife was Baptized ꝑ Do

Do 6 John, the Son of John Stevenson & Mary his Wife, was Baptized ꝑ Mr. Garden

Do Do Edward, the Son of John Smith & Mary his Wife, was Baptized ꝑ Ditto.

1724/5 [85]

March 5 John the Son of Samuel Pickering & his Wife was Baptized by Mr. Garden.

31 Josiah the Son of John Pendarvis and Hanna his Wife was Baptized by the Reverend Mr. Alexander Garden—

April 1 John Stevenson, Glazier, 29 years, was Baptized ꝑ Ditto.

Do. William Rial, Bricklayer Aged 24 years, was Baptized ꝑ Ditto

Mary the Daughter of Robert Johnson & Margaret his Wife, was Baptized by the Reverend Mr. Garden November 5th: 1724—

Elizabeth the Daughter of Vincent Pain and Elizabeth his Wife was Baptized ꝑ Ditto January the 17th: 1724/5—

1725

April 16 Judith, the Daughter of Joseph Wragg & Judith his Wife was Baptized Do

do. Gabriel the Son of Henry Gignilliat & Esther his Wife, was Baptized ꝑ Do.

23 Jacob the Son of Benjamin Godin & Mary Anne his Wife was Baptized ꝑ Do.

30 Charlotte the Daughter of Charles Lewis & Elizabeth his Wife was Baptizd. ꝑ Do.

May 7 Anne the Daughter of John Fenwick & Elizabeth his Wife, was Baptizd. Do.

June 9 David the Son of Robert Johnson & his Wife, was Baptized ꝑ ditto

July 11 Richard the Son of William Lancaster & Mary his Wife, was Baptizd: Do.

14 Edward the Son of Thomas LLoyd & Sarah his Wife was Baptized ℘ Do.

Augt. 6 James the Son of James Thompson & Mary his Wife, was Baptized ℘ Do.

do. Sophia the Daughter of Thomas Lockyer & Elizabeth his Wife was Baptd. Do.

11 John the Son of Thomas Burton & Elizabeth his Wife was Baptizd: Do.

do. Sarah the Daughter of John LLoyd & Sarah his Wife was Baptizd. Do.

Octob. 13 Sarah the Daughter of John Delabere & Jane his Wife, was Baptd. Do.

29 Rebecca the Daughter of Richard Day & Mary his Wife was Baptd. Do.

Novr. 3 Samuel William the Son of Samuel Grassett & Jane his Wife was Baptized by the Reverend Mr. Garden—

Janry: 1 Sarah the Daughter of William Rhett & Mary his Wife was Baptd: Do

do. Philippa a Parish Child was Baptizd. Do

Septr. 6 Alice the Daughter of Thomas Morritt & Margaret his Wife was Baptized Do

Janry. 5 Francis the Son of Ferdinando Geÿer & Angelica his Wife was Baptizd. Do.

14 Hanah the Daughter of Othniel Beal & Catherine his Wife was Baptized Do.

19 Sarah the Daughter of Jonathan Collings & Sarah his Wife was Baptizd: Do

21 Elias the Son of George Lea & Lydia his Wife, was Baptized ℘ Ditto

21 Elizabeth the Daughter of James Banbury & Judith his Wife was Baptd:

Febry Thomas, Sirnamed Stanyarn an Adult Person was Baptized ℘ Do.

11 Benjamin the Son of Morrice Harvey & Mary his Wife, was Baptized ℘ Do.

24 Mary the Daughter of Job Rothmahler & Anne his Wife, was Baptized ℘ Do.

24 Job the Son of Job Rothmahler & Anne his Wife was Baptized ℘ Do.

[86] Christnings continued — —

March 4 Alexander the Son of William Mackenzie & Sarah his Wife was Baptized ℘ Mr. Garden.

1726 30 Sarah the Daughter of William Blakewey Esqr. & Sarah his Wife was Baptized ℘ Do.

May 25 Elizabeth the Daughter of Edward Croft & Elizabeth his Wife was Baptized, by the Reverend Mr. Garden

June 10 William the Son of William Byrem & Mary his Wife, was Baptized by the Reverend Mr. Garden

July 31 Sarah the Daughter of Joseph Warmingham & Sarah his Wife, was Baptized by Ditto—

Do. 31 John the Son of John Moor & Rachel his Wife was Baptd. ℘ Ditto—

Augut. 17 George the Son of Philip Delagal & Eleanor his Wife was Baptd. Do

Do. 26 John the Son of Edmund Robinson & Anne his Wife was Baptized Do:

Octobr. 6 George the Son of Elias Hancock & Mary his Wife was Baptiz'd by Mr. Thomas Morritt

Do. 6 Mary Magdalen the Daughter of Henry Gignilliat and Esther his Wife was Baptized by Mr. Morritt—

Do: 12 Benjamin the Son of Benjamin Clifford & Sarah his Wife was Baptized by the Reverend Mr. Varnod—

Do. 12 Lydia the Daughter of John Laurens & Esther his Wife was Baptized by Mr. Varnod—

Do. 12 James the Son of James Rows and Sabina his Wife, was Baptized by Mr. Varnod—

Do. 14 Samuel the Son of Joseph Palmer and Patience his Wife was Baptized by the Reverend Mr. Alexr: Garden—

Do. 14 Joseph the Son of Joseph Palmer & Patience his Wife was Baptized by the Revd. Mr. Alexr. Garden

Novemr: 11 John the Son of Francis Wood of Black River & Sarah his Wife, was Baptized by the Reverend Mr. Alexr: Garden

27 Elizabeth the Daughter of Joseph Morgan & Elizabeth his Wife was Baptized by Mr. Garden

Decemr 4 William the Son of James Wilkie & Loveridge his Wife was Baptized by the Revd. Mr. Garden

9 Elizabeth the Daughter of John Stevenson Glazier & Mary his Wife was Baptized by the Revd. Mr. Garden.

14 Jane the Daughter of Capt. William Warden & Margaret his Wife, was Baptized

27 Samuel the Son of John Wood & Prudence his Wife was Baptiz'd

28 Martha the Daughter of the Revd. Alexander Garden and Martha his Wife was Baptized by the Revd. Mr. Guy

Januy. 11 Elizabeth the Daughter of Dr. John Hutchinson & Charlotte his Wife was Baptized by the Reverend Mr. Alexr: Garden

Do. 11 Joseph the Son of the said Dr. Hutchinson & Charlotte was Baptizd.

8 John the Son of John Shelf & Hanah his Wife was Baptized

1726/7 Christnings continued [87]

Janury. 18 Elizabeth the Daughter of Samuel Prioleau & Mary his Wife was Baptized by the Reverend Mr. Alexr: Garden

March 1 Mary the Daughter of Thomas LLoyd & Sarah his Wife was Baptiz[d]

8 Sarah the Daughter of John Fenwicke Esq[r]. and Elizabeth his Wife was Baptized

8 Mary the Daughter of William Pinckney and Ruth his Wife was Baptized

10 Hanah the Daughter of William Wattson & Mary his Wife was Baptized

12 Anne the Daughter of Richard Splatt and Anne his Wife was Baptized

22 Martin the Son of Jacob Motte and Elizabeth his Wife was Baptized

22 Jacob the Son of Samuel Pickering and Martha his Wife was Baptized—

1727

April 5 Eleana the Daughter of John Wright and Jane his Wife was Received into the Church, Baptized 24th May 1726.

28 Anne the Daughter of Thomas Westlyd & Margaret his Wife was Baptized

May 3 Sarah the Daughter of Robert Hawkes & Mariann his Wife was Baptized

12 Joseph the Son of William Yeomans Merchant and Mary his Wife was Baptized

Sept[r]: 8 Esther the Daughter of Samuel Grasset and Jane his Wife was Baptized

13 John the Son of John Conyers and Hanah his Wife was Baptized

20 Margaret the Daughter of Henry Parsons and Martha his Wife was Baptized

20 John the Son of the said Henry Parsons Joyner and Martha his Wife was Baptized—

29 Mary the Daughter of William Byrem and Mary his Wife was Baptized—

Nov[r]: 9 Robert Son of James Thompson & Mary his Wife was Baptized.

26 Charles the Son of Jonathan Collins and Sarah his Wife was Baptized—

[88] Month Day Year Christnings continued

Decemb. 1. 1727 Thomas the Son of William M[c]Kenzie & Sarah his Wife was Baptized by the Rever[d]. M[r]. Garden

15 John the Son of John Neufville Cooper & Elizabeth his Wife was Baptized

17 William the Son of William Rhett Esq[r]. & Mary his Wife was Baptized—

Feb[y]. 18 John the Son of John Wright Esq[r]. & Jane his Wife and Thomas the Son of the said John Wright and Jane his Wife, Twins. were this Day Baptized—

22 William the Son of Ebenezer Wyatt and Mary his Wife was Baptized—

March 12 Benjamin the Son of Christopher Smith and Susanna his Wife was Baptized—

22 Susanna the Daughter of Mr. Benjamin Godin Merchant & Mary Ann his Wife was Baptized—

22 Anne the Daughter of the said Mr. Benjn: Godin and Mary Ann his Wife was also this Day Baptized—

Rachael the Daughter of John Moore Esqr & his Wife was Baptized—

April 12 1728 John the Son of Henry Gignilliat & Esther his Wife was Baptized—

Sept 22 1728 Mary the Daughter of James Talbert & Mary his Wife was Baptized by the Revd. Mr. Lambert.

April 27 1728 Richard the Son of Thomas Wigg and Mary his Wife was Baptized by the Revd. Mr. Garden

Febry 27 1727/8 Gregory Moore the Son of Gregory Hains & Alice his Wife was Baptized by the Revd. Mr Tho: Curphey

Marc. 6 1727/8 Sarah the Daughter of John Sharp & his Wife was Baptized by the Revd. Mr. Garden

8 1727/8 John the Son of John Neufuille & Elizabeth his Wife was Baptized by the Revd. Mr. Garden—

Decr. 27 1727 Susanna the Daughter of Isaac Holmes & Susanna his Wife was Baptized by the Revd. Mr. Garden—

do. 29 1727 Prudence the Daughter of Rebeka (who had no Husband,) was Baptized by Mr. Garden

Month Day Year Christnings continued [89]

Augt. 2 1727 Jane the Daughter of Thomas Weaver & Ruth his Wife was Baptized by the Revd. Mr. Alexr. Garden

2 1727 Miles the Son of Captn. Edward Crofts & Elizabeth his Wife was privately Baptized ℘ Ditto—

April 3 1728 James the Son of James Loydell and Anne his Wife was Baptized—

Augt Elizabeth the Daughter of Capt. William Warden and Margaret his Wife was Baptized

July 3. 1728 George the Son of Elias Ball & Mary his Wife was Baptized by the Reverend Mr. Garden—

5 1728 Cathèrine the Daughter of Childermas Croft and Catherine his Wife was Baptized—

12 1728 Mary the Daughter of Michael Jeane and Mary his Wife was Baptized

12 1728 Mary the Daughter of Michael Jean and Mary his Wife was Baptized—

Augt. 14 1728 Abraham the son of Mr. William Youmans and Mary his Wife was Baptized

14 1728 Elizabeth the Daughter of Joseph Lea & Isabella his Wife was Baptized—

16 1728 Thomas the Son of William Pinckney and Ruth his Wife was Baptized—

28 1728 Sarah the Daughter of Jacob Motte & Elizabeth his Wife was Baptized

Sept[r]. 4 1728 Mary the Daughter of M[r]. Richard Splatt and Anne his Wife was Baptized—

12 1728 Damaris Elizabeth the Daughter of Peter S[t]. Julien and Sarah his Wife was Baptized—

Oct[r]- 4 1728 Elizabeth the Daughter of Edmund Holland & Henrietta his Wife was baptized:—

Sarah the Daughter of Ellis and his Wife was baptized.—

October 9th. 1728 Sarah the Daughter of Roger Moore & Catherine his Wife was baptized—

13„ 1728„ William John the Son of William John Linthwaite & Eleanor his Wife was baptized—

16„ 1728„ Susanna the Daughter of John Huchinson & Charlotte his wife was baptized.—

[90] Christnings continued

Month Day Year Elizabeth the Daughter of Capt. William Worden and Octob[r]. 9 1728 Marget his Wife was baptized.

Novem[r]. 29„ 1728„ Gibbon the Daughter of Robert Wright & Gibbon his wife was baptized.

Decem[r] 6 1728 George the Son of George Bampfield & Elizabeth his Wife was baptized.

11 1728 Robert the Son of Thomas Fairchild & Elizabeth his 1728 Wife was Baptized.

13 1728 Mary Esther the Daughter of Paul Douxsaint and Jane his Wife—was baptized.

January 23 1728 Susan Mary the Daughter of Steven Duval & Esther his wife was baptized.

27 1728/9 Elizabeth the Daughter of Isaac Lewis & Sarah his wife was baptized.

31 1728/9 John the Son of Maurice Harvey & Mary his wife was baptized.—

febry. 14 1728/9 Anne Clemens the Daughter of William Watson & Mary his wife was baptized.

20 1728/9 Mary Jane the Daughter of William Rhett & Mary his wife was baptized.

20 1728/9 Charlotte the daughter of John Hutchinson & Charlot, his wife, was baptized.

28 1728/9 Mary the Daughter of Thomas Weaver and Ruth his Wife was baptized.

April 9„ 1729„ Hannah the Daughter of Richard Miller & Judith his wife—was baptized.

25 1729„ David the Son of John Davies & Anne his Wife Was baptized—

May 2,, 1729,, Mary the Daughter of Elias Hancock & Mary his wife, was baptized—

October 24 1729,, Edward the Son of Edward Croft & Elizabeth his wife was baptized

April 2,, 1730: Susanna the daughter of Rob[t]. Hume & Sophia his Wife was baptized

D[o]: Alexander the Son of S[d] Robert Hume & Sophia his wife was also y[n] baptized

William Kilpatrick, y[e] Son of James Kilpatrick & Elizabeth his wife was also then Baptized—

Anne the daughter of S[d]- James Kilpatrick & Elizabeth his wife was also then Baptized..

William Jefferis Hill Son of Charles Hill & Elizabeth his wife was

April 1730 baptized y[e] April 1730 — —

April 14 1730,, Willoughby Son of Benj[a] Bate & Esther his wife was baptized

Christnings Continued [91]

Month Day Year

July 22,, 1730 Maria Delvincourt, daughter of Edward Richart & Ann his wife, was baptized.

D[o] 24,, 1730 Elizabeth the daughter of Edmond Holland & Henrietta his wife, was baptized.

D[o] 24 1730 Mary Daughter of Edmond Holland & Henrietta his wife baptized.—

August,, 19,, 1730,, Charles the Son of James Crokatt & Esther his wife baptized. . .

D[o].,, 14,, 1730,, Susanna, daughter of Thomas Townsend & Abigail his wife was baptized

Catherine*

Septem[r].,, 4,, 1730,, Hannah the daughter of William Warden & Mary his wife, baptized

Octo[r]-,, 1730,, John The Son of Edward Croft, & Elizabeth his wife, was baptized

D[o]. ,, 7,, 1730 James the Son of James Banbury & Judith his wife was baptized.—

D[o]. ,, 7,, 1730 Prudence Mary daughter of John Bonine & Mary Magdalen his wife baptized.

D[o]. 14,, 1730,, Mary daughter of Richard Bodycot & Anne his wife baptized.

D[o] 20,, 1730,, Breton Son of Thomas Cooper & Marget his wife was baptized.

D[o] 28,, 1730,, John Son of John Bounetheau & Frances his wife baptized.

---

* **Catherine is interlined between Susanna. and Hannah and one or the other was evidently a slip of the pen, but in correcting neither name was scratched.**

Novemr,, 30,, 1730,, Stephen Son of Stephen Duval & Hester his wife was baptized.

Decemr. „ 23,, 1730,, Robert Son of Thomas Weaver & Ruth his wife was baptized.

Susanna & Mary daughter of Stephen Duval & Hester his wife baptized

Janury,, * 1730,, Mariam daughter of George Bampfield & Elizabeth his wife baptized.

Do 29,, 1730,, David Son of Peter Hoppe & Mary Magdalen his wife was baptized.—

April 29th 1730 John Son of William Gibbes & Alice his wife was baptized

febry- 19,, 1730 Samuel Son of Maurice Harvey & Mary his wife was baptized.

May 11,, 1731,, Thomas Son of Willm: Linthwaite & Eleana his wife was baptized.

febry 19,, 1729,, John Son of John Moultrie & Lucretia his wife was baptized

Decemr. 24,, 1730 William Son of John Moultrie & Lucretia his wife was baptized—

Decemr 10,, 1730,, David Son of Peter Hoppe & Mary Magdalen his wife was baptized—

Sepr. „ 30,, 1731,, Thomas Son of Samuel Pucham & Ann his wife was baptized.

Septemr,, 10,, 1731,, Sarah & Anne 2 daughters of Stephen Proctor & Hanah his wife was baptized

10,, 1731,, Elizabeth daughter of Paul Douxsaint & Jane his wife was baptized—

22,, 1731,, Lydia daughter of George Lee & Lydia his wife was baptized

Octr. 21 1729,, Mary Wragg daughter of Joseph Wragg & Judith his wife was baptized

July 16,, 1731,, Ann daughter of Joseph Wragg & Judith his wife was baptized—

febry- „ 10,, 1730,, Sarah daughter of William Yeomans & Mary his wife baptized

October 21,, 1731,, Caroline daughter of Capn. Thomas Arnold & Eliza. his wife baptized

Decmr,, 18,, 1730 Samuel Son of Maurice Harvey & Mary his wife was baptized

March 19,, 1730 Thomas Son of Thomas Hargrave & Mary his wife was baptized

Janry. 24,, 1730,, James Son of John Stevenson & Mary his wife was baptized

---

* Undecipherable.

March 26,, 1731,, James Son of James Withers & Mary his wife was baptized

May 18 1731,, Elizabeth daughter of Jacob Motte & Elizabeth his wife baptized

April 11 1731,, Edmond Son——of John & Hannah Scott was baptized—

March 23 1730,, Elizabeth daughter of Archbald Young & Martha his wife was baptized—

Decem[r] 28 1729 Jacob Son of Jacob & Elizabeth Motte was baptized.—

[92] Christnings Continued

January 20th 1730 John francis son of John Fountain & Lucia his wife was baptized

July 14,, 1731,, Jane daughter of James Dothon & Katherine his wife was baptized

July 4,, 1731,, Jonathan Son of John Turner & Mary his wife was baptized

July 16 1731,, Daws Son of John Vickaridge & Elizabeth his wife was baptized

October 27 1731,, Sarah daughter of Childermas Croft & Katherine his wife was baptized.

Jan[ry]. 19 1731 Benjamin Son of Thomas Blundell & Martha his wife was baptized.—

May 16 1729,, Stephen Son of John Stevenson and Mary his wife was baptized

October 28,, 1729,, Anne the daughter of the Rever[d] Alexand[r]. Garden & Martha his wife was baptized—

29,, 1729,, Anne the daughter of William Yeomans & Mary his wife was baptized

Novem[r],, 5,, 1729 Elizabeth daughter of Ebenezar Wyatt & Mary his wife was baptized—

D[o] 16,, 1729 George the Son of James Dickson & Elizabeth his wife was born

April 22 1730 John Son of Isaac Holmes & Susanna his wife was baptized

Septem[r]. 2 1730 Deborah Sharp an Adult Person was baptized

Decem[r] 1 1731 Marian daughter of Henry Gignilliat & Hester his wife was baptized

January 5,, 1731 Mary daughter of the Rever[d] M[r]. Garden & Martha his wife was baptized

february 4 1731 Peter the son of Gabriel Manigault & Anne his wife was baptized

febr[y] 13 1731 William Son of George Bampfield & Eliz[a] his wife was baptized

Ditto 24,, 1731 James Son of John Greenland & Elizabeth his wife was baptized

March,, 8,, 1731,, Miles Son of Robert Brewton & Mary his wife was baptized

Do. 17 1731,, Anne daughter of John Eves & Hannah his wife was baptized

Do- 17,, 1731,, James Son of Charles & Deborah Read was baptized—

Do 22,, 1731 Margaret daughter of Isaac Holmes & Susanna his wife was baptized

April 3,, 1732,, Jane daughter of John Owen & Marian his wife was baptized—

Ditto 5 1732 Mary daughter of William Smith & Elizabeth his wife was baptized

Do 5 1732 Rebekah daughter of sd. William Smith & Elizabeth his wife was baptized

Do 15 1732,, Jane daughter of Samuel Grasset & Jane his wife was baptized—

Decr:— 16 1730 Mary the Daughter of William Watson & Mary his wife was baptized.

May. 28. 1732 Mary Anne daughter of Paul Mazyck & Katherine his wife baptized

Christnings Continued. [93]

July 28,, 1732 Trevor Son of Thomas LLoyd & Sarah his wife was baptized.

19,, 1732,, Thomas Son of John Collins & Hannah his wife was baptized.

Septemr 20,, 1732 Margaret daughter of Moses Wilson & Margaret his wife was baptized

Septemr 8 1732,, Dorothy daughter of James Tomson & Mary his wife was baptized

Ditto 27,, 1732 Martha Daughter of Jacob Motte & Elizabeth his wife was baptized

May 27,, 1730: Ann the daughter of Moses Wilson & Margaret his wife was baptized

April 28 1732,, Charles Son of William Pinckney & Ruth his wife was baptized.

Septemr. 8,, 1732,, David John Son of Lewis Tuber & Mary his wife was baptized

Septemr 22,, 1732 Mary Anne daughter of Philip Shesheau & Jane his wife was baptized.

Septemr 8 1732,, Catherine daughter of Stephen Randoll & Elizabeth his wife was baptized

Septemr 8,, 1732,, Richard Son of Richard Miller & Judith his wife was baptized.

October 12 1732,, Mighells Son of Capt. John Gascoign Commandr: of his Majesties Ship Alborough by his wife Mary Anne Eldest daughter of The Honorable: James Mighells Esqr. Comptroller of His Majestys Navy was baptized.. October 12th:. 1732.——

October 11th 1732 Childermas Son of Abraham Croft & Mary Ann his wife was baptized

O—— 29 1732,, Mary daughter of John Edmonson & Mary his wife was baptized.

August 27,, 1732 Mary daughter of Samuel Bullock & Elizabeth his wife was baptizd.

Novemr,, 17,, 1732,, John Son of Thomas Weaver & Ruth his wife was baptized.

March 7,, 1732,, Mary Daughter of John Hext & Hannah his wife was baptized.—

1732 Anne Daughter of Childermas Croft & Katherine his wife was baptized

173 ,, Mary Daughter of Edward Croft & Elizabeth his wife was baptized—

March 13,, 1733,, Elizabeth daughter of John Vicaridge & Elizabeth his wife was baptized.

febry. 2,, 1732,, John Son of Joseph Miller & Mary his wife was baptized.—

April 25 1733,, Joseph Son of John Lee & Susannah his wife was baptized—

April 27 1733,, Meler Daughter of David Hext & Ann his wife was baptized.—

May 14,, 1733,, John the Son of Stephen Graves & Mary his wife was baptized.—

May 16 1732,, John Son of John Bruce & Jane his wife was baptized..—

April 12,, 1732,, Mary daughter of James Crokat & Hester his wife was baptized.—

July 25,, 1733,, James Son of John Owen & Marian his wife was baptized.

May 16,, 1733,, Anne Daughter of John Staynford & Mary his wife was baptized.

[94] Christnings Continued

March 21,, 1732,, Daughter of John & Elenor his wife was baptized

16 1732,, Benjamin Son of Archbald Young & Martha his wife was baptized

April 26,, 1732,, Richard son of Charles Codner & Anne his wife was baptized

february,, 7 1732,, Edward Son of Moreau Sarazin & Elizabeth his wife was baptized

May 27 1730,, Edward Son of John Neufville & Elizabeth his wife was baptized—

May 27: 1730,, Anne Daughter of Moses Wilson & Margaret his wife was baptized

July 28,, 1732,, Trevor Son of Thomas LLoyd & Sarah his wife was baptized

June 20,, 1733,, Anne Daughter of James Sotherland & Mary his wife was baptized

february 14,, 1732,, Sarah Daughter of Andrew Hellerd & Hannah his wife was baptized

febry- 14,, 1732,, Jerrom of Andrew Hellerd & Hannah his wife was baptized

June 20,, 1733,, Anne Daughter of James Sotherland & Mary his wife was baptized—

August 1,, 1733,, Frances Daughter of Robert Brewton & Mary his wife was baptized

Septemr 30,, 1733,, Thomas son of Thomas Brown & Hester his wife was baptized

Septemr 26 1733,, Thomas son of Thomas Blundel & Martha his wife was baptized

October 3,, 1733,, Rachel daughter of John Fairchild & Rachel his wife was baptized

October 7 1733 daughter of Charles Read & Deborah his wife was baptizd

Novemr,, 21,, 1733,, Anne Daughter of Capt: Thomas Henning & Anne his wife was baptized

Novemr 14,, 1733,, Daniel Son of John Savy & Elizabeth his wife was baptized

Novemr 16,, 1733, Charlotte daughter of Joseph Wragg & Judeth his wife was baptized

Novemr 12 1733,, Elizabeth Millett daughter of Francis le Brasseur & Anne his wife was baptized

January 3,, 1733,, Mary daughter of William Pinckney & Ruth his wife was baptized

Richard Son of James Withers & Mary his Wife was baptized

febry 1, 1733,, Robert Son of C Sharp & Sarah his wife was baptized

Janry 9,, 1733,, James Batterson Son of John Batchelor & Eliza. his wife was baptized

febry 22 1733,, Richard Son of Richard Brickles & Sarah his wife Was baptized

March 6th 1733 Alberick Son of Alberick Brown & Mary his wife
Sh od be Almerick
was baptized

March 17 1733 John Son of Joseph Wilson & Mary his wife was baptized

April 19 1734,, Catharine daughter of Jacob Woolford & Elizabeth his wife was baptized

April 15 1734„ Elizabeth daughter of Peter Jeyer & Mary his wife was baptized

April 14 1734„ William Son of William Kerr & Elizabeth his wife was baptized

July 3„ 1734„ Anne Daughter of Edw[d]. & Catharine Stephens was baptized

feb[ry]. 14, 1734, Moreau Son of Moreau & Elizabeth Sarazin was baptized—

Sep[r]. 13„ 1734„ James Son of Archbold & Martha Young was baptized—

Christnings Continued [95]

Novem[r]„ 17„ 1734 James Son of Doc[r]: John Moultrie & Lucretia his wife was baptized.

Novem[r] 11„ 1734 Son of Thomas & Frances Goodin was baptized

July 3„ 1734 Peter Son of Joseph & Charity Pearce was baptized—

March 28„ 1735„ Mary daughter of John & Theodora Davis was baptized.

March 1„ 1734„ Frances daughter of Robert & Anne Miller was baptized.

Novem[r].„ 29„ 1734„ Gilson Son of Gilson Clapp & Sarah his wife was baptized—

Novem[r]„ 7„ 1734 Martha Daughter of Thomas & Sarah Sharp was baptized

May „ 12„ 1734„ Margaret daughter of Thomas & Margaret Cooper was baptized.

August„ 9„ 1734„ Anne Daughter of John & Deborah Colcock was baptized.

January. 4„ 1734„ of David Brown & Henrietta his wife was baptized.

June 17 1734 Mary Daughter of William Yeomans & Mary his Wife was baptiz'd

June 24 1734 Peter Son of Joseph Prew & Charity his Wife was baptiz'd

Aug[st]:— 14 1734 Ann Daughter of Jacob Motte & Elizabeth his Wife was baptiz'd

Decem[r] 2[d] 1734 Ann Daughter of Abraham Croft & Ann his Wife was baptiz'd

Dec[r]: 3[d] 1734 Martha Daughter of Benj[a]: Godin & Mary Ann his Wife was baptiz'd.

Febr[y] 19th 1734 Francis Son of Francis le Brasseur & Ann his Wife was baptiz'd.

July 23 1735 Martha Daughter of Martin Kean & Martha his Wife was baptiz'd

July 23 1735 Moses Son of John George Stricker & Ann Barbara his Wife was baptiz'd.

May 17 1735 Robert Son of Robert Poling & Elizabeth his Wife was baptiz'd

Augst 6th 1735 William Son of William Perryman & Rebekah his Wife was baptiz'd

Augst: 16 1735 William Son of James Withers & Mary his Wife was baptiz'd

Octor: 15th 1735 Peter Son of Peter Dalles & Rachel his Wife was Baptiz'd

Novr. 7th 1735 Eleanor Daughter of William Yeomans & Mary his Wife was baptiz'd

Novr: 16th 1735 Jonah Son of Michael Millure & Mary his Wife was baptiz'd.

Novr— 19 1735 Anne Daughter of Thomas Blundel & Martha his Wife was baptiz'd

Novr: 24 1735 Elizabeth Daughter of Robert Colles & Elizth: his Wife was baptiz'd

Novr. 28 1735 Elizabeth Daughter of John Bassnett & Elizth: his Wife was baptiz'd

Decr: 1st 1735 Charles Hill Son of John Guerard & Elizabth: his Wife was baptiz'd

Decr: 10th 1735 James Son of James Crockatt & Hester his Wife was baptized

Decr: 10th 1735 Martha Daughter of Collens Sharp & Sarah his Wife was baptiz'd

Decr: 10th 1735 Ann Isabella Daughter of John Cleland & Mary his Wife was baptiz'd

Januy 1st 1735 John Abraham Son of Jacob Motte & Elizabeth his Wife was baptiz'd.

Jany 6 1735 Sarah Daughter of Richard Wright & Mary his Wife was baptized

Jany 6 1735 Jane Daughter of Rice Price & Jane his Wife was baptized.

Jany 7 1735 Catherine Daughter of Benja: Godin & Mary Ann his Wife was baptiz'd

[96] Christning Continued

Januy 14 1735 John Son of John Scott and Mary his Wife was Baptized

ffebry 6 1735 John Son of James Sutherland & Mary his Wife was Baptiz'd

April 14th 1736 Robert Son of John Beswicke & Silence his Wife was baptized

April 14 1736 Lucy Daughter of Giles Holliday & Elizabeth his Wife was baptiz'd

April 14 1736 Sarah Daughter of John Hearn & Elizabeth his Wife was baptiz'd

April 17th 1736 Henry Son of Henry Hurramond & Mary his Wife was baptiz'd

July 4th 1736 Hester Daughter of Anthony Pereira & Ann his Wife was baptiz'd

Augst 13 1736 Barnaba Son of John Owen & Mariamne his Wife was baptiz'd

Augst: 25 1736 John Milner Son of John Colcock & Deborah his Wife was baptiz'd

Septr 10th 1736 George Son of George Higgins & Ann his Wife was baptiz'd

Septr 10th 1736 Anne Daughter of William Pinckney & Ruth his Wife was baptiz'd

Septr 15 1736 Joel Son of Isaac Holmes & Susannah his Wife was baptiz'd

Septr 15 1736 Sarah Daughter of Richard Wigg & Ann his Wife was baptiz'd

Decr: 1st 1736 Thomas Son of Benjamin Pool & Sarah his Wife was baptiz'd

Decr 1st 1736 George Son of James Tompson & Mary his Wife was baptiz'd

Decr 1st 1736 Charlotte Daughter of Francis LeBrasseur & Ann his Wife was baptized

Decr 5 1736 William Son of Mary Adams Illegitimate was baptiz'd—

Decr. 17 1736 Margarett Daughter of George Beard & Elizabeth his Wife do.—

Decr: 17 1736 Elizabeth Daughter of Joseph Wragg & Judith his Wife was baptiz'd

Decr: 29 1736 Thomas Son of Lawrence Ryall & Sarah his Wife was baptiz'd

Januy 1st 1736 Hannah Daughter of Jacob Motte & Elizabeth his Wife was baptiz'd

Januy 5 1736 Hannah Daughter of Henry Cassells & Margaret his Wife was baptiz'd

Januy 14th 1736 Elizabeth Daughter of John Green & Phebe his Wife was baptiz'd

Januy 21st 1736 Martha Daughter of Archibal Yong & Martha his Wife was do:—

ffebry 9 1736 Peter John Son of Andrew Darbalestier Monclar & Amey his Wife do:—

ffebry 9 1736 James Son of James Howell & Elizabeth his Wife was baptiz'd

Januy 6th 1736 Elizabeth Daughter of Mary Robinson Illegitimate was baptiz'd

Janry: 9th 1736 { Elizabeth / John and } Twins of Lawrence & Mary Coulliette was baptiz'd

ffebry 16 1736 Patrick Son of Henry Duffy and Deborah his Wife was baptiz'd

ffebry 16 1736 Andrew Son of Peter Olivier and Margaret his Wife was baptiz'd

Christning Continued [97]

March 18 1736 Mary Daughter of Thomas Harris and Elizabeth his Wife was baptiz'd Mr Orr

do:— 25 1737 Rebeca Daughter of Thomas Brown & Hester his Wife; by Mr Orr—

do:— 30 do John Son of John Dunn & Ketherina his Wife by Mr Garden—

April 12- do- Mary Ann Daughter of John Scott & Mary his Wife by Ditto—

do- 15- do- John Son of Peter Laroche and Rose his Wife——— .... Ditto—

do:- 25- do- Mary Daughter of Thomas Wigg & Mary his Wife— Mr Orr—

May 13th- do:—Robert Son of Robert Pringle & Jeane his Wife—by Mr Orr—

Augst: 2d 1734 James Son of James Osmond & Mary his Wife was baptiz'd—

April 7 1736 Thomas Son of James Osmond & Mary his Wife was baptiz'd.

May 25 1737 Martha Daughter of James Osmond & Mary his Wife by Mr. Orr—

May 23 do John son of Richard Lampart & mary his Wife............by Mr: Orr—

do 22 do. William Son of Edward Simpson & Sarah his Wife by ditto—

do. 23 do: Mary Daughter of Thomas Dale & Mary his Wife by ditto—

do 30th do John Son of George Vane & Sarah his Wife—by Commissary Garden

Jany 30th: 1733 Marianne Daughter of Samuel Prioleau & Mary his Wife by Mr Milichamp

Jany 12th 1732|3 Mary Daughter of Peter Benoist & Abigal his wife by Mr Garden

June 17 1737 Elizabeth, Daughter of Jacobus Keife & Elizabeth his Wife by Mr. Orr

do. 26 1737 Jacob, son of Benjn. Godin and Mary Ann his Wife by Mr. Orr.

do. 28 1737 Mary, Daughter of Henry Kelley & Elizabeth his Wife by mr. Orr—

do. 29 1737 Anne, Daughter of James Withers & Mary his Wife, by Mr. Orr.

April 17 1737 Benjamin, Son of Commissary Alexander Garden and Martha his Wife was Baptiz'd

Augt. 22d 1737 Mary Daughter of Edward Stephens & Cathrina his Wife was Baptized

July 15 1737 Edward Son of Capt. Edward Lightwood & Margaret his Wife

July 17 1737 Rebecca, Daughter of Robert Brewton & Mary his Wife
April 26 Elizabeth Daughter of William Pool & Lucrecia his Wife
July 18 1737 Anne Daughter of Edward Orom & Elizabeth his Wife
July 22 1737 Jean, Daughter of Thomas Awert and Elimon his Wife
Octob 27 1737 Thomas, Son of Thomas Hollins & his Wife
Febry. 2 1737 Henrietta Daughter of Joseph Wragg & Judith his Wife
do 10 1737 Francis Bathurst Son of Francis Piercey & Mary his Wife
do. 15 1737 John Son of John Cleland and Mary his Wife
do. 24 1737 Son of Peter Birol and Sarah his Wife
do. 24 1737 Elizabeth, Daughter of William Day and Anne his Wife
[98] Christning's continued
March 4 1737 Anne, Daughter of John Beswicke & Silence his Wife
17 1737 Anne, Daughter of William Stone & Anne his Wife
24 1737 Sarah Daughter of George De la Pierre & Elizabeth his Wife
1738 29 1738 Anne, Daughter of Christopr Hopkins and Anne his Wife
April 3 1738 Mary, Daughter of Thomas Honahan and Rose his Wife
do 4 1738 William, Son of Elizabeth Lindsey Illegitimate was Baptized
do. 5 1738 Francis, Daughter of John Miller and Julia his Wife
do. 16 1738 John, Son of William Mc.kenzie and Sarah his Wife
do 25. 1738 Mary, Daughter of William Harvey & Sarah his Wife
May 3 1738 Susannah, Daughter of George Tabart & Rebecca his Wife
5 1738 Peter, Son of Thomas Goodman and Barbara his Wife
24 1738 Mary Hester, Daughter of Archibald Young & Martha his Wife
26 1738 William, Son of John Dunn & Katherine his Wife
June 7 1738 Joseph, Son of Joseph Griffith, and Mary his Wife
July 28 1738 John, Son of Charles Fanshawe & Elizabeth his Wife
Novemr 20 1737 Thomas, Son of Thomas Gadsden and Alice his Wife
1738
July 31 1738 Anne, Daughter of Thomas Douglas and Mary his Wife
Augut 11 1738 Thomas, Son of Thomas Cooper & Margaret Magdalen his Wife
Septr. 15 1738 Susannah, Bassett, a free Negro Girl born in Bermudas was Baptized
Sarah, Daughter of John Lewis Poyas & Susannah his Wife
ditto 23 1738 Priscilla, Daughter of Samuel Glazier & Sarah Louisa his Wife

Octob^r^. 18 1738 William, Son of Richard Mason & Margaret his Wife
ditto d^o^. 1738 William, Son of Richard Floyd and Maryanne his Wife
1730
Septem^r^. 26 1730 Daniel, Son of Daniel Bourget & Susanna his Wife
1737
Janu^ry^. 25 1737 Rachel, Daughter of Daniel Bourget & Susanna his Wife
1738
May 23 1738 Mary Ester Daughter of Archibald Young & Martha his Wife
Novemb: 10 1738 Mary the Daughter of James Osmond and Mary his Wife
Decemb^r^: 8 1738 Henry Christopher, Son of Christopher Row and Margaret his Wife
15 1738 John, Son of Captn. Henry Scott (of the Seaford Man of Warr) & Elizabeth his Wife
15 1738 Sarah, Daughter of John Sharp and Deborah his Wife

Christnings continued [99]

Decemb 28 1738 Henry Son of John Scott and Mary his Wife was Baptized
January 3 1738 Martha, Daughter of James Michie and Martha his Wife
17 1738 Lydia, Daughter of John Beckman & Ruth his Wife
17 1738 Anne, Daughter of Charles Sheppard and Anne his Wife
30 1738 James, Son of John Watson and Abigal his Wife
Febru^y^ 21 1738 Thomas, Son of James Reid & Dorothy his Wife
March 4 1738 Elizabeth Daughter of John Daniel & his Wife
16 1738 Isaac, Son of Jacob Motte and Elizabeth his Wife
23 1738 John, Son of John Brathwaite and Silvia his Wife
April 4 1739 Anne Daughter of Jordan Roche & Rebecca his Wife
11 1739 Mary, Daughter of George Cocker and Elinor his wife
26 1739 William, Son of William Woodrope and Elizabeth his wife
May 9 1739 Ellinor, Daughter of George Austin and Anne his Wife
9 1739 John Brand, Son of Peter Jeys and Mary his Wife
June 1st. 1739 William Son of William Dean and Anne his Wife
8 1739 Elizabeth Daughter of John Owen and Meriam his Wife
15 1739 Thomas, Son of Henry Harramon and Mary his Wife

July 3 1739 Richard, Son of Richard Lampart and Mary his Wife
5 1739 Anne, Daughter of David Mallice & Anne Harris
13 1739 Anne, Daughter of George Vane & Sarah his Wife
27 1739 Nathaniel, Son of Benj[a]. Clifford & Sarah his Wife
27 1739 Elizabeth Ann Daughter of Maurice Lewis & Jean his Wife
August 1 1739 Mary, Daughter of Robert Collis and Elizabeth his Wife
Novemb. 14 1739 Anne, Daughter of Barshabah Tattle
14 1739 Sarah Charlot Daughter of Rebecca Tattle
14 1739 Rice Price, Son of Rice Price and Jane his Wife
14 1739 Joseph Taylor, Son of William Christiana Williamson & Sophia his Wife
28 1739 Charles, Son of Charles Patchelbel and Hannah his Wife
Decemb. 18 1739 John, Son of John Hollybush and Sarah his Wife
25 1739 Robert, Son of John Remington and Margaret his Wife
26 1739 Daughter of Peter Horry and Martha his Wife
Januy. 1st 1739 Mary the Daughter of William Stone and Anne his Wife

[100] Christnings continued

1739
Decembr 25 Robert the Son of John Remington & Margaret his Wife was Baptized
26 Daughter of Peter Horry and Martha his Wife, do—
Janury: 1st. Mary the Daughter of William Stone and Anne his Wife was Baptized
11 William the Son of William Pinckney and Ruth his Wife
30 Peter the Son of Robert Johns and Anne his Wife
Februy: 27 Josias the Son of Thomas Tatnell and Elizabeth his Wife
March 5 John the Son of Archbald Young and Martha his Wife
5 Walay Edmund, the Son of Charles Sheppard and Anne his Wife
14 Mary the Daughter of Jacob Motte and Elizabeth his Wife
April 2 John the Son of James Howell and Elizabeth his Wife
2 Mary the Daughter of Martin Coleman and Mary Ann his Wife
23 Thomas Loughton Smith Son of Benj[n]: Smith & was Baptized
24 Mary the Daughter of Daniel Wood and Mary his Wife was Baptized
25 William the Son of William Harris and Sarah his Wife
25 David the Son of John Mackall & Martha his Wife

May 23 Mary the Daughter of William Comer & Mary his Wife
23 Benjamin, the Son of John Guerard & Elizabeth his wife was Baptized
23 John, the Son of John Guerard & Elizabeth his Wife } Ditto
23 David, the Son of John Guerard & Elizabeth his Wife }
27 John, the Son of Peter Oliver and Margaret his Wife was Baptized

August 8 William, Son of William Yeomans & Mary his Wife was Baptized—

1740

Septemr. 12 Ann, Daughter of Samuel Prioleau & Providence his Wife was Baptized.—

Octob: 3d Ann, Daughter of Cornelius Wren & Hester his Wife, was Baptized.—

Novemr. 5 James Watsone Son of John Watsone & Abigail his Wife, was Baptized—
12 Sarah Daughter of Samuel Legen & Mary his Wife was Baptized
14 Abraham Son of Peter Shaw & Martha his Wife was Baptized

Decemr. 3d. William, Son of John Miller & Julia his Wife was Baptized
do: Thomas, Son of Dr: John Moultrie & Lucrecia his Wife was Baptized
do: Sarah, Daughter of Capt John Colcock & Deborah his Wife, was Baptized
10 Teresa Elizabeth, Daughter of William Trueman & Elizabeth his Wife was Baptized
31 Joseph, the Son of John Scott and Mary his Wife, was Baptized

January 9 Christian the Daughter of John Robertson & Margret his Wife was Baptized
14 Rebecca, the Daughter of Jordan Roche & Rebecca his Wife was Baptized

Christning's continued [101]

1740.

January 16 Robert, the Son of Robert Harvey & Mary his Wife was Baptized

Ditto 21 William, Son of Thomas Crosthwaite & Mary his Wife was Baptized

Ditto do. Elizabeth, Daughter of James Withers & Mary his Wife, was Baptized

Ditto 24 Rebecca the Daughter of William Ridggill & Rebecca his Wife was Baptized privately——

Februry: 4 Elizabeth, the Daughter of Capt. James Sutherland & Mary his Wife was Baptized

Ditto 4 Joseph, the Son of Antonio Perare & Hanah his Wife, was Baptized

Ditto 4 Hanah, the Daughter of William Passwater & Hanah his Wife, was Baptized—

Ditto 18 Richard, the Son of Richard Howard & Sarah his Wife was Baptized

March 13 John, the Supposed Son of Francis Thompson & Mary Slater was Baptized——

1741

April 27 William, the Son of William Farrow and Rachel his Wife was Baptized

May 13 Cornelia Amorentia, Daughter of Daniel Welchuyson & Catherine his Wife was Baptiz'd

Augut. 2 Susannah Charlotte the illegitimate Daughter of Francis Holmes by Susannah Monroe was Baptized

10 Thomas, the Son of Thomas Heathey & Susannah his Wife, Baptiz'd.

24 Thomas the Son of John Hollybush & Sarah his Wife was Baptized—

Octob. 23 Susannah the Daughter of Thomas Lee & Mary his Wife was Baptized.—

23 Jane Carolina, the Daughter of John Wathen & Ann his Wife was Baptized

23 John (Thompson) the Son of John Thompson & Anne his Wife was Baptized

Novemr. 5 Richard, the Son of Richard Shubrick & Elizabeth his Wife was Baptized

8 William Thomas Son of William Williamson & his Wife was Baptized

27 Sarah the Daughter of William Mc.Carty & Maryann his Wife was Baptized

Decemr. 2 Mary the Daughter of Zech: Brazier & Maryann his Wife was Baptized

Januy. 1 George the Son of George Austin & Anne his Wife, was Baptized

2 Sarah the Daughter of Dr. John Lining & Sarah his Wife was Baptized

8 Rice Price Son of Rice Price & Jane his Wife was Baptizd.

22 Ann the Daughter of John Nightingale & Ann his Wife was Baptized

20 William the son of William Stone & Ann his Wife was Baptized

29 Hannah the Daughter of Jeremy: Leacroft & Ann his Wife was Baptized

Februy. 3 Mary Elizabeth ye Daughter of Alexr. Dingwell & Mary his Wife was Baptized

28 Mary, the Daughter of George Vane & Sarah his Wife was Baptized

March 18 John the Supposed Son of Thomas Buckle by Kathrine Bird was Baptiz[d]

1742

April 7 Joseph the Son of Dr. John Dewicke & Anne his Wife was Baptized

9 William George, Son of George Avery & Mary his Wife was Baptized

14 Mary, the Daughter of Robert Harvey & Mary his Wife, was Baptized

15 Benjamin the Son of William Hare & his Wife, was Baptiz'd

May 14 Benjamin the Son of Benja[n]. Burnham & Ann his Wife, was Baptized

[102] Christnings continued

1742

May 26 Martha Ladson was Baptized being about 22 years old.

26 Ann Bassett was Baptized being about 19 years old

June 23 William the Son of John Scott & Mary his Wife was Baptized

25 William the Son of William Farrow & Rachael his Wife was Baptized

25 Isaac Amiand the Son of Childermus Croft & Kather[n]: his Wife was Baptiz'd

July 26 Alexander the Son of Doctor John Moultrie & Lucrece his Wife was privately Baptized by Commissary Garden——

Augu[t]—. 4 Jane, the Daughter of John Townsend & Hannah his Wife was Baptized

6 Ann the Daughter of Richard Power & Esther his Wife, was Baptized

6 Elizabeth Bee was Baptized near 18 years of Age

6 Elizabeth Poole was Baptized being 28 years of Age

Sept[r]. 6 Cooper **Dicker**, the Son of Benja[n]: Whitaker Esq[r], & Saran his Wife was Baptized

Grace the Daughter of Charles Codner & Ann his Wife was Baptized 11th Augu[t]. 1742

Augu[t]. 24 Elizabeth, the Daughter of Will[m]: Smith & Ann his Wife was Baptized

Sept[r]. 29 William Brounchurst, the Son of Hillman Hutchins & Sarah his Wife was then Baptized—

Octob. 1 Thomas, the Son of Thomas Honyhorn & Sarah his Wife was Baptized—

July 1 Mary, the Daughter of William Harris & Sarah his Wife was Baptized

Octob. 1 Edward the Son of Griffith Bullard & Hephzi-beh his Wife was Baptized

6 Mary the Daughter of William Harris & Sarah his Wife was receiv'd into the Congregation of Christ's Flock

15 John a negro man of about 24 years of Age belonging to Mr. Benjamin D' harriette merchant was Baptized

22 Sarah, the Daughter of Dr. John Rutlidge & Sarah his Wife was Baptizd:

Novemr. 3 Martha, the Daughter of Jacob Motte and Elizabeth his Wife was Baptized

26 Samuel the Son of Samuel Prioleau & Providence his Wife was Baptized.

Decemb: 8 Mary, the Daughter of William Smith & Elizabeth his Wife was Baptized by Commissy Garden.

10 Joseph the Son of Joseph Norton & Mary his Wife was privately Baptized by the Revd. Mr. Mc:gillchrist.

14 Margret the Daughter of John Berksdale & Ann his Wife was privately Baptiz'd ℘ Do

28 Samuel the Son of William Smith & Elizabeth his Wife was Publickly Baptized by the Reverend Commissary Garden

29 Elizabeth the Daughter of Henry St. Martin & Philipine his Wife was Baptized.—

Januy. 5 Martha Isabell the Daughter of James Wright Esqr. & Sarah his Wife was Baptized

9 Thomas the Son of Jordan Roche & Rebecca his Wife was Baptized by the Commissary

Feby: 13 Mary the Daughter of Joseph Hutchins & Cath'rine his Wife was privately Baptized by the Reverend Mr. Wm Mc.gillchrist.

Feby 11 William the Son of Richard Lamport & Mary his Wife was privately Baptized by the Reverend Mr. Mc.gillchrist—

Christnings continued [103]

1742

Februy 24 Esther the Daughter of William Boone & Jane his Wife was Baptized.

March 4 Peter the Son of John Bonnetheau & Mary his Wife was Baptized by the Revd. Commissary Garden

March 5 Sarah the Daughter of John Smith and Sarah his Wife was privately Baptized, by the Reverend mr. William Mc:gillchrist.—

Ditto 9 Hannah the Daughter of Joseph Norton and Mary his Wife was privately Baptized by the Reverend Mr. William Mc:gillchrist.—

January 25 Mary the Daughter of Doctor John Lining and Sarah his Wife was privately Baptized by the Reverend Mr. William Mc.-gillchrist—

March 27 Elinor the Daughter of William Watkins and Rachel his Wife was privately Baptized by the Revd Mr. Garden Commissary

1743

April 8 Thomas the Son of James Howell & Elizabeth his Wife was Baptized.

8 John the Son of John Francis & Anne his wife was privately Baptized by the Revd. Mr. Garden Commissary.

22 Joseph the Son of Alexr. Dingwell & Mary his Wife was privately Baptized by the Revd Mr McGillchrist.

May 6 Margaret the Daughter of John Remington & Margaret his Wife was privately Baptiz'd

11 Elizabeth the Daughter of William Comer & Mary his Wife was publickly Baptized—

12 Peter, the Son of Peter Shaw and Martha his Wife, was Publickly Baptized

13 Joseph the Son of Thomas Lee and Mary his Wife, was Publickly Baptized

8 William the Supposed Son of William Laws by Mary Howard was privately Baptized by the Reverend Mr. William Mc.Gillchrist.

17 Anne the Supposed Daughter of John Swain by Mary Haddock was privately baptized by the Reverend Mr. William .Mc.Gillchrist—

20 Anne the Daughter of John Craston & Julia his Wife was privately Baptized by the Rev.d Mr. Mc.Gillchrist—

12 Elizabeth the Daughter of Peter Laurens and Lydia his wife was privately Baptized by the Reverend Mr. Mc. Gillchrist—

26 Elizabeth the Daughter of James Osmond & Mary his Wife was privately Baptized by the Reverend Mr. William Mc.Gillchrist

June 15 Thomas the Son of Benjamin Burnham & Anne his Wife was Baptized.

17 John the Son of Jacob Fidling & Rebecca his Wife was Publickly Baptized—

July 1 Charles Thomas the Son of John Beckman & Ruth his Wife was Publickly Baptized

6 Elizabeth Esther Bellinger, the Daughter of John Watsone and Abigail his Wife was publickly Baptized by the Reverend Mr. Alexander Garden Commissary.—

10 Samuel Royer and Hannah, Two Twins of Dr: Henry Dewicke and Anne his Wife was privately Baptized by the Reverend Mr. William Mc.Gillchrist—

31 Thomas the Son of Roger Jones and Phebe his Wife, was privately Baptized by the Reverend Mr. William Mc:Gillchrist—

August 9 Joseph, the Son of Cornelius Rand and Esther his Wife was privately Baptized by the Reverend Mr. William Mc.Gillchrist.—

17 Charles, the son of Charles Peele and Jane his Wife was Publickly Baptized.

Septemr. 2 John the Son of Robert Harvey & Mary his Wife was Publickly Baptized—

ditto 2 John the Son of John Hume & his Wife was Publicly Baptized

August 18 Catherine Keith, Daughter of Hugh Anderson and Elizabeth his Wife was privately Baptized by the Revd. Mr. Mc.gilchrist

[104] Christnings continued

1743

Octob 21 William the Son of Edward Richardson & Elizabeth his Wife was Publickly Baptized by the Reverend Alexander Garden Commissary

26 Joseph the Son of George Avery & Mary his Wife was publickly Baptized ℘ ditto

28 Evelin the Daughter of Daniel & Mary Pepper, was publickly Baptized ℘ ditto

28 Robert the Son of Richard & and Sarah Howard, was publickly Baptized ℘ ditto

Decemr. 8 William the Son of John Bee and Martha his Wife was Baptized by the Reverd.Mr. Mc.gilchrist privately—

28 Adam the Son of Henrick & Margaret Metz was Publickly Baptizd. ℘ Mr. Garden

Januy. 15 Anne the Daughter of Robert & Mary Wright was Baptized by Mr. Mcgilchrist

25 John the Son of Benjamin & Anne Smith was Publickly Baptized ℘ ·ditto

Febry.. 8 Elizabeth the Daughter of William & Rachael Farrow was Baptizd. ℘ ditto

18 Mary the Daughter of William Stone & Anne his Wife was privately Baptized by the Revrd. Mr. Alexander Garden Commissary

25 Elizabeth the Daughter of John Lancaster and Mary his Wife was privately Baptized by the Reverend Mr. Mc.-gilchrist.

29 Mary the Daughter of John Houghton & Mary his Wife was Baptized by Mr. McGilchrist—

Marc. 2d Amey the Daughter of Jacob Motte Esqr & Elizabeth his Wife was publickly Baptized by the Revd. Mr. Garden

7 Elizabeth the Daughter of James Lesesne and Sarah his Wife was publickly Baptized by the Revd. Mr. Mc.gilchrist

9 John the Son of Henry Middleton and Mary his Wife was publickly Baptized by the Revd. Mr. Garden

16 Richard the Son of John Guerard and his Wife, was
1744 was publicly Baptized by the Revd. Mr. Mc gilchrist.
April 12 Thomas the Son of John & Lucy Hanson was Publickly Baptized by the Revd. Mr McGilchrist..........
..........27 Ann the Daughter of James Smith & Elizabeth his wife was ....Publickly Baptized by the Revd Mr Garden..........
May 13 Margaret the Daughter of Peter Oliver and Margaret his Wife was Publickly Baptized by the Revd Mr McGilchrist......
Feby. 21 Mary the Daughter of Henry Harramond & Eliza his Wife was Publickly Baptized by the Revd Mr Garden - -
May 18 Wm Ward Son of Thomas & Mary Croswaite & Mary Croswaite was Publickly Baptized by ye Revd Mr McGilchrist

1744 Christnings Continued [105]

June - -1 Mary Daughter of Thomas Smith & Mary his Wife was ....Privately Baptized by the Revd Mr McGilchrist..........
ditto. 8 Mary Daughter of Thos & Martha Ryebout was Publickly Baptized by Mr. McGilchrist
ditto 23 Susanah Daughter of Elisha & Catherine Poinset was Baptized
July 4 Henry the Son of Thomas & Sarah Frankland was Publy Baptized by
Augt 3 Sarah Daughter of James & Sarah Wright was Baptized by
11 Sarah Daughter of George & Sarah Vane was Privately Baptized
15 Samuel Jeremiah Son of Michall (& Margeret Row) Christopeth was Baptized -
17 Elizabeth Daughter of Benjamin & Anne Burnham was Baptized-
Septr. 5 John the son of John & Deborah Colcock was Baptized - -
12 John the son of William & Anne Moat was Baptized
26. Mary Anne the Daughter of Michall & Barbarah South was Baptized
Octor 3 Sarah the Daughter of John & Martha McCall was Baptized
5 Anne the Daughter of William & Elizabeth Smith was Baptized
5 Moses Heasel son of Jos & Anjulinah Semor was Privately Baptized by G
3 Rebeckah Daughter of Thomas & Mary Lee was Baptized
3 Rebeckah Daughter of William & Mary Gay was Baptized
24 Elizabeth Harvy Daughter of Frances & Mary Bremar was Baptized
Decr 5 Thomas the Son of Jacob & Rebeckah Fidling was Baptized
13 Sarah the Daughter of Jeremiah & Anne LeCraft[1] was Baptized
James the Son of
Jany 1 Daniel the Son of John & Susanah Crocket was Baptized

[1] Badly blurred, but looks like "LeCraft."

23 William the Son of John & Margeret Remington was Baptized
Feby 1 Isabella the Daughter of John & Susannah Hume was Baptized
6 Mary Magdalen Daughter of Samuel & Providence Prioleau was Baptized
Mar 7 John the Son of George Avery & Mary his Wife was Baptized
22 Martha the Daughter of Richard & Mary Ackerman Baptized
1745
April 24 John the Son of Samuel & Mary Leger was Baptized
11 Samuel the Son of Samuel & Jane Lacey was Baptized
20 John the Son of James & Sarah Atkins was Baptized
May 1 Mary the Daughter William & Martha Edwards was Baptized
15 Francis the Son of James & Mary Withers was Baptized
15 Sarah the Daughter of James & Mary Withers was Baptized
15 Mary the Daughter of George & Hannah Newcomb was Baptized
29 Charlotte the Daughter of Jacob & Elizabeth Motte was Baptized
June 18 Mary Daughter of James & Martha Michie was Baptized
.... by The Revd Mr Quincey.................. ....
July 3 William the Son of Richard & Hester Powers was Baptized
[106] Mo. day yr Christnings Continued
Febry.. 24 1744 William the Son of William & Elizabeth Woodhouse was Baptized by the Revd. Mr. Alexr Garden
July 17th 1745 Ann the Daughter of John & Martha Coleman was Baptized—
Septr. 13th 1745 Ann the Daughter of William & Rachel Farrowe was Baptized—
Octr. 4th 1745 Rodger the son of Thomas & Sarah Smith was Baptized——
Octr.. 16th 1745 John Houghton the Son of Charles & Ann Sheppard was Baptized——
Octr 16. 1745 Charles the son of Charles & Ann Sheppard was Baptized—
Octr 16. 1745 Mary Christiana the Daughter of Willm. & Sarah Hopton was Baptizd
Septr. 26 1736 Martha the Daughter of William & Mary Coomer was Baptized—
Janry. 16 1744 Sarah the Daughter of William & Mary Coomer was Baptized——
Janry 3d 1745 Mary the Daughter of William & Ann Stone was Baptized—
Janry 3d 1745 Christian the Daughter of Willm: & Ann Stone was Baptized———

Janry 10h 1745 Thomas the Son of Thomas & Mary Doughty was Baptized——

Janry 17 1745 John the son of Philip Jacob & Mary Elizabeth Ernst was Baptized

Janry 17 1745 Mary Elizabeth, the Daughter of Mark & Rachel Smith was Baptd

Feb:ry. 21 1745 Henrietta, the Daughter of Henry & Eliza: Harramond was Baptiz'd

March 5th. 1745 Catharine, the Daughter of John & Deborah Colcock was Baptized

March 27 1746 Sophia Maria Henrietta, the Daughter of John & Susannah ———— Crokatt was Baptized. pr Revd. Mr Garden ————

March 15th 1745/6 Sarah, the Daughter of William & Marian Kirk was Baptized

April.. 9t 1746 Sarah, the Daughter of Hillman and Sarah Hutchins was Baptiz'd

April 16t: 1746 John William a Negroe, was Baptized. pr Revd Mr Garden

April 18. 1746.. Childermas, the son of John & Catherine Harvey was Baptized pr. Mr Garden

April 25 1746 Henry, the Son of Peter & Lydia Laurens was Baptized ———— by the Revd. Mr Betham

April 30t 1746 Anne, the Daughter of Benjamin & Anne Smith was ———— Baptized by the Revd Mr. Garden

May 2d. 1746 Timothy, the Son of Timothy & Mary Briton was ———— Baptized by the Revd Mr Garden

May 16 1746 Charles Cotesworth, the Son of Charles & Elizabeth ———— Pinckney was Baptized by the Revd Mr Garden ————

May 28 1746 James the Son of James & Sarah Lessene was Batized by the ———— Revd. Mr. Betham ————

June 28 1746 Mary the Daughter of Meller & Mary St John was privately ———— Baptized ꝑ. do:

July 2d 1746 Mary the Daughter of Peter & Elizabeth Sanders was ———— Baptized by the Revd Mr Betham

July 3d. .1746 Isaac Walker, son of Isaac & Elizabeth Lesesne was ——— ——— Baptized by the Revd Mr Robt Betham- ————

Christnings Continued [107]

1746 29 June Nathaniel, Son of Henry & Charlotte Izard was privately ———— Baptized by the Revd. Mr Robt Betham ————

1746 25 June Gabriel, Son of John & Mary Bounetheau was Baptized ———— by the Revd MrRobt Betham ————

1746 18 July Susannah, Daugher of Edward & Elizabeth Richardson was ———— Baptized by the Rev[d]. Mr Robt. Betham——

1746 25 July Catherine, Daughter of John & Ruth Beekman was ——— Baptized by the Rev[d] Mr Robt Betham————

1746 25 July Robert, Son of James Wright Esq[r] & Sarah his Wife was———— Baptized by the Rev[d]. Mr Rob[t] Betham————

1746 30 July James, Son of Francis & Mary Clarke was Baptized by y[e] Same

1746 4th. Aug[t]. Mary, Daughter of Benjamin & Anne Smith was privately ———— Baptized by Rev[d]. Mr Betham

1746 .27th Aug[t]. Richard, Son of Richard & Esther Powers was Baptized by d[o]:

—— — ——— Hepsibah, Daugh[r] of Thomas & Bulah Rose was Baptized by d[o]:

1746 22[d] May Elizabeth, Daughter of William & Margaret Shepard was ———— privately Baptized by the Rev[d] Mr Betham ————

1746 12th Sept[r]. Isaac, Son of John & Marian Guerard was privately Baptized by do:

1746 5th. Sept[r]. David Thomas, Son of William & Grace Roper was publickly —— —— Baptized by the Rev[d]: Mr: Betham ————

1746 25 Oct[r]: William, Son of William George Freeman & Jane his Wife was privately Baptized by the Rev[d]. Mr Betham ———

1746 25 Oct[r]: Samuel Son of Samuel Carne & Elizabeth his Wife was privately Baptized by the Rev[d]. Mr Rob[t] Betham ————

1746 26 Nov[r] James Son of John & Martha McCall was publickly Baptized by the Rev[d]: Mr Rob[t] Betham ————

1724|5 9th Jan[ry] Estienne, fils D'Estienne et de Marie Mounier éte Baptizé par Mons[r]. Poudrou Ministre de Santee —

1727 5th D'Avril Jean Glaude, fils D'Estienne et de Marie Mounier éte Baptizé par Mons[r]. Delapierre Ministre de S[t] Dennis.

1746 13th: Feb[ry]: Margaret, Daughter of Kenneth Michie & Mary his wife. was publickly baptized by the Rev[d]. Mr Robt Betham

1746 14 Feb[ry] Morreau, Son of Morreau Sarracen & Elizabeth his Wife was privately baptized by the Rev[d] Mr Robert Betham

1746 17th Feb[ry]: Martha, Daughter of Thomas Weaver and Martha his Wife was privately baptized by y[e] Rev[d]. Mr. Rob[t] Betham——

1746 13 Feb[ry] Mary, Daughter of Maurice & Mary Keating was privately Baptized by y[e] Rev[d] Mr Rob[t] Betham ————

do. . 18 Feb[y] Elizabeth Ann, Daughter of Peter & Ann Timothy was privately Baptized by Mr Rob[t] Betham ————

[108] Christnings

1746 Jan[ry]: 21. Alexander & Ann Sharpe Son & Daughter of Colen & Sarah Sharpe were privately Baptized by the Rev[d]. Mr Rob[t] Betham

1746 Sept 17th: George, Son of George & Mary Avery was privately Baptized by d[o]:

1746 Nov^r: 27 Ashby, Son of Thomas & Ann Easton was privately Baptized by d^o

1746 Mar 1 Elizabeth, Daughter of Frederick & Elizabeth Strubel was privately Baptized by d^o: ——————

1746 Mar 2^d James, Son of John & Sarah Lining was priv: baptized by d^o:

—————— 7th: Providence, Daughter of John Paul Grimke & Ann his Wife was privately baptized by the Rev^d: Mr Robert: Betham

—————— 21st: James, Son of John & Susannah Hume, was priv baptized by d^o:

1747 Mar 25th: Charlotte, Daughter of Thomas & Mary Roybould was publickly baptized by ditto ——————

1746 Febr^y 18 William, son of William & Marian Kirk was priv: Baptized

1746 Febr^y 16 Elizabeth, Daught^r. of Robt. & Mary Harvey was priv Bap^d:

1747 April 6th Elizabeth Ann, Daug^r: of Thomas & Anne Greene was priv Baptized

1747 April 12th: William, Son of John & Abigail Watsone was priv Bapt^d.

1746 Mar 9 Elizabeth, Daughter of Samuel & Mary Leger was Bapt^d.

1747 May 6 Richard, Son of Richard & Mary Peak was Baptized

1747 May 8 William, Son of Thomas & Mary Doughty was Baptized

1747 May 13 Elizabeth, Daughter of Edward & Martha Fenwicke was Baptized

1747 May 15 Jane, Daughter of Hugh & Ann Anderson was Baptized

1747 June 21st Roger & Rebeccah } Twins, Son & Daughter of John & Sarah Champneys was Baptized by the Rev^d. Mr Alexander Garden

June 24^h. George Lucas, Son of Charles & Elizabeth Pinckney was privately Baptized by the Rev^d. Mr Alex^r Garden

1747 April 25 Jane, Daught^r. of Roger & Jane Saunders was baptized

1747 July. 1st. Mary, Daught^r. of Benj^a: & Anne Burnham was baptized

..................................10 Sarah, Daugh^t. of Samuel & Hannah Lacey was baptized

..................................29 Margaret, Daugh^t of William & Jane Duthy was baptized

..........................Augt. 12 Elizabeth Daught^r. of Henry & Elizabeth Harramond was Baptized

..........................Augt. 31 Charlotte, Daughter of Daniel & Catherine Welshuysen was Baptized ——

..................Septem^r 4th. Susannah Elizabeth, Daughter of George & Sarah Vane was Baptized.

1747. Christnings [109]

October 2^d Charlotte, Daug^r; of Henry & Charlotte Izard was Baptized

Octr.... 2d Phillis, a Negroe of the sd Henry Izard was also Baptized & & Charlotte Letour Charlotte Izard & Henry Izard were Sponsors

November 18 Catherine Daugr. of James & Mary Kirkwood was Baptized

November 18th Rebecca, Daugr. of Jacob & Elizabeth Motte was Baptized

Novemr. 18th. Catherine, Daugr: of William & Margaret Shepard, was privately Baptized

Novemr 27. Sophia, Daughter of the Revd. Mr John Snow by Sophia his Wife was Baptized by the sd. Mr Snow.

Novemr 30 James Samuel, Son of Peter & Margaret Olivier was publickly Baptized by the Revd. Mr Quincy.

Decemr 11th: Elizabeth, Daughtr of Elias & Mary Snell was Baptized by the Reverend Mr John Snow.

Novem 28 George Hall, Son of Hall & Mary Richardson was privately Baptized by the Revd. Mr. Quincey.

Decem 16th Sophia Snow, Daughter of the Revd. Mr. John Snow by Sophia his Wife was received into the Congregation of Christs Flock by the Revd: Mr. Alexr: Garden. The Revd: Mr. Saml Quincy Mrs: Elizabeth Motte Miss Margt. Glen being Sponsors.

October 2d. Tucker, son of William & Sarah Harris was Baptized

Novr: 8th Richard, Son of Richard & Susannah Butler was Baptiz'd

Decem 16th. Thomas, Son of William & Rachael Farroe was Baptized

Decem 17th Ruth, Daughter of Alexr. & Jane Hext was privately Baptized

Janry 6th. James Son of James Wright Esqr by Sarah his Wife was publickly Baptized—

1747

Octr... 14 Thomas, Son of John & Susannah Crokatt was baptized.

Janry 14 Mary Ann, Daughter of Thomas & Sarah Newton was Baptized by the Revd. Mr. Quincey

1747 Novr... 20 Elizabeth, Daughter of Frederick & Rose Holzendorf was Baptized by the Revd. Mr. Fras Guichard

Janry 22 William Son of Peter & Mary Edwards was Baptized
1747 Septr 6. Jane Daughter of George & Hannah Duckett was Baptized
Janry 15 David, Son of David & Katherine Caw was Baptized
17th William, Son of Peter & Mary Cattel was Baptized.
1747 Janry 1st William, Son of Thomas & Mary Lee was Baptized
} by Mr. Garden

Febry. 5th= Amee, Daughter of Thomas & Ann Easton was priv: Baptd. by the Revd Mr Quincey

1747 October Esther Daughter of Richd: & Esther Power, was pub: Baptizd-

1745——Jordan, Son of Jordan & Rebecca Roche was Baptized by the Revd. Mr Durant Min: of Christ Church Parish

1747 Febry... 17, John, Son of Samuel & Sarah Perkins was Baptized

[110] Christnings

1747 Febry: 26th Luke, Son of Luke & Sarah Stoutenburgh was pub: Baptd.

do.. do.. 27 Edward, Son of John & Grace Fitzgerald was priv: Baptd:

do. March 2d. Martha, Daughter of Samuel & Providence Prioleau was priv: Baptized by the Revd. Mr A: Garden—

do March. 15th Jane McLaughlan, Dr: of Daniel & Catherine Roulain was Baptized—

do Decemr 1st. Charles, Son of George & Mary Avery was Baptized—

do. March.. 9 Anthony, Son of Levinus & Elizabeth Van Schaik was Bap:

1748 April 30 Elizabeth, Daughter of John & Sarah Nelson was Bap:

1747/8 Mar. 16 Mary, Daughtr. of Frederick and Francis Grienzweig was Bapd:

1748 May.. 4 Martha, Daughtr. of Lionel & Martha Chalmers was Baptiz'd

1748 June.. 3 Ann Daughter of John & Catherine Harvey was Baptized.

1748 June 12 Elizabeth, Daughter of Thomas & Elizabeth Poole was Baptized

1748 July 23 Thomas Son of Thomas & Sarah Smith was Baptized.
Sarah Daughtr. of John & Sarah Wheeler was Baptized

1748 Augt- 4 Susannah Daughtr. of Chas: Jacob & Susannah Pischard was Baptized by the Revd- Mr. Guishard

1748 Septr. 21st Jacob, Son of John & Margaret Remington was privately baptized by the Revd Mr Alexr. Garden

1748 Septr. 22 William, Son of William & Ann Cattell was Baptiz'd

1748 Octr. 12 Robert, Son of Richard & Susannah Muncreef was baptized

1747/8 Janry. 10th Marian, Daughter of Joseph & Hannah Cook was baptized

1748 Septr 24 Francis, Son of Francis & Anne Roche was Baptized

1748 Decr 9 John, Son of John & Susannah Crokatt was Baptized

1748 Decr 7th Mary, Daughter of Elisha & Catherine Poinsett was Baptized
Jane, Daughter of Thomas & Sarah Shubrick was Baptiz'd
Thomas, Son of Thomas & Sarah Shubrick was Baptiz'd

1748 Octr 28 Robert, Son of Robert & Ann Waller was Baptized

1748 Decr: 7th. Jane, Daughter of Hugh & Ann Anderson was publickly Baptized by Mr: Garden jun;

1748 Janry 20 Henrietta Carroll Daughter of Charles & Easter Carroll was priv Baptized

1749 June 11 Then was Baptized Charles Cordes a Negroe Man, in the parish of St Johns by the Revd. Mr. ;Samuel Bowman, William Keith & Hester Dwight were Sponsors—

[111]

1749 Novem 3d Mary, Daughter of Thomas & Mary Doughty was Baptized by A. G

Novem 3d Mary, Daughter of John & Mary Corbett was Baptized

Decr. 3 Mary, Daughter of James & Penelope Edes was Baptized by Mr Bell Presbyterian Minister

Rachael, Daugr. of Hugh & Ann Anderson was Baptized by the Revd. Mr Garden.

Ann Stewart — On the twenty third day of March 1749/50 was Publickly Baptized by the Revd. Mr. Alexr Garden. Ann Daughter of Col. William Stewart & Ann his Wife

---

Corbett Freeman — On the 22d day of Febry 1749/50 was Baptized by the Revd Mr Alexr Garden Corbett Freeman Son of Willm. George Freeman & Jane his Wife—

Wm. Air. — On the 28th. day of April 1749 was Baptized by the Revd. Mr Alexr Garden. William Son of William & Ann Air—

Mary Air — On the 6th. day of April 1750. was Baptized Mary Daughter of William & Ann Air.——

John Bryan — On the 27th day of April 1750 was Baptized John the son of John & Sarah Marguerita Bryan ——

George Vane — On the 4th day of May 1750. was Baptized George the son of George & Sarah Vane.——————

Sush Snell Colleton — On the 13th. day of December 1750. was Baptized Susannah Snell the Posthumous Daughter of the Honble. John Colleton Esqr; by Susannah his Wife———

Thomas & John Caw — On the 25th. Day of January 1748, was Baptized Thomas, & on the 8th Day of January 1750. was Baptized John, the Sons of Doctr. David Caw by Catherine his Wife; The first by Mr Garden & the Latter by the Revd. Alexr. Keith

[112] Christnings

Ann McQueen — On the 15th. August 1750 Ann the Daughter of John and Ann McQueen was Baptized

---

Saxby Dymond — On the 1st. November 1750. Saxby son of George & Abigail Dymond was Baptized.

Elizabeth Pomer — On the 14th. November 1750. Elizabeth Daughter of Michael & Dorothy Pomer was Baptized

---

Elizabeth Churchwell	On the 14th November 1750. Elizabeth Daughter of John & Mary Churchwell was Baptized.
Thomas Hall	On the 30th. November 1750. Thomas Son of William & Susannah Hall was Baptized.
David Oliphant	On the day of 1750. David Son of David Oliphant & Hannah his Wife was Baptized
Charles Doughty	On the fourth day of April 1751. Charles Son of Thomas & Mary Doughty was Baptized priv—
Ann Harman	On the 31st- Day of May 1751 Ann Daughter of John Harman & Margaret his Wife was baptized
William Searug	On the 18th. Day of October 1751. William the Son of William & Mary Searug was Publickly Baptiz'd
Robert Rutherford	On the 20th. Day of December 1751 Robert Son of Robert & Isabella Rutherford was Baptized by Mr Keith
Elizabeth Remington	On the 13th Day of November 1751 Elizabeth Daughter of John & Margaret Remington was Baptized by Mr Keith
Mary— Deas—	On the 8th: Day of November 1751 Mary Daughter of David & Mary Deas was Baptized by Mr Keith
William Coomer	On the 3d- Day of March 1749. William Son of William & Mary Coomer was Baptized by Mr Keith
William Raper	On the 16th: Day of April 1750 William Raper an Adult Mulatto was publicly Baptized in St. Philips Church by the Revd- Mr Alexr Garden Rector ———

Christnings [113]

James Air	James Son of William & Ann Air was Baptized the day of 1752— ꝑ Mr Keith
Joel Poinsett	Joel Son of Elisha & Catherine Poinsett was Baptized the 13th- Day of March 1752 ———
Daniel Brunett	Daniel son of Esaie & Susannah Brunett was Baptized the 6th. November 1752 ———
Mary Campbell	Mary Daughter of William & Mary Campbell was Baptized the day of
William Oliphant	William Son of David Oliphant by Hannah his Wife was Baptized the
Philip Neyle	Philip Son of Sampson & Martha Neyle was Baptized the 14th February 1752 ꝑ Mr Keith
William Irving	William Son of James & Elizabeth Irving was Baptized the 11th. April 1751

Elizabeth James & Amelia Irving	Elizabeth Irving James Irving Amelia Irving } Son & Daughters of James & Elizabeth Irving were publickly Baptized on the 8th. day of May 1752. /
Mary Cooper	Mary Daughter of John & Mary Cooper was Baptized the 10th day of July 1752. /
John Doughty	John Son of Thomas & Mary Doughty was Baptized the 2d. November 1752 by the revd Mr Alexr Keith
Peter Stevenson	Peter Son of Charles & Mary Stevenson was Baptized the by the revd Mr A Garden
Mary Stevenson	Mary Daughter of Charles & Mary Stevenson was Baptized the by the revd Mr A Keith—
John Howell	John Son of John Howell & Elizabeth his Wife was Baptized the 20th= June 1753 by the Revd Mr A. G:
Martha Coomer [114]	Martha Daughter of William & Mary Coomer was privately Baptized the 7th March 1753 by the Revd. Mr Keith Christnings
Ann Corbett	On the 30th: day of October 1752 Ann the Daughter of John & Mary Corbett was Baptized ——
James Doughty	On the 29th. day of November 1753 James the son of Thomas & Mary Doughty was Baptized by the Revd Mr. Andrews Assistant to the Rector.
Mary Pickering	On the 13th. day of November 1753. Mary Daughter of Joseph & Ann Pickering was Baptized
Coll Mac Donald	On the 30th— day of November 1753. Coll MacDonald Son of Coll MacDonald & Ann Elizabeth his Wife was Baptized by the Revd. Mr Richard Clarke Rector
Ann Burnham	On the 15th Day of March 1754 Ann Daughter of Thomas & Mary Burnham was Baptized ℘ the Revd Mr Clarke
John Christian Henning	On the third day of April 1754. John Christian Henning Son of Philip & Catharina Henning was Baptized by the Revd. Mr Clarke
Henry Laurens	On the Nineteenth day of October 1753 Henry Laurens Son of Henry & Eleanor Laurens was Baptized by the Revd. Mr Alexr Garden then Rector &c
Ann Gibbes	On the day of January 1751/2 Ann, Daughter of William & Elizabeth Gibbes was Baptized by the Revd. Mr. Keith Assistt- to the Rector ————

William Gibbes	On the day of March 1754. William Son of William & Elizabeth Gibbes, was Baptized by the Rev[d]. M[r] Andrews Assist to the Rector
Ann Air	On the fifteenth Day of March 1754 Ann Daughter of William & Ann Air was Baptiz'd by M[r] Andrews
Sarah Smith	On the 31st day of October 1753, Sarah, Daughter of Thomas & Sarah Smith was Baptized by M[r]. Garden.
Thomas Cole	On the 5th day of June 1754, Thomas Cole an Adult mulatto was publickly Baptized by the Rev[d] M[r] Clarke
Paul Kolien	On the 7th. day of June 1754. Paul son of Michael and Elizabeth Kolien was baptized by the Rev[d] M[r] Clark

Christnings [115]

Harriot Clarkson	On the fifth day of January 1755. Harriot, Daughter of Thomas Clarkson & Elizabeth his Wife was privately Baptized by the Rev[d] M[r] Clarke Rector &c—
Jane Oliphant	On the day of November 1754, Jane Daughter of D[r] David Oliphant & Hannah his Wife was Baptized.
Mary Burrows	On the 16th :— day of April 1755 Mary Daughter of William Burrows & Mary his Wife was Baptized
Fra[s] Claudia Lewis Will[m]: Timothy	On the 20th. Day of June 1755—Frances Claudia & Lewis William the Daughter & Son of Peter Timothy & Ann his Wife were Baptized ————
Eleanor Linthwaite	On the 16th July 1755 Eleanor Daughter of Thomas & Ann Linthwaite was Baptized ———
Grissell & Louisa Susanna Wells	On the 18th May 1754 Grissel a Daughter and on the 30th day of November 1755. Louisa Susanna another Daughter, of Robert Wells & Mary his Wife were Baptized by the Rev[d]. M[r]. Cha[s] Lorimer, Ministr of the Scotch Meeting Entred at request of s[d] Rob[t]. Wells by J[no] Remington registr
Mary Dewar	On the 5th Day of April 1754 Mary the Daughter of Charles & Elizabeth Dewar was Baptized ℘ the Rev[d] M[r], Alexander Garden, Rector
Rob[t]. Dewar	On the 21st. Day May 1756 Robert Son of Charles and Elizabeth Dewer was Baptized ℘[r]. the Rev[d]. M[r]. Durant
Eliz[a] Dewar	On the 30th Day January 1758 Elizabeth Daughter of Charles & Elizabeth Dewar was Baptized ℘ the Rev[d]. M[r]. Clarke Rector
William Elfe	On the 1st. Day July 1754 William Son of Thomas & Rachel Elfe was Baptized ℘ the Rev[d], M[r]. Clarke

Eliza Elfe — On the 1 Day October 1756 Elizabeth Daughter of Thomas and Rachel Elfe was Baptized ꝑ the Revd Mr. Andrews

Hannah Elfe — On the 25th July 1758 Hannah Daughter of Thomas & Rachel Elfe was Baptized ꝑ the Revd Mr. Smith

[116] Christnings

Benjamin — Benjamin Godfrey Son of Benjamin & Mary Godfrey was Baptized ꝑ the Revd Mr. Clarke on the

Mary & — Mary Godfrey Daughter of Benja, & Mary Godfrey was Baptized ꝑ the Revd Mr.   On the

Robert Godfrey — Robert Richard Son of Benjamin & Mary Godfrey was Baptized ꝑ the Revd, Mr.   on the

---

John Pringle — John Pringle Son of Robert Pringle Esqr and his Wife was Baptized ꝑ the Revd, Mr.   26th October 1753

Robt Pringle — Robert Pringle S of Robert Pringle Esqr. & his Wife was Baptized ꝑ the Revd. Mr 16th December 1755

Eliza. Pringle — Elizabeth Pringle Daughter of Robt. Pringle Esqr & his Wife was Baptized ꝑ the Revd, Mr.   25 January 1758

Susannah Trezevant — Susannah Daughter of Daniel & Elizabeth Trezevant was Baptized ꝑ the Revd. Mr.

Martha Trezevant — Martha Daughter of Daniel & Elizabeth Trezevant was Baptized ꝑ the Revd. Mr.

Ann Simmons — Ann Daughter of Ebenezer & Jane Simmons was Baptized ꝑr. the Revd, Mr. Andrews Assistant to the Rector on ye.

James McQueen — James Son of John McQueen & Ann his Wife was Baptized ꝑ the Revd. Mr. Andrews Assistant to the Rector

Alexr. McQueen — Alexander Son of John McQueen & Ann his Wife was Baptized ꝑ the Revd, Mr, Andrews

George McQueen — George Son of John McQueen & Ann his Wife was Baptized ꝑ the Revd, Mr, Robert Smith Assistant to the Rector

---

William Brailsford — William Son of Samuel and Elizabeth Brailsford was Baptizd, ꝑ the Revd. Mr. Harrison of St James's Goose Creek on the 4 Day Novr. 1753

Christnings [117]

Ann Williams — On the   day of   175   Ann Daughter Mr. Robt Williams and Elizabeth his Wife was Baptised ꝑ Mr Andrews

Margaret Williams	On the Day of 175 Margaret Daughter of Mr Robt. Williams was Baptized ℘ Mr. Sergant
Elizabeth Williams	On the Day of 175 Elizabeth Daughter of Mr Robt. Williams was Baptized ℘ Mr. Clarke Rector
Wm Roper	On the 2d. Day of December 1758 William Son of William Roper Esqr. & Grace his Wife was Baptized ℘ the Revd. Mr. Samuel Quincy
Ann Roper	On the Day of Sepr. 1750 Ann Daughter of William Roper Esqr. & Grace his Wife was Baptized ℘ Mr. Keith
Martha Roper	Martha Daughter of Ditto was Baptized ℘ Mr. Keith
Broughton Laurens	On the 1st. Day of November 1753 N S Broughton Son of James Laurens & Mary his Wife was Publickly Baptized in St. Philips Church ℘ the Revd. Mr. Alexr. Garden Rector
Hext and Philip Prioleau	On the Day of Hext Prioleau son of Samuel and Providence his Wife was Baptized ℘ Mr. Andrews On the Day of Philip Prioleau son of Samuel and Providence his Wife was Baptized ℘ Ditto
Mary Mc,kenzie	On the 1st Day of December 1753 Mary Daughter of Robert and Johanna Mc,kenzie was Baptized ℘ Mr. Charles Lorrimer
Dennes Desmond Catherine Desmond	On the 1 Day of October 1755 Dennis son of John Desmond and Martha his Wife was Baptized ℘ Mr. Andrews On the 30 Day of September 1758 Catherine Daughter of John and Martha Desmond was Baptized ℘ Mr. Smith
Lloyd	On the day Sarah Daughter of William Lloyd and Martha his wife was Baptized ℘ Mr Zubly William Son of Ditto was Baptized ℘ Mr. Andrews Decr. 10th: 1755 Elizabeth Daughter of Ditto was Baptd, ℘ Mr. Andrews Feby, 25th. 1757 Henrietta Ditto..of Ditto was Baptd. ℘ Mr. Clarke Feby 16. 1758

[118] Christnings

Cathrina and Edward Stephens Sinclair	On the Day of 1755 Cathrina Daughter of Mr. Daniel Sinclair was baptized ℘ the Reverend Mr. Charles Lorimer of the Scotch Meeting On the Day of 1756 Edward Stephens Sinclair was Baptized ℘ the Revd, Mr. Clarke Rector

William On the 5 Day of June 1749 William son of Thomas and Anna Maria Hoyland was Baptized ꝑ

Thomas & On the 21st Day of April 1753 Thomas Son of Thomas and Anna Maria Hoyland was Baptized ꝑ

Elianor Sarah Hoyland On the 2d. Day of September 1758 Elianor Sarah Daughter of Thomas & Anna Maria Hoyland was Baptized

---

Elizabeth Webb On the 5 Day of May 1757 Elizabeth Daughter of Wallace John Webb and Mary his Wife was Baptized ꝑ

Eliza Muncrief On the Day of Elizabeth Daughter of Richard Muncrief and Susannah his wife was Baptized ꝑ the Revd, Mr. Keith

Richd Muncrief On the Day of Richard Son of Richard Muncrief & Susannah his Wife was Baptized Mr. Garden Senr.

Susannah Muncrief On the Day of Susannah Daughter of Richd. and Susannah Muncrief his Wife was Baptized ꝑ Mr. Clarke

---

Christnings[1] [119]

Marriages [149[2]]

James Allen & Susa: Currant On the Eighteenth Day of July 1753, were Married James Allen, of Christ Church Parish, Planter, and Susannah Currant, Widow, ꝑ Licence by the Reverd Mr: John Rowan Minister Acting in Christ Church Parish—— Jno= Remington Regtr— of St Philip Charlestown

---

Jno Ernt Poyas & Eliza Grant On the 20th day of May 1753 were married John Ernest Poyas & Elizabeth Grant ꝑ Lic by the Revd Mr. A Garden

---

Mayrant & Stone— On the twenty seventh day of September 1753 were Married Mr John Mayrant & Miss Ann Stone Spinster by Licence by the Revd Mr Alexr Garden

Marriages [151[3]]

Screven & Cooke On the 29t- day of November 1753 were Married Robert Screven and Elizabeth Cooke ꝑ Licn. by the Revd Mr Richard Clarke Rector

---

[1] The rest of p. 119 is blank.

[2] Page 120 is blank, and the pagination there skips to 145, and 145 to 148 are blank.

[3] Page 150 is blank.

McGaw & Ireland	On the 11th day of February 1754 were Married James Mc-Gaw & Gartwright Ireland ꝑ Licence by the Revd. Mr Richd Clarke Rector——
Linthwaite & Withers	On the 31st. Day of March 1754 were married Thomas Linthwaite and Ann Withers pr. the Revd. Mr. Andrews Assistant to the Revd. Mr. Clarke Rector, pr. Licence
Bringhurst & Shute	On the Eighth day of April 1754 were Married John Bringhurst & Elizabeth Shute Spinster ꝑ Lic by the Revd Mr. Richard Clarke Rector

[152] Marriages ——

Palmerin & Glover	On the first day of May 1754 were Married Samuel Pal-merin & Jane Glover Wido: ꝑ Lic by the Revd Mr Richard Clarke
Cowell & Yeomans	On the fourth day of May 1754 were Married Henry Cowell & Ann Yeomans ꝑ Lic: by the Revd Mr. Richard Clarke Rector [3]

Marriages [153]

Waters & Sinclair	On the 29th October 1754 were Married Richard Waters & Margaret Sinclair ꝑ Licence ꝑ the Revd Mr. Clarke [1]

[154] Marriages

Williams & Hext	On the first Day of Jany. 1755 Robt. Williams Esqr & Elizabeth Hext Spinster was married ꝑ Lic ꝑ Revd. Mr. Richd, Clarke Rector of St. Philips Parish Chs. Town So, Carolina
Poyas & Portall	On the seventeenth of February 1755 James Poyas and Eliza-beth Portal Spinster were married ꝑ Licence by the Revd. Mr Richard Clarke Rector as afsd[2].

Marriages [155]

Davis & Campbell	On the Eleventh day of March 1755 William Davis & Mar-garet Campbell ꝑ banns were Married by Mr Clarke
Poyas & Bourgett	On the 20th day of May 1755 were married John Ernest Poyas & Rachael Bourgett ꝑ Lic ꝑ the Revd Mr Clarke
Manigault & Wragg	On the Eighth Day of June 1755 were married Peter Mani-gault & Elizabeth Wragg ꝑ Lic. ——

[3] The rest of page 152 is blank.

[1] The rest of page 153 is blank.

[2] The rest of page 154 is blank.

Easton & Nelson — On the Eighth day of June 1755 were Married Christopher Easton & Jane Nelson ℘ Lic by the revd Mr Clarke

---

Wilson & Beckett — On the 6 Day of December 1755 were married John Wilson Mariner and Mary Beckett Spinster was married ℘ the Reverend Mr. the Revd. Mr. Clarke ℘ Banns [3]

Marriages. [165[4]]

1720—

April 26th Then was Maried, Henry Bossard & Elizabeth Stuart, by ye: Revd: Mr: Garden, ℘ Licence Governr: Johnson.

May 14th: Then was Maried, James Mc:Cune & Mary Goold, by Do: ℘ Licence of Govr: Johnson

29 Then was Maried, Edward Pied & Mary Pounds, by Do:, ℘ Banns &ca:

June 16 Then was Maried, Joseph Blake & Sarah Lyndrey, by Do: ℘ Licence of G: Johnson

17 Then was Maried, John Finlay & Mary Sparks, by Do: ℘ Do:

29 Then was Maried, Ebenezer Peekham & Lydia Adams, by Do:, ℘ Banns &ca:

July.. 7 Then was Maried, John Hind and Jane Wilson, by Do:, ℘ Licence of G: Johnson

27 Then was Maried, George Melekin & Janet Melekin, by Do:, ℘ Banns &ca:

31 Then was Maried, John Fowles & Frances Gifford, by Do:, ℘ Do: &ca:

August 2 Then was Maried, William Bonner & Marjory Wilkins, by Do:, ℘ Do: &ca:

13 Then was Maried, James Howe and Mary Yarder, by Do:, ℘ Licence of G: Johnson

18 Then was Maried, Robert Tough & Hannah Bennet, by Do:, ℘ Do:

Septembr. 15 Then was Maried, Robert Miller & Elizabeth Hains, by Do:, ℘ Do:

27 Then was Maried, Nicholas Hamerser Cramer & Sarah Coats, by Do:, ℘ Do:-

29 Then was Maried, John Stevenson, & Mary Allen, by Do:, ℘ Banns &

October 2d Then was Maried, John Croskeys, & Sarah Mathews, by Do: ℘ Licence of G: Johnson

---

[3] The rest of page 155 is blank.

[4] Pages 156 to 164, inclusive, are blank.

20 Then was Maried, Hill Crofft, & Priscilla Mariner, by Do:, ℘ Do:-

Janry: 2 Then was Maried, James Jouneau & Magdalen Beauchamp, by Do:, ℘ Do:-

19 Then was Maried. Ralph Jerman & Margaret Graham, by Do:, ℘ Do:

26 Then was Maried, Nicholas Stevens & Elizabeth Garnet, by Do:, ℘ Do:

February 8 Then was Maried, Thomas Clifford & Martha Guerard, by Do:, ℘ Do:

13 Then was Maried, Hugh Stot & Elizabeth Williams, by Do:, ℘ Do:-

14 Then was Maried, David Allen & Mary Mitchel, by Do:, ℘ Do:-

19 Then was Maried, Thomas Barker & Vertue Mardoh, by Do:, ℘ Do.

21 Then was Maried, John Perdriau & Jane Laurans, by Do, ℘ Do:

March 8th Then was Maried, Nathaniel Mariner, & Anne Leverage, by Do:, ℘ Do:

10 Then was Maried Oliver Ditmere & Christian Laroche, by Do:, ℘ Do.

Do: Then was Maried, Henry Mews & Anne Thornton, by Do:, ℘ Do:.

13 Then was Maried, Anthony Mathews Junr: & Anne Brandford, by Do:, ℘ Do:.

April 22 Then was Maried, Edmond Robinson & Anne Butler, by Do:, ℘ Do:.

23 Then was Maried, Joseph Bertoin & Elizabeth Rambert, by Do:, ℘ Do:-

[166]

1721

* ye: 7th: Then was Maried, William Betson & Mary Pinckney als Evans, by the Revd: Mr: Garden, by Licence of Governr: Johnson.

* 11 Then was Maried, John Clement, and Patience Utbert, by Do:, ℘ Licence of G: Johnson.

* Do. Then was Maried, Jeremiah Cogswell, & Mary Wyet, by Do: ℘ Do:.

* 13 Then was Maried, John Pendarvis & Hannah Keys, by Do:, ℘ Do:.

* 15 Then was Maried, Robert Hume & Sophia Wiggington, by Do:, ℘ Do:.

* ly—27 Then was Maried, Elias Ball, and Mary Dellamare, by Do:, ℘ Do:,

---

* Months destroyed.

August 8 Then was Maried, Thomas Grimbal, & Sarah Pert, by Do:, ꝑ Do:.

17 Then was Maried, Edward Vanvellsen, & Catherine Spencer, ꝑ Do:, ꝑ Do:.

20 Then was Maried, Nicholas Haynes & Martha Fryar, by Do:, ꝑ Do:.

Septembr: 1 Then was Maried, Eleazer Allen & Sarah Rhett, by Do:, ꝑ Do:.

15 Then was Maried, Joseph Morgan, & Anne Watkins, ꝑ Banns &ca:.

October 6 Then was Maried John Hodgson & Esther Randles, by Do:, ꝑ Licence.

10 Then was Maried, Roger Moore, & Catherine Rhett, by Do:, ꝑ Do:-

Decembr: 6 Then was Maried, Thomas Holton, & Anne Mindemen, by Do:, ꝑ Do:.

January 12 Then was Maried, William Obroley, & Rachel Robinson, by Do:, ꝑ Banns.

Febry: 8th: Then was Maried, Henry Toomer, & Mary West, by Do:, ꝑ Licence.

March 8 Then was Maried, Francis Holmes, & Elizabeth Symmons, by Do:, ꝑ Do:.

1722.

25 Then was Maried, Othniel Beale, and Katharine Gale, by Do:, ꝑ Do:.

28 Then was Maried, John Caswell, & Sarah Bee, by Do:, ꝑ Do:.

April 13 Then was Maried, George Ford, & Sarah Oliver, by Do:, ꝑ Do:.

15 Then was Maried, Jonathan Brown, & Margaret Booth, by Do:, ꝑ Banns.

18 Then was Maried, William Bollaugh, & Mary Britten, by Do:, ꝑ Licence.

26 Then was Maried, Alexander Hall, & Henrietta Ward, by Comissry: Bull, ꝑ Do:.

June 25 Then was Maried, Philip Gouron, & Charlotte Jortin, by Mr: Garden, ꝑ Do:

July 10 Then was Maried, John Heard, & Esther La Pierre, by Do:, ꝑ Do:.

July 17 Then was Maried, Robert Stantin, & Eliza: Nash, by Do:, ꝑ Banns &ca:.

19 Then was Maried, Edwd: Crofft, & Eliza: Brewton, by Do:, ꝑ Licence.

August 4 Then was Maried, James Searles & Christian Scott, by Do:, ꝑ Do:.

21 Then was Maried, Samle: Sleigh, & Mary Oldfield, by Do:, ꝑ Do:.

Novbr: 21 Then was Maried, Thomas Carman, & Deborah Palmetor, by Do:, ℔ Do:.

23 Then was Maried, Samuel Woodwards, & Eliza: Vaughan, by Do:, ℔ Do:.

Decbr: 3 Then was Maried, James Thomson, & Mary Waters, by Do:, ℔ Do:.

Febry: 10 Then was maried, Herrald Bly & Mary Jerum, by Do: Do:.

Decbr: 9th: Then was married, Job Rothmahler & Anne Dubose, by Do: Do:

18 Then was married, George Smith & Elizabeth Allen ℔ Do: Do:

20 Then was married, Ebenezer Simmons & Eliza: Jones ℔ Do: Do:

1722/23 [167]

Febry: 2d: Then was married John Bruce & Jane Holbeatch ℔ Licence, ℔ Mr: Garden

3 Then was married David Abbot & Katherine Hall ℔ Do. Do:

9 Then was married Benjamin Carter & Eliza: Carrant ℔ Do: Do:

19 Then was married Lawrence Mackay & Deborah Honour ℔ Do: Do:

25 Then was married John Blunt & Jane Jones ℔ Do: Do:

March 3 Then was married Samuel Fairread & Mary Aires ℔ Do, directd: to Mr: Garden

1723

Septemr: 26 Then was Married, William Wattson and Mary Kemp ℔ Lic by the Reverend Mr. Alexander Garden

Octob: 27 Then was Married Captn: William Martin, and Anne D'la Con [*] ℔ Licence, by Mr. Garden

Novemr: 18 Then was Married John Arnoll & Lidia Reynolds ℔ Ditto

Decr: 19 Then was Married Thomas Butler and Elizabeth Elliott

26 Then was Married Andrew Hellerd & Hanah Jerome ℔ Licence

Janury: 15 Then was Married James Gray and Mary Simmons ℔ Ditto

16 Then was Married William Mackenzie and Sarah Founds ℔ Do:

19 Then was Married Isaac Holmes and Elizabeth Peronneau ℔ Do.

23 Then was Married John Perriman & Mary Snypes ℔ Ditto ℔ Do.

23 Then was Married Edward Scott and Mary Hopkins ℔ Ditto ℔ Do.

---

* Rest broken off.

30 Then was Married Job Wiggins and Mary Langley ꝑ Banns ꝑ Ditto

Febry: 3 Then was Married John Fogarty and Mary Harris ꝑ Licence ꝑ Do.

15 Then was Married Samuel Seamans and Mary Nutton ꝑ Banns ꝑ

March 5 Then was Married James Fowler & Martha Widdicomb ꝑ Licence

9 Then was Married John Smith and Anne Odingsells ꝑ Licence ꝑ do:.

May 28 Then was Married Nicholas Newlin & Mary Roberts ꝑ Ditto ꝑ Ditto

1724

July 8 Then was Married Francis Gracia and Anne Bisset ꝑ Ditto ꝑ Ditto

19 Then was Married John Fowler and Dorothy Gary ꝑ Licence ꝑ Ditto

25 Then was Married Thomas Boulton & Elizabeth Miller ꝑ Ditto P Ditto

30 Then was Married Thomas John Elliott & Mary Pendarvis ꝑ Ditto

Do Then was Married Joseph Warmingham & Sarah Lea ꝑ Ditto

Novr. 5 Then was Married Wm- Hayes and Mary De Filleau ꝑ Banns ꝑ Ditto

Decembr: 10th Then was Married James Sadler and Mary How widow ꝑ Licence ꝑ Do.

21 Then was Married Dr. John Hutchinson Widower and Charlotte Foislin Spinster ꝑ Licence of His Excellency Governr. Nicholson, ꝑ the Reverend Mr. Garden

January.30 1724/5 Then was Married James Laurens Batchelor, and Hanah Rivers Widow ꝑ Licence of His Excelcy.. the Governor, ꝑ the Reverend Mr. Alexr: Garden

31 Then was Married Captn. John Sharp Widower and Deborah Gough Spinster, ꝑ Licence of Ditto ꝑ Mr: Garden

Februry: 9 Then was Married George Melligan Batchelor & Mary Hambleton Spinster, ꝑ Licence of the Governor, ꝑ the Reverend Mr. Garden—

24 Then was Married John Ladson & Charlotte Bew ꝑ Licence ꝑ Ditto

April 12 Then was Married Edward Marriner & Mary Harris ꝑ Ditto Do.

30 Then was Married William Byrem & Mary Rogers ꝑ Ditto Do.

[168] Marriages Continued

* 13 Then was Married Thomas Langley & Mary Mitchel ꝑ Licence ꝑ Mr Garden.

* 15 Then was Married Benjamin Romsey & Martha Crook ꝑ Ditto Ditto

20 Then was Married William Tutton & Mary Cogswell ꝑ Ditto Do. . . .

June 2 Then was Married Thomas Farley & Mary Morrice ꝑ Ditto Do. .

6 Then was Married Thomas Weslyd & Margaret White ꝑ Ditto Do.

8 Then was Married the Reverend Alexander Garden and Martha Guerard ꝑ Licence, by the Reverend Mr. Thomas Morritt.

July 2 Then was Married John Levins and Elizabeth Thornton ꝑ Bans ꝑ Mr. Garden

† Then was Married Edward Wyatt and Joanna Ellis ꝑ Licence ꝑ Mr. Garden

† Then was Married Charles Bisson & Anne Sanson ꝑ Ditto Do.

* 29 Then was Married John Wright and Jane Keays ꝑ Ditto Do.

* 29 Then was Married James Tarbet & Frances Chalcroft ꝑ Do. Do.

Septr. 26 Then was Married Joseph Hosford & Hanah Pendarvis ꝑ Ditto Do.

Octob: 10 Then was Married Samuel LLuellin & Sarah Crosskeys ꝑ Do. Do.

12 Then was Married Thomas Ellery & Anne Moore ꝑ Ditto Do

30 Then was Married James Willke & Loveridge Brown ꝑ Do. Do

Novemr: 3 Then was Married Clodius Raguley & Rachel Braley ꝑ Do. Do.

4 Then was Married Stephen Taveroon & Sarah Turner ꝑ Do. Do

16 Then was Married Thomas Cooper & Eleanr. Wright ꝑ Ditto Do

Decbr. 14 Then was Married Thomas Goring & Martha Wigfal als D'Oily ꝑ Do. Do.

15 Then was Married Joseph Danford & Margaret Gray ꝑ Ditto Do.

29 Then was Married Richard Miller & Judith Lambol ꝑ Do. Do.

30 Then was Married John Davis & Anne Parris ꝑ Do. Do

---

* Month destroyed. † Whole date destroyed.

Janry. 1 Then was Married Jacob Motte & Elizabeth Martin ℘ Do. Do.

6 Then was Married William Pinckney & Ruth Brewton ℘ Do. Do

20 Then was Married William Elliott & Frances Gearing ℘ Do. Do.

22 Then was Married John Fling & Judith Butler ℘ Do. Do.

Febry. 9 Then was Married James Still & Mary Wigmore ℘ Do. Do

10 Then was Married Thomas Stone & Elizabeth Fryer ℘ Do. Do.

17 Then was Married George Bampfield & Elizabeth Delamere ℘ Do. of the Deputy Governr. Married ℘ the Reverend Mr. Jones

22 Then was Married Benjamin Godfrey & Margaret Fossin ℘ Licence, Married by the Reverend Mr. Alexr. Garden—

22 Then was Married John Brand Junior & Jane Meadows ℘ Do. Do.

March 2 Then was Married Benjan D'Hariette & Anne Smith widow ℘ Do. Do.

1725/6 Marriages Continued [169]

March 18 Then was Married Joseph Freers & Eleanor Gibson ℘ Licence ℘ Mr: Garden

April 28 Then was Married Childermas Croft & Katherine Parteridge
1726 by Licence of The Honble: Arthur Middleton Esqr. ℘ Mr. Garden

May 11 Then was Married Jonathan Murrel & Eliza: Vardell ℘ Ditto, Do.

14 Then was Married Hezekiah Russ & Kathern: Douglas ℘ Ditto Do.

June 2 Then was Married Hill Croft & Rebekah Corbin ℘ Ditto Ditto

July 1 Then was Married James Bullen & Mary Poinsett ℘ Ditto Do.

21 Then was Married Ebenez Wyatt & Mary Fullard ℘ Do ℘ Mr. Morritt

22 Then was Married Ralph Rodda & Anne Pawley ℘ Do ℘ Mr. Garden

Augt. 11 Then was Married Richard Scott & Grace Walker ℘ Ditto ℘ Ditto

Septr: 2 Then was Married Henry Livingston & Anne Harris ℘ Ditto Ditto

14 Then was Married Thomas Weaver & Ruth Roberts ℘ Ditto Ditto

21 Then was Married James Pain & Mary Bellamy ℘ Ditto Do.

22 Then was Married, Benjan: Mellens & Sarah Price ℘ Ditto Do.

23 Then was Married James Hartley & Mary Needland, belonging to the Parish of Christ Church, ℘ Licence, ℘ Mr. Garden

Octr: 23 Then was Married, Thomas Mountjoy & Hester Conyers ℘ Do: Do.

Novr: 25 Then was Married Lawrence Couliette & Mary Williams ℘ Ditto.

Decr. 4 Then was Married John Conyer & Hanah Marriner ℘ Ditto

8 Then was Married John Noufuille & Elizabeth Marston ℘ ditto

28 Then was Married Samuel Bullock & Elizabeth Bollard ℘ ditto

Jany: 12 Then was Married John Gregory & Elizabeth Williams ℘ ditto.

18 Then was Married Thomas Sharp & Sarah Corke ℘ ditto.

28 Then was Married Isaac Holmes & Susanna Poinset ℘ ditto

Feb: 10 Then was Married Thomas Lovelace & Susanna Wood by the Reverend Mr. Dyson ℘ Licence

16 Then was Married Thomas Wigg & Mary Evans ℘ the revd: Mr Garden

17 Then was Married William Lancaster & Elizabeth Currant ℘ ditto.

24 Then was Married Samuel Ash & Katherine Clements both of Christ Church Parish, ℘ the Revd. Mr. Alexr: Garden

28 Then was Married John Arnold & Martha Bee ℘ ditto..

Mar. 1 Then was Married Daniel Fleurison & Cybil Neufuille ℘ ditto

14 Then was Married William Fairchild & Martha Elliott ℘ ditto

April 2 Then was Married Joseph Lea & Isobel Sherriffe ℘ ditto

1727 5 Then was Married Thomas Hutt & Esther Leper ℘ ditto ℘ Banns

12 Then was Married John Jenkins & Elizabeth Adams ℘ Mr. Morritt

27 Then was Married Joseph Hurst & Margaret Cartwright ℘ revd: Mr Garden

May 3 Then was Married John Witter & Anne Marriner ℘ ditto.

4 Then was Married James Kilpatrick & Elizabeth Hepworth ℘*

7 Then was Married Experience Howard & Rachel Bee Widow ℘*

[170] Marriages Continued

1727

May 10 Then was Married John Bonin & Mary Magdalen Dess by the Revernd Mr: Dyson, ℘ Licence

18 Then was Married Richard Mason Batchelor & Susanna Sumner spinster by the Reverend Mr. Alexander Garden ℘ Licence

* Rest destroyed.

23 Then was Married John Jenkins Junior & Mary Adams ℘ Revd.. Mr Morritt
June 1 Then was Married Peter St. Julien & Sarah Godin ℘ Revd. Mr Garden
July 9 Then was Married John Sergeant & Elizabeth Johnson ℘ ditto
Augt: 8 Then was Married Tweedie Somerville & Elizabeth Cawood ℘ ditto
Sept 24 Then was Married Edmund Holland & Henrietta Hall ℘ ditto
Oct. 8 Then was Married William Fullwood & Alice Wells ℘ ditto.
21 Then was Married Peter Shepheard & Elizabeth Hitchcock ℘ ditto
31 Then was Married Anthony Pottevine & Hanah Atkins ℘ ditto
Novr. 1st Then was Married James Talbert & Mary Jolly ℘ Banns ℘ ditto.
Decr. 11 Then was Married Francis Larkin & Martha Card ℘ Ditto ℘ ditto
22 Then was Married James Withers & Mary Cartwright ℘ Licence ℘ do.
24 Then was Married Richard Salter & Anne Sullivan ℘ ditto ℘ ditto
Janry: 9 Then was Married John Fountain & Jane Lewis Chapnis ℘ Banns ℘ ditto
Feby: 10 Then was Married William Tunley & Elizabeth Lockyer ℘ Licence ℘. ditto
17 Then was Married Robert Ellis & Cathrine Abbot ℘ ditto
21 Then was Married Richard Murphy & Hanah Anderson ℘ ditto
do. Then was Married William Randall & Mary Muncreef ℘ ditto
23 Then was Married David Mellory & Rebeka Smith ℘ ditto—
Marc. 4 Then was Married Nicholas Trott Esqr: & Sarah Rhett ℘ ditto- —
do. Then was Married Robert Collins & Elizabeth Waters ℘ ditto
1728. 25 Then was Married Peter Crewett & Unity Neal ℘ ditto
April 5 Then was Married the Revd. Richard Ludlam & Anne Carter ℘ ditto
11 Then was Married Thomas Gadsden & Collins Hall ℘ ditto
22 Then was Married John Moultrie & Lucrecia Cooper ℘ ditto
26 Then was Married John Greenland & Elizabeth Forrest ℘ ditto

May 7 Then was Married John Skene & Hanah Palmer ꝑ ditto
10 Then was Married Robert Randall & Anne Mathews ꝑ ditto
June 13 Then was Married William Wilkins & Sarah Crosskeys alias LLuellin
July 2 Then was Married Thomas Palmster & Anne Duval ꝑ ditto
11 Then was Married Abel Pimell & Mary Tutton ꝑ ditto—
17 Then was Married John Arnott & Hanah Gull ꝑ ditto
* Then was Married Jacob Woolford & Elizabeth Tunley ꝑ ditto
* Then was Married William Osborn & Hellena Mackie ꝑ ditto
* Then was Married Thomas Cooper & Margt. Magdalen Beauchamp, do.
* Then was Married Isaac Mazyck & Jane Mary St Julien ꝑ ditto
* Then was Married James Dixon & Elizabeth Wilson ꝑ Do. L
* Then was Married Francis Baker & Mary Shepherd ꝑ L.
* Then was Married Thomas Tuson & Mary Varien ꝑ L,
* Then was Married Garrat Vanvelsin & Hannah Johnson ꝑ L.

Marriages Continued [171]

1728/9
March 14 Then was Married Henry Coyle & Anne Young ꝑ L.
1729.
April 10 Then was Married John Reynolds & Penelope Stollard ꝑ L.
15 Then was Married Robert Brewton & Mary Loughton ꝑ L.
17 Then was Married John Lewis & Judith Lee Roche ꝑr L.
22 Then was Married Joseph Prince & Jemima Webb. ꝑ L—
May 7 Then was Married James Hitchins & Margaret Longhair ꝑ L.
20 Then was Married John Scott. & Hannah Fogartie ꝑ L.
June 30 Then was Married Claudius Boulee & Magdalen Meinson ꝑ B.
July 18,, Then was Married John Arnold & Mary Haskett. ꝑ L—
Augt. 28,, Then was Married Robert Gillcrist & Rebekah Underwood ꝑ L
Septemr 7,. Then was Married Joseph Summers & Elizabeth Roll. ꝑ L.
October 6,, Then was Married James Dalton & Katherine Martin ꝑr L.
16,, Then was Married Peter Oliver & Margaret Duval ꝑ L.
27,, Then was Married Gabriel Peyrand & Magdalen Rant ꝑ L.

---

* Dates destroyed.

28,, Then was Married Thomas Robins & Francis Lowrie ꝑ L

Novem^r 14,, Then was Married John Stone & Susanna Marshe ꝑ L

30 Then was Married Philip Arnold & Margaret Gardenor ꝑ L

Decem^r. 2,, Then was Married Joseph Townsend & Mary Burnham ꝑ L

6,, Then was Married Thomas Squire & Mary Sanders ꝑ L

20 Then was Married Thomas Hargrave & Mary Cox ꝑ L

22,, Then was Married Stephen Leepard & Martha Parsons ꝑ L.

Jan^ry- 1st- Then was married James Cordes, & Eliz^a. Simmons.... ꝑ L—

14,, Then was married William Carwithen & Mary Bisset ꝑ L

29,, Then was Married William Carr & Elizabeth Shute ꝑ L—

Feb^ry- 2,, Then was Married John Savy. & Elizabeth Green ꝑ L—

4,, Then was Married David Christian & Frances Rochonet ꝑ L—

10 Then was Married John Vicaridge & Elizabeth Ashby ꝑ L—

March,, 5,, Then was Married Paul Cherright & Rebekah Magee ꝑ L—

1730

April 2,, Then was Married Samuel Fley and Elizabeth Poinset ꝑ L

1730 ,, Then was Married Thomas Bertran & Mary Hancock ꝑ L—

.... 9,, Then was Married Richard Fowler & Catherine Grant ꝑ L—

May 2 Then was Married James Dolphin & Margaret Rowlin ꝑ L—

July 3,, Then was Married Adam Beauchamp & Joannah Corbet ꝑ L—

April 9,, Then was Married Andrew Lawrimore & Mary Mackdowel ꝑ L

July 9,, Then was Married Isaac Chardon & Mary Mazyck ꝑ L—

August 2,, Then was Married Thomas Blundell & Martha Clews ꝑ L

[172] Marriages Continued.

1730

Septem^r,, 3,, Then was Married John Hanover & Deborah Sharpe ꝑ L

D^o. 17,, Then was Married George Young & Anne Carlisle ꝑ L

Octo^r.,, 18,, Then was Married Francis Sureau & Mary Mackpherson ꝑ L

X^ber— 31,, Then was Married Peter Leger & Mary Evans ꝑ L.

Janry. 14,, Then was Married John Moore, & Elizabeth Smith ꝑ Banns—

Ditto 22,, Then was Married David Lullams & Patience Palmer. ꝑ L—

Ditto 31 Then was Married Francis LeBrasseur & Anne Splatt. ꝑ L—

Februaryy,, *,, Then was Married Robert Nesbit & Mary Hepworth ꝑ L ꝑ mr. Varnon-

March 2,, Then was Married William May & Elizabeth Harding ꝑ L

Ditto,, 14,, Then was Married William Morgan & Eliza. Smith ꝑ L—

1731

April 27,, Then was Married Stephen Bull & Martha Godin ꝑ L—

May ,, 16,, Then was Married Pons Ollier & Jane Satur ꝑr L—

Ditto 19,, Then was Married Thomas Stocks & Rachel Howman ꝑ L—

Ditto 20,, Then was Married Robert Booth & Martha Dandridge ꝑ L—

June 5,, Then was Married William Hall & Sarah Taveroone ꝑ L—

Ditto 6 Then was Married Michael Moore & Martha Currant ꝑ L—

Ditto 7,, Then was Married John Bee & Martha Miller ꝑ L—

July * Then was Married Joseph Maybank & Mary Ann Dupuy ꝑ L—

Ditto * Then was Married Thomas Snow & Elizabeth Cartwright ꝑ L—

July 8 Then was Married Aaron Cheesborough & Eliza- Wanlys ꝑ L—

Ditto 25,, Then was Married Abraham Croft & Anna Maria Marston ꝑ L—

Ditto 29,, Then was Married Charles Read, & Deborah Honor Petty ꝑ Banns—

August * Then was Married John Goldsmith & Rebekah Mallory ꝑ Banns—

Ditto,, 11,, Then was Married Charles Codner & Anne Barnet ꝑ L.—

31,, Then was Married Francis Padget & Anne Pointset pr L—

Septemr 13,, Then was Married Richard Baker, and Sarah Glaze ꝑ L

20,, Then was Married Paul Bruneau & Elizabeth Pair pr L—

22,, Then was Married John Bonnetheau, & Angelica Caier ꝑ L—

23,, Then was Married John Sullivant & Hesther Nelson ꝑr L—

---

* Undecipherable figure.

Octo^r „ 12 Then was Married William Heathly & Mary Vinin ℘^r L
24„ Then was Married Jeremiah Gregory & Margaret Dennis ℘ L
28„ Then was Married John Fryer, & Rachel Gray ℘ L—
Novem^r„ 9„ Then was Married John Neilson, & Susannah Edgar ℘ L
20„ Then was Married Peter Erving & Jane Leecroft ℘^r L
28„ Then was Married John Hicks, & Hannah Murdock- ℘ L
Decem^r 14„ Then was Married Alexander Wood & Mary Slokum. p^r L.
16„ Then was Married Peter Benoist & Abigail Townsend. ℘ L—

Marriages Continued [173]

1731
Decem^r„ 23„ Then was Married Joseph Butler & Mary LeRoach ℘ L—
29„ Then was Married William Hales & Rebekah Ireland ℘ L—
January 1„ Then was Married Robert Shaw, & Eleanor Mills ℘ L—
4„ Then was Married Alexander M^cpherson & Sarah Bray ℘ L—
8 Then was Married John Kingland & Elizabeth Flood ℘ L—
14„ Then was Married John Spencer & Dorothy M^cgregory. ℘ L—
27„ Then was Married George Colleton & Elizabeth Peterson ℘ L—
27„ Then was Married John Thomson & Mary Jones .. ℘ L—
31„ . Then was Married Samuel Summers & Anne Snow ℘ L—
February 16 Then was Married Henry Wools & Grace Poole ℘^r L.
20„ Then was Married William Macgie & Rebekah Fell ℘ L—
21„ Then was Married William Leander & Marian Stewart ℘ L—
22„ Then was Married, Daniel Murphey & Jane Wilson, ℘ L—
March .6„ Then was Married Samuel Glasier &' Sarah Louisa Roy ℘ L—
6„ Then was Married William Daxter & Anne Holton ℘ L—
14„ Then was Married Robert Johnston & Sarah Collins. ℘ L—

1732
March 27„ Then was Married Isaac Cutforth & Martha Powel ℘ L—

April 16,, Then was Married Francis Murriel & Elizabeth Price ℔ L.
Do 22,, Then was Married Docr. Wm. Cleveland. & Margaret Macnobney Wido. ℔r L—
27 Then was Married Edward Haselwood & Elizabeth Mills. ℔ L—
29 Then was Married James Atkins & Mary Gray ℔ L.
May 4,, Then was Married Peter Jayes & Martha Nash ℔ L—
9,, Then was Married David Robinson & Elizabeth Bruer ℔ L—
19,, Then was Married John Davis & Theodorah Cook. ℔ L—
28,, Then was Married Thomas Harwood & Jane Johnston ℔ L:
June * Then was Married Elias Foissin & Mary L Roche ℔ L—
30,, Then was Married John Frampton & Hannah Adams ℔ L
July 13 Then was Married John Colcock & Deborah Milner ℔ L—
25 Then was Married Thomas Gadsden & Alice Mighells ℔ L—
27,, Then was Married Thomas Crosthwaite & Mary Ward ℔ L
Septemr,, † Then was Married William Mills & Grace Parker ℔ L
8,, Then was Married James Kerr & Mary Bertram ℔ L
9,, Then was Married John Barrat & Alice Wiliams ℔ L
10,, Then was Married Lawrence Withers & Eliza. Beauchamp ℔ L
24,, Then was Married James Lewis & Jane Atkins ℔ L
Octor 9,, Then was Married John Vaughan & Eleanor Shaw ℔ L—
12 Then was Married James Mackgirt & Priscilla Davison ℔ L

[174] Marriages Continued

1732
October 17,, Then was Married Collin Sharp & Sarah Devall ℔ L
Novemr 15,, Then was Married Peter Currant & Susanna Hope ℔ L
Decemr 20 Then was Married Francis Goddard & Mary Pight. ℔ L
21 Then was Married William Greene & Martha Sams ℔ L
January † Then was Married Richard Brickles & Sarah Warmingham ℔ L.
4 Then was Married Henry Williams & Mary Cart. ℔ L.
6 Then was Married John Batchelor & Eliza. Batterson ℔ L—

---

* Day gone.

† Undecipherable figure.

13 Then was Married Hobart Stanbrough & Marget Millent ℔ L

31 Then was Married James Dupree & Mary Bullein. ℔ L—

febry- 4 Then was Married Thomas Tatnel & Mary Ward ℔ L

19 Then was Married Stephen Douse & Sarah Stewart ℔ L

January 18 Then was Married Richard Wigg & Sarah Mayne ℔ L. Mr Winterly

1733

March 28 Then was Married Thomas Dale & Mary Brewton ℔ L—

Ditto 29 Then was Married William Roper & Mary Wilson ℔r L—

April 2 Then was Married Garrat Valvensin & Rebecca Croft Wido ℔ L·

9 Then was Married John Munroe & Susanna Stewart ℔ L

12 Then was Married James Sutton & Mary Hutchins ℔ L

27 Then was Married Hewark Peacock & Sarah Smith ℔ L

12 Then was Married Manly Williamson & Hannah Hogg. Exiled[1] By the Reverd. Mr. Guy ℔r. L.

May 15 Then was Married Phannet Cooke & Anne Haddock ℔ L

June 10 Then was Married Peter Jeyes & Mary Brand ℔ L

12 Then was Married Thomas Rose & Beuler Elliott ℔ L

17 Then was Married Thomas Galloway & Anne Winigood ℔ L

29 Then was Married Jacob Craggs & Mary Welsh ℔ L

28 Then was Married Thomas Clemens & Anne Morgan ℔ L

July 2 Then was Married Martin Rease & Martha Morgan ℔ L

3 Then was Married Robert Duke & Maria Phillis Dudly ℔ L

25 Then was Married Edward Wills & Susanna Hope. ℔ L

August 2 Then was Married John Barton & Jane Perryman ℔ L

2 Then was Married Samuel Holmes & Elizabeth Morgan ℔ L

28 Then was Married Francis Gratia & Mary Scriven ℔ L

Septemr 8 Then was Married William Calvert & Mary Steinson ℔ L

[2] [175]

1733

Septemr * Then was Married John Tampleroy, and Veronica Wedgworth ℔ L

Ditto * Then was Married John Fountain & Susanna Matthews ℔ L

Ditto * Then was Married Nathaniel Gittins & Mary Lawrens ℔ L—

October * Then was Married William Bresben & Margaret Stewart

Ditto 18 Then was Married John Ferguson & Mary Bowman ℔ L—

---

[1] Appears to be. [2] Heading to page gone. * Day of month broken out of page.

Novem^r 6 Then was Married William Anderson & Catharine Lane ℘ L—
Decem^r 13 Then was Married John M^cacgilvery & Elizabeth Hassard ℘ L—
Ditto 14 Then was Married Tweedie Somerville & Sarah Wigg ℘ L—
Ditto 31 Then was Married Thomas Fisher & Henrietta Holland ℘ L—
Ditto 31 Then was Married Charles Grinnin & Dorothy Whitaker ℘ L—
January 2 Then was Married Arthur Johnston & Martha Taylor ℘ L—
Ditto 20 Then was Married Philip Massey & Jane Hopkins ℘ L
Ditto 24 Then was Married Robert Rawling & Elizabeth Cole ℘ L—
Ditto 24 Then was Married Robert Collis & Elizabeth Ellis ℘ L—
Ditto 29 Then was Married Gilson Clapp, and Sarah Ward ℘ L—
Febry- 16 Then was Married John Aldridge and Rachel Laywood ℘ L—
Ditto 16 Then was Married Jordan Roche and Rebecca Brewton ℘ L—
Ditto 29 Then was Married William Risby & Mary Sams ℘ L—
Ditto 24 Then was Married William Gibson & Margaret Arnold ℘ L—
Ditto 24 Then was Married Christian Heidelberg & Isabel Oliver ℘ L—
Ditto * Then was Married William Finch & Isabel Lea ℘ L—
March * Then was Married William Manning, and Jane Blunt ℘ L—
1734—
April * Then was Married Richard Wright & Mary Rhett ℘ L—
April * Then was Married Thomas Croftman & Mary Cooms ℘ L—
May * Then was Married John Chevillette & Sarah Yanham ℘ L.
April * Then was Married John Lepper & Elizabeth Painter ℘ L—
June * Then was Married Edward Arden & Eleanor Forth ℘ L—
June * Then was Married Richard Woodward, & Susanna Mazyck ℘ L—
June 10 Then was Married Stephen Shrewsbury & Catharine Driskill ℘ L—
July -8 Then was Married Joseph Robertson & Anne Neves ℘ L—
Ditt^o. 8 Then was Married Thomas Butler & Elizabeth Gibbes ℘ L—
Ditto 9 Then was Married James Smalwood & Charlotte Hutchinson ℘ L—
Ditto 18 Then was Married Thomas Yonge & Mary Box ℘ L—
Ditto 18 Then was Married Robert Pringle & Jane Allen ℘ L—
Ditto 21 Then was Married George Higgins & Anne Collis ℘ L

[176] [2]

[3] Then was Married Archibald Sinclare & Isabel Ma[4]
July 29 Then was Married Hobart Stanbrough & Margaret H[4]
August 11 Then was Married the Honorable: Henry Scott Esqr: & Elizabeth Fenw[4]
October 10 Then was Married Michael Millure & Mary West ℔ L—
October 11 Then was Married Thomas Edgley & Penelopy Middleton ℔[4]
Novemr 18 Then was Married Griffith Bullard & Hibaba Young ℔[4]
Do: 18 Then was Married Gideon Ellis & Eliza- Henley ℔ L
25 Then was Married Ribton Hutchinson & Providence Dennis ℔ L—
Decemr.. 9 Then was Married John Scott & Mary Cray ℔ L—
15 Then was Married John Charville & Anne Mackay ℔ Banns
January 23 Then was Married William Gumbles & Elizabeth Partridg[4]
Ditto 23[1] Then was Married William Bulmer & Elizabeth Rogers ℔ L
Febry- 3 Then was Married John Ulrick Myllur, & Anne Stopfar ℔ L—
Do 4 Then was Married, Richard Wigg, & Anne Smallwood ℔ L—
Do 13 Then was Married John Guerard & Elizabeth Hill ℔ L
Do 23 Then was Married John Richards & Mary Thomlinson ℔ L
March 5 Then was Married Richard Martin & Mary Clarke ℔ L—
Do.. 5 Then was Married James Elsinor & Rebekah Boggs ℔ L—
Do 6 Then was Married John Allen & Mary Bellamy ℔ L—
Do 19 Then was Married Willm. Verplank, & Anne Lorey ℔[2]
1735
April 8 Then was Married Henry Harramond, & Mary Fisher ℔[2]
May 4 Then was Married Richard Floyd, & Anne Howard[2]
6 Then was Married William Croft, & Jane Richard[2]
June 2 Then was Married Joseph Panton, & Mary Howard[2]
Do.. 10 Then was Married Willm. Griffin, & Eliza- Stevens[9]
Do.. 21 Then was Married James Pollard & Anne Stittsm[2]
27 Then was Married Benjamin Osborn & Mary Brown ℔ L[2]
July 29 Then was Married Gideon Norton & Anne Thomas ℔ L ℔[2]
Augt. 8 Then was Married, Wm. Leperre & Eliza- Henderson ℔ L ℔[2]
Do. . 18 Then was Married, David Dalbiac & Catharine Coulet ℔ L ℔[2]

---

[2] Heading of page broken off. [3] Date broken off. [4] Rest broken off.

[1] "January 25th" interlined between "January 23" and "ditto 23."

[2] Rest broken off.

Do. . 21 Then was Married Joseph Thornton & Mary Middleton ꝑ L ꝑ Mr Jon[2]

Do. . 22 Then was Married Thomas Goodman, & Barbara Parry ꝑ L ꝑ Mr Jon[2]

Septemr 6 Then was Married Wm- Comer & Mary Jeffrys ꝑ L ꝑr Mr Mellich[2]

Marriages Continued. [177]

1735

October 3 Then was Married Reynold Cox & Margaret Bryan ꝑ L ꝑr Mr Millechamp

Ditto 16 Then was Married George Curry & Allen Fletcher ꝑ L ꝑr Mr. Thomson

Ditto 24 Then Was Married Nicholas Mullet & Mary Brown ꝑ L ꝑ Mr Leslie.

Decemr 23 Then was Married Richd. Cartwright & Kesiah Skinner ꝑ L ꝑ Mr Garden

January 10 Then was Married Edward Fisher & Prudence Nash ꝑ L—

January 11 Then was Married William Bryan & Mary Bennet ꝑ Banns—

January 25 Then was Married Paul Jenys & Elizabeth Raven Widow by the Revd Mr. Wm. Guy

February 13 Then was Married James Lusk & Hannah Williamson ꝑ L ꝑ Mr Garden

February 22d Then was Married William Weekley, & Martha Stocks ꝑ L ꝑ Mr. Garden

March 4th Then was Married Isaiah Brunet & Alice Thomson ꝑ L ꝑ Mr Garden

March 16th Then was Married[1] Jacobus Kipp & Elizabeth Millen ꝑ L ꝑ Mr Garden

1736

April 10th Then was Married Daniel Bingil & Catherina Kigleman ꝑ L ꝑ Mr Garden

April 27th Then was Married John Burford & Ann Berches ꝑ L ꝑ Mr Garden

April 27th Then was Married Jacob Axon & Ruth Glazbrook ꝑ L ꝑ Mr Garden

May 3d Then was Married Maurice Lewis & Jane Hill ꝑ L ꝑ Mr Garden

June 10th Then was Married Peter Stanley & Elizabeth Ward ꝑ L ꝑ Mr Garden

June 28th Then was Married John Bruder & Eleanor Anneshele ꝑ L ꝑ Mr Garden

---

[1] Just above these words is interlined: "cant find it."

July 14th Then was Married George Vane & Sarah Tattle ℘ L ℘ Mr. Garden
July 19th Then was Married Nathaniel Burt & Rebekah Goldsmith ℘ L ℘ do:—
July 22d Then was Married Thomas Hollins & Hannah Moore ℘ Mr Garden
July 27th Then was Married Joseph Whitne & Mary Coit ℘ Mr: Garden
July 29th Then was Married Edward Clarke & Lydia Viart ℘ Mr Garden
Septr: 8th Then was[2] Married Michael Scully & Elizabeth Sergeant ℘ ditto
Septr 15th Then was Maried Thomas Harden & Anne Nelson ℘ L ℘ do:
October 22d Then was Maried John Tozer and Mary Sparks ℘ L ℘ Mr Thompson
do 27 Then was Maried John Nelme and Elenor Whitte ℘ L ℘ Mr Garden
do 29 Then was Maried Daniel Smith and Ruth Goodin ℘ L ℘ do:—
do 31st Then was Maried William Frost and Mary Townshend ℘ L do:—
Novemr 4 Then was Maried Richard Woodward and Elizabeth Godin ℘ L do

[178] Marriages Continued

1736

Noevmr 9 Then was maried John Gibbens and Elizabeth Bennett ℘ L pr Mr: Garden
10 Then was maried William Mathews and Mary Loughton ℘ L do:-
13 Then was maried Christopher Hopkins and Ann Cadell ℘ L do:—
17 Then was Maried George Austin and Ann Dawes— ℘ L do:—
Decr: 16 Then was Maried John Clifford and Martha Dandridge ℘ L do:—
22 Then was maried Richard Wainwright and Mary Joice ℘ L do:—
25 Then was maried David Skinner and Hannah Clifford—℘ L do:—
29 Then was maried Frederick Bathan & Margaret King ℘r Banns do-
30 Then was maried Pierre Courtonne & Mary Magdalena Peltro ℘ do:-

---

[2] Just above is interlined: "cant find". "Do." is interlined above next five entrys.

Jany 13 Then was maried George Dennistone & Mary Risby........
℘ L do:-
19 Then was maried Jenkin Hughes & Margaret Danford -
℘ L do:-
30 Then was maried George Dela Pierre & Elizabeth Loyd......
℘ L. do:-
ffebry 8 Then was maried Peter Birot and Sarah Leste ....
℘ L do:-
27 Then was Maried Thomas Wright and Ann Hutchinson -
℘ L. do:-
March 24 Then was Maried John Whittesides and Sarah Dashwood
℘ L: do:-
ffebry: 9th Then was Maried William Chambers & Isabella Maceant.
℘ L do

1737
April 19th Then was maried William Smith & Elizabeth Smith - -
℘ L. do
23d Then was Maried John Roche & Jane Romage — — —
℘ L do
May 3d Then was Maried John Hambleton & Patience French ℘
L do
3 Then was Maried William Woodrop & Elizabeth Crokat
℘ L Mr Garden
7th Then was Maried John Tanner & Barbara Rumph ℘ L
Mr Orr
22d Then was maried Thomas Lambson & Martha Stone ℘ L
Mr Garden
June 23d Then was Maried Peter Horry & Martha Romsey - -
℘ L
July 5th Then was Maried James Grayall & Charity Fickling ℘ L
20th Then was Maried Christopher Smith & Susannah Huddleston ℘ L
Augst: 7th Then was Maried Seamour Mallery & Mary Scrogins - -
℘
16th Then was Maried Thomas Crotty and Jane Mackgrew
℘ L
Septr 8th Then was Maried Samuel Clase & Martha Remy ℘ L.
10th Then was maried Richard Masson & Margaret Morgan
℘ L
11th Then was maried William Harris & Mary Wilkinson ℘ L

Marriages Continued [179]

1737
Septr 17th Then was Maried David Fox and Mary Dill ℘ L ℘r Mr Garden
Octor 4th Then was Maried John Tipper & Mary Parrot ℘ L
13th Then was Maried Jonathan Bryan & Mary Williamson
℘ L

Novr 3d Then was Maried James Michie & Martha Hall — — ℔ L
24th Then was Maried Henry Christian Mackrodd & Susannah Maria Durousseaū — — — — — — — — — — — — — ℔ L
24th Then was Maried Abijah Russ and Rachel Moore— ℔ L-
28th Then was Maried Alexander Dingwell & Mary Middleton ℔ L
Decr: 21st Then was Maried Henry Karlington and Margaret Winter ℔ B.
21st Then was Maried Michel Christopher Row & Margaret Hesy ℔ B.
23d Then was Maried Daniel Hunt & Christian Thompson ℔ L
Jany 3d Then was Maried John Cattel & Margaret Levingstone ℔ L
6th Then was Maried John Rivers & Hannah Tathom ℔ B.—
12th Then was maried Benjamin Roberts and Mary Holton ℔ L
16th Then was Maried Benjamin Savage & Martha Pickering ℔ L:
ffebry 11th Then was Maried Elsworth Darvil & Elizabeth Storey ℔ L:
13th Then was Maried Martin Coleman & Marian Leander ℔ L
16th Then was Maried John Beekman & Ruth Watson — — ℔ L
16th Then was Maried Charles Theodore Patchelbel & Hannah Poitevin ℔ L.......... } ℔ L
25th Then was Maried John Deveaux & Sarah Sullivant- ℔ L
28th Then was Maried Horatio Samuel Middleton & Anne Sutton ℔ L
Mar: 4th Then was maried Adam Beauchamp & Jane Mackqueen ℔ L
20th Then was maried Francis Bishop & Jane Goodin ℔ L
25th Then was Maried James Tucker & Kusiah Mallory ℔ B:

1738
April 2 Then was Married John Lacy & Anne Miller per L.
April 2 Then was Married Thomas Charnock & Sibell Milner ℔ L
April 2 Then was Married William Luter & Elizabeth Holworth ℔ L
17 Then was Married William Orr & Isabella Scott per L.
May 7 Then was Married Samuel Smith & Jehosubeth Morris ℔ L
16 Then was Married Charles Reid & Mary Cannon ℔ L

[180] 1738 Marriages Continued

May 23 Then was Married Joseph Batsford & Bridget Hughes ℔ Licence

June 3 Then was Married William Evans & Sarah Cox per License
5 Then was Married Peter Coutua & Mary Middleton ⅌ L
22 Then was Married Artimus Elliott & Mary Burnham ⅌ L
26 Then was Married Berrisford Bacon & Sarah Montgomrie ⅌ L
27 Then was Married John Prosser and Anne Harris ⅌ L
July 4 Then was Married John Menson & Margaret Snelling ⅌ Banns.
7 Then was Married Phanuel Cook & Elizabeth Woodward ⅌ L.
18 Then was Married George Helm & Anne Mc:Cullock ⅌ L.
28 Then was Married Alexander Sands & Mary Wells per Licence.
August 7 Then was Married Ralph Rodda & Dorothy Evans ⅌ L———
31 Then was Married John Houghton & Mary Sheppard ⅌ L———
Septemr. 14 Then was Married Alexander Wood & Anne Partridge ⅌ L———
Octobr. 23 Then was Married John Watson and Sarah Pigot per Licence
Novemr. 5 Then was Married Edward Fowler & Elizabeth Yates ⅌ L—
do. 5 Then was Married Samuel Hyde & Sarah Moncrieff ⅌ Licence
6 Then was Married George Coker and Eleaner Thomas ⅌ L—
16 Then was Married Kenedy Obryan and Mary Wigg ⅌ Licence
26 Then was Married Thomas Dale Esqr and Anne Smith, ⅌ L:———
Decmr 23 Then was Married John Oliver and Sarah Russell per Licence
January 7 Then was Married Thomas Pool and Elizabeth Tootle ⅌ L.
do. 8 Then was Married Philip Prioleau & Anne Etheridge ⅌ L
29 Then was Married Richard Cook and Hannah Willeby per Banns
29 Then was Married Thomas Lomitt & Martha Watkins per Licence
30 Then was Married John Vantutrÿ and Mary Shumlevin ⅌ L
30 Then was Married Lionel Chalmers & Martha Logan ⅌ L—
31 Then was Married Robert Stede and Martha Watkins ⅌ L

Februy: 17 Then was Married Andrew Deveaux & Magdalen Juneau ℘ L

18 Then was Married William Williams & Mary Mackenzie ℘ L

19 Then was Married Alexander Rattery & Hannah Shell ℘ L

March 1 Then was Married Francis Bremare and Martha Laurens ℘ L

1739

April 7 Then was Married Israel Deveaux & Elizabeth Martin ℘ L

17 Then was Married Gabriel Collea and Catherine Davis ℘ L

22 Then was Married Samuel Leger and Mary Tucker ℘ L

22 Then was Married John Mackall and Martha Hext ℘ L

29 Then was Married William Ward and Mary Pearse ℘ L

29 Then was Married William Edwards & Martha Watkins ℘ L

May 1 Then was Married John Smith and Sarah Rice ℘ L

17 Then was Married Patrick Blair and Mary Stathams ℘ L

21 Then was Married Richard Howard and Sarah Hawkins ℘ L

22 Then was Married Joseph Brown and Mary Hudson ℘ L

1739 Marriages Continued [181]

June 5 Then was Married James Bobby and Catherine Smith. per Licence

d°. 13 Then was Married Nassau Hastie and Mary Still ℘ L

27 Then was Married Samuel Higginson & Margery Hamilton ℘ L

July 18 Then was Married John Conyer and Anne Stone ℘ L

22 Then was Married Joseph Norton & Maryann Archibald ℘ L

24 Then was Married Cornelius Rand and Hester Orems ℘ Banns

August 2 Then was Married James Donohow & Judith Clark ℘ Licence

2 Then was Married John Thompson & Cybell Dyngle ℘ Licence

7 Then was Married John Lacy and Anne Lowe ℘ L.

16 Then was Married William Trueman and Elizabeth Gleadorse ℘ L

19 Then was Married William Harris and Sarah Tucker per Licence

Septr. 9 Then was Married Peter Shaw and Martha Blundall widow ℘ L

Octob. 3 Then was Married Peter Boquet & Barbara Sence, ℘ L

14 Then was Married Samuel Prioleau & Providence Hext ꝑ L

17 Then was Married Benjamin Webb and Mary Matthyson ꝑ L

Novem^{r} 11 Then was Married John Yarmouth and Sarah Bridge ꝑ L

Decem^{r}. 1 Then was Married James Smith & Elizabeth Harris ꝑ L

6 Then was Married David Adams and Anne Jenkins ꝑ L

8 Then was Married Azariah Sandwell & Elinor Linthwaite ꝑ L

15 Then was Married John Martin & Margaret Reid ꝑ L

16 Then was Married William Farrow & Rachel Callebeuff ꝑ L

Janu^{ry}: 3 Then was Married James Collins and Mary Thomson ꝑ L

14 Then was Married John Murray and Lucy Smith ꝑ L

15 Then was Married, William Passwater & Hannah Pezaza ꝑ L

16 Then was Married, Robert Harvey and Mary Stevenson ꝑ L

18 Then was Married John Tipper and Susannah Orem, ꝑ L

Febru^{y} 12 Then was Married, John Johnson & Catherine Stevens ꝑ L

12 Then was Married John Townshend and Hannah Holland ꝑ L

13 Then was Married William Smith and Anne Linter ꝑ L

March 22 Then was Married John Mackoy & Elizabeth Lee ꝑ L

1740

April 7 Then was Married Zachariah Brazier & Mary Anne Fairfax ꝑ L

8 Then was Married Henry Dewick and Anne Dymes ꝑ L

11 Then was Married John Devant & Izabella Watson ꝑ L

17 Then was Married William Stewart and Anne Hall ꝑ L

22 Then was Married John Drayton and Sarah Newberry ꝑ L

26 Then was Married John Johnston & Sarah Glazier ꝑ Licence

[182] Marriages Continued

1740

April 29 Then was Married John Allen and Anne Scott by Licence

29 Then was Married Thomas Oliver and Anne Vanvelsen ꝑ L

May 6 Then was Married Benjamin Russ and Elizabeth Parker ꝑ L

24 Then was Married John Francois Triboudett & Lucreece Musard ꝑ L

31 Then was Married Richard Haselton and Susanna Gilbert ꝑ L

June 4 Then was Married Richard Freeman and Anne Loroach ꝑ L

4 Then was Married John Mack and Sarah Brickles ꝑ L

12 Then was Married William Westberry and Elizabeth Upham ꝑ L

29 Then was Married Samuel Jones and Rebecca Holmes ꝑ L

July 5 Then was Married Thomas Atwell and Martha Cox ꝑ L

9 Then was Married John Sallens and Jane Morgan ꝑ L

17 Then was Married William Webb and Sarah Peronneau ꝑ L

August 25 Then was Married Hugh Surrey and Hanah Smith ꝑ L

Septemb. 3 Then was Married Samuel Macquoid & Abigail Goble ꝑ L

5 Then was Married William Tilly and Mary Gibbs ꝑ L

9 Then was Married George Newcombe & Hannah Skinner ꝑ L

28 Then was Married Thomas Hardin and Angel Scott ꝑ L:

Octobr. 12 Then was Married Jeremiah Leaycroft & Anne Sterling ꝑ L.

12 Then was Married Thomas Chapman and Anne Helm ꝑ L:

15 Then was Married Richard Shubrick & Elizabeth Viccaridge ꝑ L

25 Then was Married Arthur Nash and Mary Coleman, ꝑ L

Novembr. 5 Then was Married William Hartman & Ruth Scanlen, ꝑ L

6 Then was Married Albert Ditmere and Mary Craige ꝑ L

12 Then was Married George Page and Catherine Clements ꝑ L

23 Then was Married James Wedderburn & Susanna Frazer ꝑ L

Decembr. 4 Then was Married Thomas Humpress & Anne Armestrong ꝑ L to Mr. G.

18 Then was Married William Payne and Anne Clifford ꝑ L

19 Then was Married William Mackartey and Anne Dennis ꝑ L

22 Then was Married Thomas Innis and Unity Ridley ꝑ L

25 Then was Married Richard Powers and Esther Morgan ꝑ L

January 1 Then was Married Isaiah Brunett & Susannah Mary Leay ꝑ L

1 Then was Married Benjamin Green & Jennet Cooper ꝑ Banns

13 Then was Married Timothy Marr and Mary Dawson ꝑ Licence

13 Then was Married Grafton Déane and Mary Shrewsbury ꝑ L

15 Then was Married Joseph Hutchens & Catherine Cuttice ꝑ L

16 Then was Married William Sym and Jane Negus ꝑ Licence

1740 Marriages continued [183]

Janury. 31 Then was married William Brown & Esther Dupuy ꝑ Licence

Februy: 14 Then was married Thomas Ferguson and Mary Leay ꝑ do.

March 9 Then was married Thomas Griffith & Rebecca Ridgill Widow ꝑ ditto

19 Then was married John Robinson and Anne Jones ꝑ Licence

April 13 Then was married George Harris and Rachel Lance ꝑ ditto

1741 23 Then was married Jacob Fidling and Rebecca Edenburgh ꝑ Licence

23 Then was married Thomas Heathly and Susannah Monroe ꝑ L

May 31 Then was married George Avery and Mary Savy ꝑ Licence

June 18 Then was married Andrew Ruck and Judith Miller ꝑ L

24 Then was married Bartholomew Baptist and Hanah Wilkins ꝑ Banns

July 2 Then was married Samuel Smith Junior & Elizabeth Dill per Licence

8 Then was married Gideon Norton and Anne Proscer ꝑ L.

12 Then was married Samuel Stone Maverith & Catherine Cayer ꝑ L.

23 Then was married Francis Delgrass and Sarah Arno ꝑ L.

Augut 27 Then was married Thomas Hall and Deborah Hancock ꝑ L

Septr. 11 Then was married Thomas Rybold and Mary Thornton ꝑ L.

20 Then was married Roger Jones and Phebe Parrey ꝑ L.

Octob. 8 Then was married Samuel Hurst and Mary Henderson ꝑ L.

29 Then was Married Luke Stoutenbourgh & Sarah Mackenzie ℔ L.

Nov[r]. 1 Then was Married Joseph Alston & Margaret Cameron ℔ Banns

3 Then was Married John Akles and Margery Jordan ℔ Licence

8 Then was Married Arthur Mowbray & Mary Stanyarn ℔ L

9 Then was Married Marmaduke Ash and Elizabeth Gordon ℔ L

12 Then was Married Thomas Rhodes and Mary Blair ℔ L.

15 Then was Married Edward Jenkens and Elizabeth Savy ℔ L

19 Then was Married John Gardner and Rachael Heatley ℔ L

Decemb[r]. 8 Then was Married Felix Byrn & Deborah Mackey ℔ L.

10 Then was Married James Akin and Sarah Bremar ℔ L

13 Then was Married George Saxby and Elizabeth Seabrook ℔ L.

31 Then was Married Nicholas Burnham and Elizabeth Smith ℔ L.

Janu[ry]: 3 Then was Married Henry Harremond & Elizabeth Montcrief ℔ L.

8 Then was Married Robert Edgell and Mary Hewitt ℔ L———

10 Then was Married Henry S[t]. Martin & Philipine Henning ℔ L.

13 Then was Married Jeremiah Theis & Cathrine Elizabeth Shaumlefall ℔ L.

22 Then was Married John Cart and Rachael Dallas ℔ Licence

Febru[y]. 2 Then was married William Alexander and Deborah Mariner ℔ Banns

[184] Marriages continued —

1741

Febru[y] 9 Then was Married Florentius Cox and Sarah Lockyer ℔ Licence

24 Then was Married Thomas Honyhorn & Sarah Woodbury ℔ Licence

March 1 Then was married Peter Laurens & Lydia Laurens ℔ Licence

1742 26 Then was married James Torquit & Jane Weatherly ℔ Licence

April 2 Then was Married Nicholas Mathyson & Bridget Duncook ℔ Licence

May 1 Then was Married Joseph Mary & Jane Albert ꝑ Licence
13 Then was Married George Fickline & Jane Cammell ꝑ Licence
June 10 Then was Married John Francis & Anne Basset ꝑ Banns—
July 1 Then was Married George Galphin & Bridget Shaw ꝑ Licence
3 Then was Married John Laurens & Elizabeth Wicking ꝑ Licence
8 Then was Married Thomas Bearley & Martha Atwell, ꝑ Licence
8 Then was Married John Weems & Frances Hasell ꝑ Licence
27 Then was Married Daniel Bell & Margery Higgeson ꝑ Licence
29 Then was Married John Eycott & Mary Jeys, ꝑ Licence
Augut 24 Then was married John Wheeler & Sarah Winn ꝑ Licence
Septemr. 21 Then was married Thomas Lamboll and Mary Detmar ꝑ Licence
22 Then was married William Garnes and Rachel Mc.Daniel ꝑ Licence
25 Then mas Married William Duthy and Jane Boone ꝑ Licence
26 Then was married Thomas Ferguson and Hannah Sterland ꝑ Licence
30 Then was Married William Saxby and Sarah Hales ꝑ Licence
Octob: 11 Then was Married John Craston & Julia Miller ꝑ Licence
26 Then was married Alexander Monroe & Mary Anne Cameron ꝑ Banns—
28 Then was married Edward Mead and Catherine Salter ꝑ Licence
31 Then was Married Edward Richardson and Elizabeth Fl'y ꝑ Licence
Novemb: 11 Then was married Francis Clark and Mary Smith ꝑ Licence
20 Then was married Anthony Smith and Anne Middleton ꝑ Licence
23 Then was married Townsend Crisp and Mary Cowley ꝑ Licence
Decemr 20 Then was married Cornelius Solom & Anne Barnes ꝑ Banns
21 Then was married James Lessesne and Sarah Walker ꝑ Licence

1742

Decem^{r}. 25 Then was married Renè Gygee and Elizabeth Ker ꝑ Banns

27 Then was married William Johnsone & Anne Symmons (2 negro's) ꝑ Ban

January 13 Then was married Thomas Smith and Mary Chick ꝑ Licence

15 Then was married William Mouat and Anne Smith ꝑ Licence

20 Then was married Edward Swann and Rachel Robinson ꝑ Licence

February 3 Then was married Samuel Wainwright and Frances Goddard ꝑ Licence

23 Then was married Charles Steadman and Anne Simpson ꝑ Licence

24 Then was married Miles Brewton and Mary Payne ꝑ Licence

26 Then was married Alexander Chesolm and Judith Ratcliffe ꝑ Licence

1743

April 7 Then was married Robert Stewart and Elizabeth Clifford ꝑ Licence

10 Then was married Timothy Britten and Mary Goddard ꝑ Licence

14 Then was married John Dick and Mary Gascoigne ꝑ Licence

16 Then was married Samuel Perkins and Sarah Cartwright ꝑ Licence

28 Then was married James Ramsey and Sarah Jean ꝑ Licence

May 7 Then was married John Moore and Elizabeth Moore ꝑ Banns

25 Then was married Morgan Griffith and Mary Walford ꝑ Licence

27 Then was married Captn. Thomas Frankland and Sarah Rhett ꝑ Licence

June 19 Then was married Peter Sanders and Elizabeth Fishburn, ꝑ Licence

30 Then was married Thomas Dale and Hannah Symmonds ꝑ Licence

30 Then was married Samuel Perronneau and Elizabeth Daniel ꝑ Licence

July 3 Then was married Moses Audibert and Susanna Tozer, ꝑ Licence

Augut 11 Then was married John Witherston & Martha Perroneau ℘ Licence

25 Then was married Stephen Bedon & Ruth Nicholas ℘ Licence

27 Then was married William Smith & Mary Denistone ℘ Licence

Septr. 3 Then was married George Inglis & Elizabeth Parker ℘ Licence

21 Then was married John Croft & Magdalen Menson ℘ Licence

Novemr 3 Then was married John Coleman & Martha Bee ℘ Licence

9 Then was married Richard Akerman & Mary Brown ℘ Licence

20 Then was married William Reid & Catherine Bullen ℘ Licence

23 Then was married Adam Mc.donald & Anne Wood ℘ Licence

24 Then was married Austin Robert Lockton & Margaret Strahan ℘ Licence

Decem 15 Then was married Alexander Hext & Jane Weaver per Licence

29 Then was married James Edes & Penelope Delescure ℘ Licence

Janury. 14 Then was married James Marsh & Susannah Bisset ℘ Licence

15 Then was married John Kingston & Anne Camren ℘ Licence

[186] Marriages continued

1743

Februy 4 Then was married Francis Gotier & Isabel Gordon per Licence

9 Then was married Philip Pinyard & Anne Millar ℘ Licence

21 Then was married Nicholas Millar & Elenor Henox ℘ Licence

28 Then was married James Goelett & Mary Handcock ℘ Licence

March 11 Then was married John Menson & Anne Trusler ℘ Licence

17 Then was married Nathanel Fuller & Sarah Loyd per Licence

1744

April 3 Then was married William Hopton and Sarah Clap ℘ Licence

Then was maried Dolbiack (see folio 189) by ye French ministr

26 Then was maried Rob[t] *Couzens** & Lillies Ducket ℔ Licence

May 6 Then was maried Peter David & Anne Keating ℔ License

18 Then was married William Woodhouse & Elizabeth Fairchild ℔ Licence

June 20 There was married John Paul Grimke & Anne Grimboll ℔ Licence

4 Then was married James Rogers & Anne Edwards ℔ Licence

29 Then was married Charles Mitchell & Martha Tamilson ℔ Licence

July 25 Then was married Charles Richmond Gascoyn & Sarah Tipper ℔ Licence

27 Then was married Joseph Russill & Mary Raven ℔ Licence

28 Then was married Henry Allen & ℔ Licence

Aug[t] 4 Then was married John Moncreef & Elinor Elders ℔ Licence

8 Then was married Geo Bell to Mary Bee ℔ Licence

18 Then was married William Kirk to Mary Dolaback ℔ D[o]

Sept[r] 1 Then was married Joseph Wilcox to Elioner Miller ℔ D[o]

23 Then was married Vincent Leaycroft to Elizabeth Righton ℔ D[o]

Octo[r] 23 Then was married William Plaiters to Sarah Saller ℔ D[o]

25 Then was married Hugh Bryan to Mary Prioleau ℔ D[o]

Nov[r] 1 Then was married Peter Marcon to Mary Voloux ℔ D[o]

5 Then was married James Comerford to Mary Dering ℔ D[o]

6 Then was married Thomas Green to Anne Jenkins ℔ D[o]

8 Then was married James Thomson Margaret M[c]kay ℔ D[o]

9 Then was married John Causton to Mary Pestell ℔ D[o]

13 Then was married Humphrey Elliot Catherine Booth ℔ D[o]

29 Then was married Thomas Lamboll to Elizabeth Pitts D[o]

Dec[r]- 1 Then was married John Walker to Sarah Morren ℔ Banes

8 Then was married Thomas Hall to Elizabeth Hale ℔ Lic-

22 Then was married Edward Bushell to Mary Bull ℔ Licence

24 Then was married Alexander Peroneau to Margeret Hext D[o]

29 Then was married Rob[t] London to Frances Moungin ℔ D[o]

31 Then was marrid William Herbert to Elizabeth Oram D[o]

Jan[y] 9 Then was married Thomas Lowe to Sarah Collins ℔ D[o]

Marriages Continued [187]

1744/5

Jan[y]- 10 Then was married Luke Stoutenburgh to Susannah M[c]kenzie ℔ L

---

*"Corsan" interlined above.

17 Then was married John Harvey to Catherine Croft ℘ L
30 Then was married Thomas Rice to Elizabeth Bond ℘ L
30 Then was married Talbott Brown to Margeret Cuddy ℘ L
Feby 1 Then was married John Abbot to Elizabeth Houce ℘ L
Mar 4 Then was married Samuel Laier to Dorothy Caen ℘ L
8 Then was married Charles Bishaw & Anne Hazel ℘ L
8 Then was married Mark Haines & Eliza Porter ℘ L
11 Then was married Thomas Bint & Anne Dixon ℘ L
22 Then was married James Summers & Mary Lang ℘ L
1745 28 Then was married Rodrick Morrison & Jane Gorden ℘ L
28 Then was married Hugh Anderson & Anne Robinson ℘ L
29 Then was married Joseph Cole & Barbara Walter ℘ L
30 Then was married Joseph Singletary & Hannah Dunham Do
April 4 Then was married Nathaniel Green & Susannah Huthinson ℘ L
8 Then was married John Watts & Joppe Stuard by Banes
May- - 7 Then was married John Loup & Martha Clayter ℘ L
21 Then was married George Addis & Bethia Beesley ℘ L
O mitt ed vizt—

1744
Febry 3d Then was married Christopher Jones & Catherine Brown pr Lic
——— 7th Then was married Joseph Fenn & Elizabeth Hamean pr. Lic:
.... 21th Then was married James Hawkins & Rebekah Tipper pr Lic:
.... 24th Then was married, Thomas Newton & Sarah Hawks .... pr Licence
.... 27th Then was married, William Ball & Catherine Burrows pr Licence
Marc 2d: Then was married, William Lupton & Alice North .. pr Licence

1745
May. 9th Then was married, James Mattrass & Jane Chechez pr Licence
June 3d Then was married, Isaac Colcock & Catherine Woodman pr Licence
.... 6th. Then was married, Peter Cattel & Mary Lloyd .. pr Licence—
.... 6th. Then was married, Robert Herry & Margaret Pope pr Licence
.... 8th. Then was married, Robert Colley & Mary Kelly. .pr Licence
.... 15th: Then was married, Archibald Knox & Elizabh: Croft pr Licence
July.. 29th Then was married, Alexr: McGregor, & Hannah Bestat pr Lic:

.... 31st Then was married. John Bilby & Mary Haddock pr Licence.—
August 3d Then was married, William Dicks & Jane Hutchins pr Licence
.... 10th Then was married, George Winter & Barbara Howzen ℘ Licence
.... 31st Then was married, Michael Roche & Anne Glazebrook ℘ Licence
Septr.. 5th Then was married, William Roper & Grace Hext ℘ ; Licence
.... 7th: Then was married, Griffin Tubbs & Jane Middleton pr Licence

[188] Marriages continued

1745

Septemr 8th: Then was married, Robert Hamilton & Mary Derber pr Licence
.....................26th: Then was married, Willm: Amy & Rebekah Wainwright pr Lic
October 2d: Then was married, John Finley & Eleanor Smith pr. Licence
.... 8th: Then was married, Mark Anthony Besseliau & Martha Chichet ℘ L
.... 20th: Then was married, William Bisset & Mary Smith pr Licence
Novem— 19th: Then was married, Adam Beauchamp & Elizabeth Nichols pr Lic:
.... 19th: Then was married, Maurice Keating & Mary Jones pr Licence
Decem—: 8th: Then was married, Peter Timothy & Ann Donavan pr Licence
.... 26th: Then was married, Thomas Hoyland & Anna Maria Linthwaite ℘ Lic—
January 8th: Then was married, Thomas Weaver & Martha Shaw pr Licence
——— 28th Then was married, William Dry & Mary Jane Rhett ℘r Licence
Febry..: 4th Then was married, Kenneth Michie & Mary Clapp pr Licence
.... 9th: Then was married, Edmund Summersett & Catherine Shroseberry ℘ L
11th: Then was married, Thomas Tew, & Joan Robinson pr: Licence—
22d Then was married, John Watson & Anne Blair pr Licence
27th: Then was married, Thomas Beazley & Susannah Appleby pr Licence by the Revd Mr R: Betham *Assist to the Rector of St Philips*

March 6th: Then was married Charles Hill & Sarah Smith pr Licence by A:G

.... 15th: Then was married William Wright & Catherine Craig pr Lic—:

.... 18th Then was married John Fawkner & Anne Bint pr. Lic—:

1746. 31 Then was married Joseph Gaultier & Mary Esther Portal pr do:

April 1st: Then was married Nathaniel Wickham & Martha Stone pr do:

.... 14th Then was married Peter Larey & Elizabeth James pr Licence pr. Mr Garden ———

.... 24th Then was married John Dart & Mary Hext by Licence— ——————————By Revd. Mr. Betham

.... 26th Then was married James La Chapelle and Patience —— ——————————Hutchins pr Lic— by Revd Mr Garden.

May 8th Then was married Thomas Shubrick & Sarah Motte ——— ——————————℘r. Lic— by Mr: Garden ————

.... 14 Then was married William Morgan & Alice Smith pr Lic

.... 16 Then was married Nathaniel Burt junr & Rebeccah Mallory pr Lic:

.... 24th Then was married Alexander Livie & Catherine Philp—— Spinster by Lic by the Revd Mr. Robt Betham —————

.... 27th: Then was married James Doughty & Ann Wilson pr-Licence —————————— by the Revd. Mr Robt Betham

Marriages Continued [189]

1746

June 12th Then was married Paul Villeponteux & Mary Gantlett ——————————pr Lic: by the Revd Mr Robt Betham—

July. 3d. Then was married Joseph Cox & Hannah Liston Spinter pr Lic: by the Revd Mr Robt Betham

.... 8th... Then was mraried Peter Commett and Hannah Watson— ——————————pr Lic by the Revd. Mr Robt Betham

.... 23d Then was married Thomas Lloyd and Mary Mathews —————————— ℘ Lic by the Revd. Mr Robt Betham

.... 22d Then was married John Jones & Dorothy Christian Spinster ————— pr Lic by the Revd. Mr Robt Betham

.... 27 Then was married George Spencer & Catherine Rowland ——————————pr Lic by the Revd Mr Robt Betham

.... 28 Then was married Christopher Gadsden & Jane Godfrey Spins ————— pr Lic by the Revd Mr Robt Betham

.... 31 Then was married Jemmitt Cobley & Eleanor Wright Spins ——————pr Lic Endorsed by the Revd. Betham to the Revd. Mr Quincey-

1746
August 10 Then was married John Owen & Ann Scull Widow ℘r Lic ————by Endorsm^{t} on the Same to the Revd Mr Durant

---

1746
August 12 Then was married Francis Roche & Anne Simmons Spinster by the Revd Josiah Smith presbyter Minist^{r} According to the form of their profession ———— Remington Reg^{r}

1744/5
Febry... 5th Then was married Benjamin Mathews & Ann Holmes Spinster by the Rev^{d} M^{r}. Josiah Smith presbyter Minister According to the form of their profession ————Remington Reg^{r}

John Daniell At the Desire of M^{r}. John Daniell of Charles Town Shipwright It is Register'd, That the said John Daniell and Mary Arnoll Widow of John Arnoll were married 25th December 1732 by the Revd Mr Nathan Basset presbyter Minist^{r}. According to the form of that profession ————————Remington Reg^{r}.

1746
August 17th Then was married William Bull jun^{r}; & Hannah Beale ————Spinster p^{r} Lic by the Rev^{d}- Mr Robert Betham ———

Adrian Loyer Adrian Loyer and Catherine Dalbiac Widow were married the twenty fourth day of April One thousand seven Hundred & forty four, p^{r} Licence Endorsed by the Rev^{d} M^{r}. Alex^{r} Garden to Henry Chiffelle French Minister ————

---

[190] Marriages Continued

1746
August 19th Then was married Richard Lake & Mary Houghton Widow——p^{r} Licence by the Rev^{d}: Mr Robert Betham—

August 19th Then was married Samuel Giddens & Elizabeth Ellis Spinster——p^{r} Licence by the Rev^{d}. Mr Robert Betham—

1745
Febry: 17th Then was married John Scott & Darkes Heskett Spinster by Banns, by the Rev^{d}. Mr Josiah Smith Presbyter Minister

---

1746
Sept^{r}.. 25 Then was married John Butcher and Barbary Gas Spinster p^{r} Licence by the Rev^{d}. M^{r}. Robt. Betham

---

1746
Oct^{r}. . . 13 Then was married Isaac Liens & Martha Taylor Spinster p^{r} Licence by the Revd Mr Robt Betham

---

1746
Septr. 8 Then was married Joseph Moody & Katherine Dunn Widow

(having been three times published) by the Rev^d Mr Josiah Smith presbyter Minister According to the form of their professon —

1746
Novem—27 Then was married Doctor David Caw & Katherine Serree Widow pr Licence by the Rever^d. Mr Robert Betham

1746
Novem— 30 Then was married William Cray & Mary Gignilliat Spinster pr Lic by the Rev^d. Mr Robert Betham.

1746
Decem^r 6 Then was married James Hunter & Frances Fayssoux Widow pr Lic by the Rev^d. Mr Robert Betham.

1746
Decem^r 18 . Then was married John Mackay & Elizabeth Hamilton Spinster ℘r. Lic by the Rev^d. Mr Robert Betham

1746
Decem— 22 Then was married Jasper Hegerman and Froney Craven Widow pr Lic by the Rev^d. Mr Robert Betham.

——— 28th Then was married Mathias Johnson and Sarah Mackenzie Spinster pr Banns by the Rev^d. Mr. Betham

Jan^ry 17 Then was married Joseph Oram and Frances Wainwright Spinster pr Lic by the Rev^d. Mr Robt Betham

Jan^ry 19 Then was married Joshua Toomer & Sophia Hypworth Spinster pr Lic by the Rev^d. Mr Robt Betham

Feb^ry 6th Then was married Algernon Wilson & Sarah Daniel Spinster ℘r. Lic: by the Rev^d. Mr Robt Betham

Marriages continued [191]

1746
February 14 Then was married Thomas Smith Senr. & Ann Oliver Widow ℘r Licence by the Rev^d. Mr. Bobt Betham

Febru^y: 15 Then was married John Fitzgerald & Grace Butlar— Widow ℘r. Licence by ditto——

February 19 Then was married Daniel Roulain and Catherine McLaughling Spinster ℘r Licence by ditto——

February 22 Then was Married James Irving & Elizabeth Motte Spinster ℘ Lic by the Rev^d. Mr Levi Durant

Feb^ry.... 28 Then was Married Richard Muncreef & Susannah Cray Spinster ℘r Lic by the Rev^d. Mr Robert Betham

February 20 Then was Married William Hart & Mary Coursey Spinster ℘ Licence by the Rev^d. Mr Robert Betham

February 27 Then was married Philip Williams & Mary Magdalen

Benoist Widow pr Licence by the Revd. Mr Robt Betham

1746

Novemr 10th Then was Married Gabriel Gaignard & Frances De Lesslienne Spinster ℘r Lic by the Revd: Mr Levi Durante

1746/7

March 3d Then was married Thomas Colson & Mary OBrian pr Banns by the Revd: Mr Robt. Betham—

do. . . . 11th: Then was married Peter Miller & Anna Maria Lutzen ℘r Licence by the Revd: Mr Robt Betham— ———

1746

July.... 31 Then was married William Cattel junr; & Ann Frazer Spin— by the Revd. Mr: Timothy Mellichamp

1747

April 7th Then was married Benjamin Heape & Mary Wood Spinr. pr Lic—by the Revd. Mr Alexander Garden.

Eodem die Was married John Nelson & Sarah Warmingham Spintr pr Lic: by the Revd. Mr. Alexr: Garden

April 9th Then was married Samuel Smart & Katherine Johnson Widow by Lic by the Revd. Mr: Garden

April 12th. Then was married Levinus Van Schajck & Elizabeth Clark Widow ℘ Licence by the Revd. Mr A Garden

[192] 1747 Marriages

April 19 Then was Married John Fripp & Elizabeth Hunn Spintr: ℘ Lic by the Revd: Mr Alexr Garden — —

23d Then was Married Samuel Quincey & Elizabeth Hill Widow ℘r Licence by the Revd. Mr Alexr Garden

May 2d Then was married John Mackenzie junr & Elizabeth Green Spinstr: ℘r. Lic by the Revd: Mr Robert Betham

Eodem die Was married Stephen Bull Eldest Son of the Lieutn Governor to Judith Mayrant Spinster by the Revd. Mr A Garden ℘ Lic

May 4th Then was married Charles Jacob Pichard, (Son of Alexander & Anna Catharine Pichard, both Burgesses of the City of Yverdon in Switzerland) & Susannah, (Daughter of Daniel & Susannah Bourget both of Charles Town So Carolina) ℘r. Lic by A Garden Rector of St. Philips Chas Town—

May.. 10th Then was married William Milford & Susannah Croskey ℘r: Licence by do.—

April 28 Then was married Joseph Allen & Mary Akerman Widow ℘r Lic ℘ do:—

May 23d Then was married Daniel Gardner & Frances Hackett ℘r .Lic ℘r do :—

May 29th Then was married Abel Inman & Mary Mullet ℘ Lic ℘ do :—

June 5 Then was married Hugh Dobbin & Ann Crese ℘ Lic

8th Then was married William Burch & Carolina Langdon ℘ Banns—

26th Then was married John Vanall & Elizabeth Bonneau ℘ Lic.—

July 13 Then was married Robert Harvey & Elizabeth Mongin Spinster ℘ Lic.—

August 6 Then was married The Revd. Mr William Guy Rector of St Andrews & Elizabeth Cooper Spinster by Lic. by the Revd Mr Alexr: Garden

Marriages [193]

1747 August 17 Then was Married William Elders & Sarah Amory Spinstr. ℘r Licence by the Revd. Mr Alexr Garden

Septr... 3d Then was married Richard Wainwright and Susannah Allen ℘r Lic by the Revd. Mr Alexr Garden.

Septr 14 Then was married Giles Fitchett & Elizabeth Danford ℘ Lic by the Revd.Mr Alexr Garden.—

28 Then was married Samuel Jones & Susannah Scott Spinster ℘ Lic by the Revd. Mr Alexr: Garden

Octr.. 1st- Then was married Peter Fisher & Margaret Mcpherson Widow, ℘r Lic by the Revd. Mr Alexr: Garden.

9th Then was married Richard Glidden & Mary Barrows ℘ Licence ℘ do :—

13th Then was married Samuel Dunlop & Ann Smith ℘ Licence ℘ do :—

14h. Then was married Barnard Taylor & Susannah Bonneau ℘ Licence ℘ do :—

16th. Then was married William Abbot & Catherine Hope ℘ Licence ℘ do :—

30th Then was married Richard Warren & Frances Labri ℘ Licence ℘ do :—

Novr: 14h Then was married Edward Finnekin & Margaret Marshall Widow ℘ Lic ℘ do—

17th: Then was married Thomas Barnes & Susannah Prockter ℘ Lic ℘ do—

17 Then was married Benjamin Perdriau & Mary Barton ℘ Lic ℘ do :—

Decemr 1st Then was married William Kerk & Mary Bennoit ꝑ Lic ꝑ do——

19 Then was Married Samuel Winborn & Naomi Stiles Spinster ꝑr Lic ꝑr do:——

[194] Marriages

1747 Decemr. 23 Then was Married Benjamin Wainwright & Anna Hurst ꝑ Licence by the Revd. Mr Alexr Garden.

29 Then was Married Richard Linter & Sarah Williams ꝑ Banns by do:

January 1st. Then was Married John Williams & Elizabeth Bullard ꝑ License by do

18h. Then was Married Abraham Edings & Sarah Baily ꝑ Licence by do

23d Then was Married Francis Brown & Anne Margaret Come pr Licence ꝑ do:

Febry:.. 2d Then was married Alexander Petrie & Elizabeth Holland ꝑ Lic: ꝑ do:

7th Then was Married Daniel Crawford & Mary Holland ꝑ Lic ꝑ do:

8th Then was Married David Crawford & Isabella Maine by Banns ꝑr. Mr Bell, presbyterian Minister

9th: Then was married Andrew Newton & Martha Ladson ꝑ Licence ꝑr: the Revd. Mr Alexr Garden.

10th Then was married John Suthey & Mary Grant ꝑ Lic ꝑ do:

11th Then was Married John Yarworth & Mary Livingston ꝑ Lic ꝑ do:

17h Then was married William Woolridge & Sarah Low ꝑ Lic pr do:

23 Then was married Francis Spencer & Mary Richards ꝑ Lic pr do:

March 15 Then was married Edward Croft Jun & Mary Wilson ꝑ Lic ꝑ do

18 Then was married Allen Barnet & Ann Purle ꝑ Licence ꝑ do

1748 April.. 10h Then was Married Thomas Smith & Mary Daniell ꝑ Lic ꝑ do

13 Then was Married David Van Leuwe & Agnes Marignaç ꝑr. Banns ꝑr do:

1748 Marriages [195]

April.. 19 Then was Married John Corbett & Mary Clifford ꝑ Licence by the Revd. Mr Alexr Garden

21st Then was Married Benjamin Trapier & Hannah Thompson ℔ Lic ℔ do

28 Then was Married John Thomas & Alice Sidney ℔ Lic ℔ do

May.. 1 Then was Married John Dobell & Susannah Holmes ℔ Lic ℔ do.

1 Then was married Edward Lightwood & Ann Fishburn ℔ Lic ℔ do:

5 Then was married Thomas Broughton & Sarah Heskett ℔ Lic ℔ do:

19 Then was married Charles Stevenson & Mary Benoist ℔ Lic ℔ do:

21 Then was married William Hall & Susanna Treasvant ℔ Licence ℔ do.—

June 7h Then was married Thomas Elfe & Mary Hancock Wido: ℔ Licence ℔ do—

14th Then was married Robert Keown & Elizabeth Harvey ℔ Licence ℔ do:

16th Then was married William Screven & Sarah Stoll Spinster ℔ Licence ℔ do.——

21st Then was married Thomas Poock & Priscilla Dunn ℔ Licence ℔ do:—

23d Then was Married Hopkin Price & Martha Steil Widow ℔ Licence ℔ do:—

29 Then was Married John Moultrie & Elizabeth Mathews Widow ℔ Lic ℔ do.—

30 Then was Married Samuel Henderson & Jane Mattrass Widow ℔ Licence ℔ do—

July.. 4h. Then was Married Leonard Shevrie & Sarah Delgrass Widow ℔ Licence ℔ do—

9h Then was Married Barnard Beekman & Susannah Duval Spinster ℔ Licence ℔ do.

[196] Marriages

1748 August 1st. Then was Married Richard Cussens & Esther Thompson by Banns ℔ A G Rector &c—

Augt. 2d Then was Married Doctor Charles Wellard & Hannah Kellham Spinster ℔ Licence by the Revd. Mr Alexr Garden Rector

Augt 15 Then was Married Rawlins Lownds & Amarintha Elliott Spinstr ℔ Licence by ditto.

Septr 4 Then was married Henry Dungworth & Ann Thomson ℔ Banns . by ditto

8th Then was married John Metheringham & Elizabeth Beau-Champ, Widow ℘ Lic: by ditto

10th Then was married, John Deliesseline & Dorothy Tomson Spinster ℘ Licence. by ditto

October 2d Then was married James Robertson & Helen Innis ℘ Lic.

3d Then was married John Goldin & Mary Robertson ℘ Lic

13th Then was married William Countee & Ruth Leaycroft ℘ Licence. by the Revd. A G

16th Then was married John Thomas & Deborah Scott ℘ Lic

25th Then was married John Ragnous & Mary Davis ℘ Lic.

Novemr: 2d Then was married Christopher White & Mary Ranford ℘ Lic

15 Then was married Benjamin Stead & Mary Johnson Spinstr ℘ Licence by the Revd- A G.

22d Then was married Henry Richardson & Elizabeth Moore ℘ Lic.

Decemr 3d: Then was married Benja: Harvey & Mary Mortimore ℘ Lic

9h Then was married Solomon Dingle & Elizabeth Bodington ℘ Lic.—

15 Then was married, John Harris & Eleanor Watson ℘ Licence.—

1748 Marriages [197]

Dec— 18 Then was Married, William Wilkins & Sarah Marshall ℘ Lic

Janry 5th Then was Married John Roberson & Ann Boddicott ℘ Lic

Febry 1st. Then was Married George Brown & Mary Obart ℘ Lic

6h. Then was Married Thomas Kirk & Marian Lubbeck ℘ Lic.

9h. Then was Married Martin Binseky & Mary Stongeon ℘ Lic.

1749

March 26th Then was Married John Martin & Esther Dubberline ℘ Lic

30 Then was Married Peter Logan & Ann Langdon ℘ Lic

Mar. 28th Then was Married, Edmond Cossens & Eliza: Godfrey ℘ Lic:

April 18th Then was Married John Savage & Ann Allen ℘ Lic

20th: Then was Married William Burrows & Mary Ward ℘ Lic

May 11th Then was Married Theodore Treasvant & Elizabeth Wells ꝑ Lic.

13th Then was Married John Lewis & Sarah Linter ꝑ Lic

June 2d. Then was married William Campbell & Mary Times ꝑ Lic

18th Then was married Peter Cahusac & Mary Manzequen ꝑ Banns

22d Then was married Peter Bostock & Martha Trezvant ꝑ Licence

22d Then was married William Glover and Jane Packrow ꝑ L

22d Then was married John Anding & Francis Hirsh ꝑ L

23d. Then was married Robert Rawlings & Lydia Vouloux ꝑ L

[198] Marriages

1749

June 24 Then was married John Sinclair, Merchant and Sarah Cartwright Spinster ꝑ Lic ꝑ the Revd Mr Garden

July 1st. Then was married David Oliphant & Hannah Freeman ꝑ Lic

2d Then was married Robert Jones & Elizabeth Fly ꝑ Lic

4th. Then was married William Hildyard & Hannah Wills ꝑ Lic.

13th Then was married William Greenland & Catherine Smith ꝑ Lic.

Schermerhorn & Hildreth On the twentyeth day of January 1749/50 were married Arenout Schermerhoorne & Eddy Hildreth, Widw: ꝑ Lic by Mr: Garden Rector &c— Jno Remington Regr

Neufville & Moore On the first day of March 1749/50 were married John Neufville & Elizabeth Moore Spinster ꝑ Lic by Mr. Garden Rector &c Jno Remington Regr.

Cannon & Winn On the Eighth day of March 1749/50 were married Daniel Cannon and Martha Winn Spinr ꝑ Lic by the Revd Mr Garden Rectr. &c Jno Remington Regr

Dart & Hext On the 18th: Day of January 1749/50 were Married, Benjamin Dart & Amelia Hext Spinster ꝑ Lic. by the. Revd. Mr Garden Rectr &c Jno Remington Regr

Graham & Amory On the Eighteenth day of October 1749 were married Mungo Graham & Sarah Amory. ꝑ Lic by the Revd. Mr. Alexr Garden &c— JnoRemington Regr.

Marriages [199]

Hawkes & Coleman On the 30th- Day of July 1749 were Married William Hawkes & Martha Coleman ꝑ Lice by the Revd- Mr. Garden Rectr. &c— Jno Remington Regr.

Mathews & Godin	On the 29th. day of March 1750. were married James Mathews & Charlotte Godin ꝑ Lic by the Revd. Mr. Garden Rectr &c— Jno Remington Regr:
Cooper & Morris	On the 21st day of April 1750 were married John Cooper & Mary Morris ꝑ Lic by the Revd. Mr. Garden Rectr &c— Jno Remington Regr.
Phillips & Herbert	On the 13th. day of September 1749 were married William Phillips & Elizabeth Herbert ꝑ Lic by the Revd. Mr. Alexander Garden Rectr- &c— Jno Remington Regr.
Raven & Holmes	On the sixth Day of November 1750. were married Mr. John Raven & Mrs. Sarah Holmes Spinster ꝑ Licence by the Revd. Mr. Alexr. Keith.... Jno Remington Regr.
Lambton & Walters	On the twenty seventh day of November 1750 were Married Richard Lambton & Ann Walters Widow ꝑ Licence by the Revd. Mr. Alexander Garden Rectr. &c- Jno Remington Regr;
Beekman & Mienson	On the fourth Day of November 1750 were married John Beekman and Ann Mienson widow ꝑ Licence by the Revd Mr Alexr Garden Rector &c Jno Remington Regr;
Hill & Gregory	On the first Day of November 1750. were married James Hill & Susannah Gregory, ꝑ Licence by the Revd Mr Alexr. Garden Rector &c— Jno Remington Regr
Deas & Michie	On the twelfth Day of ffebruary 1750. were married David Deas of Charles Town Merchant and Mary Michie Widow and Relict of Kenneth Michie, Mercht. Deced ꝑ Licence By the Revd Mr Alexr Garden Rector &c Jno Remington Register

[200]

Marriages

Milner & Petty	On the sixteenth day of December 1749 were Married Solomon Milner and Mary Petty Widow by the Revd Mr Alex Garden Rector &c- Jno Remington Regr ꝑ Licence
Neyle & Garden	On the fourteenth day of February 1750. Were Sampson Neyle of Charles Town Merchant and Martha Garden Spinster, Daughter of the Revd- Mr- Alexander Garden Rector of the Parish of St Philips Charles Town ꝑ Licence ꝑ the Revd. Mr: Jno Remington Regr.
Chaddock & Christian	On the first day of August 1749 were Married Thomas Chaddock & Ann Modiner Christian ꝑ Lic by the Revd. Mr. Garden Rector &c— Jno Remington Regr.
Fry & Charity	On the 15h day of August 1749 were married Paltor Fry and Martha Charity ꝑ Licence.

Burk & Vance	On the 18 day of August 1749 were married Tobias Burk & Mary Vance ℘ Licence
Screven & Stoll	On the 22^{d} day of August 1749 were married William Screven and Catherine Stull ℘ Licence
Hiscock & Wickers	On the 11th. day of September 1749 were married Martha Wickers & Edward Hiscock ℘ Lic
Roche & Watkins	On the 18^{h} day of September 1749 were married Dominick Roche & Mary Watkins ℘ Licence
Jones & Norris	On the fourth day of October 1749 were married Joseph Jones & Mary Norris ℘ Licence
McGilvery & Laroche	On the twelfth day of October 1749 were married Alex^{r}. McGilvery & Mary Laroche ℘ Licence

Marriages [201]

Frazer & Harvey	On the tenth day of November 1749 were Married Alexander Frazer & Ann Harvey ℘ Lic.
Outerbridge & Clemens	On the Nineteenth day of November 1749 were married White Outerbridge & Ann Clemens Watson ℘ Lic
Millekin & Watson	On the Nineteenth day of November 1749 were Married George Millekin & Mary Watson ℘ Licence
Thompson & Hutchins	On the twentyeth day of November 1749 were Married John Thompson & Sarah Hutchins ℘ Licence
Nightingale & Elder	On the thirtieth day of November 1749 were Married Thomas Nightingale & Sarah Elder ℘ Licence
Moultrie & De St Julian	On the 10th. day of December 1749 were married William Moultrie & Elizabeth Damaris De St Julian ℘ Licence
Brown & Guerin	On the 13th. day of December 1749 were Married Francis Brown & Mary Guerin ℘ Licence
Roulain & Hutchins	On the 25^{h} day of December 1749 were married Abraham Roulain & Mary Hutchins ℘ Licence

Butler & Graham — On the 27th Day of Feby- 1749 were married Peter Butler and Elizabeth Graham Spinster ℘ Licence

Brailsford & Holmes — On the 2d. April 1750 were married Samuel Brailsford & Elizabeth Holmes ℘ Lic

[202] Marriages

Sheed & Wilkins — On the 23d. May 1750 . were Married George Sheed and Eleanor Wilkins ℘ Lice

McGilveray & Patchable — On the fourth day of June 1750 were Married Alexander McGilveray & Elizabeth Patchabel ℘ Licence

Laurens & Ball — On the 25th. day of June 1750 were Married Henry Laurens and Eleanor Ball ℘ Licence

Henderson & Cook. — On the 25th: day of November 1750. were Married William Henderson & Sarah Cook ℘ Lic

Corker & Hill — On the 27h day of November 1750 were Married Thomas Corker & Mary Hill ℘ Lic

Cleiland & Simpson — On the 18th. December 1750. were Married Doctr. John Cleiland & Ann Simpson ℘ Licence

Marriages [203]

Banbury & Bonnetheau — On the 30h day of December 1750. were married William Banbury & Jane Bonnetheau ℘ Licence

Pickering & Lebrasseur — On the tenth day of January 1750 were Married Joseph Pickering & Ann Lebrasseur ℘ Licence

Morril & Burney — On the 19h February 1750 were Married Green Morril & Mary Burney ℘ Licence

Pringle & Bull — On the 16h day of April 1751 were Married Robert Pringle & Judith Bull ℘ Lic

Brandford & Savage — On the 24h day of April 1751. were Married William Brandford & Elizabeth Savage Spinster ℘ Licence

[204] Marriages

Seaman & Allen — On the Second Day of May One thousand seven Hundred & fifty One Mr. George Seaman of Charles Town Merchant & Mrs. Mary Allen Widow of Wm. Allen deced were Married ℘ Licence by the Revd Mr. Alexander Garden Rectr. of St Philips Chas town ———

Jno Remington Regr.

Kennan & Godin — On the third day of June 1751. Mr. Henry Kennan & Mrs Susannah Godin were married ℘ Licence by the Revd. Mr. Alexander Garden Rectr &c

Howell & Philips — On the 29h July 1751. were married, John Howell and Elizabeth Philips ℘ Licence. by Mr.- A Garden Rector &c—

Welch & Amey — On the 31st: July 1751 were married William Welch and Rebeccah Amey ℘ Licence by Mr Garden

Marriages [205]

Meynier & Playstowe — On the 5th: day of September 1751 were Married Peter Meynier and Dorothy Playstowe by Licence by the Revd Mr Alexr Garden Rector &c—

Mathews & Knelson — On the 2d day of November 1751. were married William Mathews & Sarah Knelson ℘ Licence

Lownds & Cartwright — On the 23d December 1751 were Married Rawlins Lownds Esqr; & Mary Cartwright ℘ Lic

[206] Marriages

U'hl & Lydston — On the 10h. day of January 1752 were Married Washington U'hl & Mary Lydston ℘ Licence

Marrino & Gaultier — On the 18th. day of January 1752 were Married Charles Marrino & Mary Henriette Gaultier ℘ Licence

Snelling & Jones — On the 5th day of February 1752 were married John Snelling & Mary Jones ℘ Lic

Carne & Borland — On the 23d February 1752 were Married Samuel Carne & Jannet Borland ℘ Lic

Laurens & Broughton — On the 10th March 1752 were Married Mr. James Laurens and Mary Broughton ℘ Licence ℘ the Revd, Mr. Levi Durand of St. Johns Berkley County

Marriages [207]

Reid & Cossens — On the 16h April 1753 were Married Patrick Reid & Elizabeth Cossens Widow ꝑ Lic by Mr Keith

Bedon & Baker — On the 18th. April 1752 were Married John Raven Bedon & Elizabeth Baker ꝑ Licence—

Mathews & Brodie — On the tenth day of May 1753 were married John Mathews & Mary Brodie ꝑ Licence

Peronneau jun & Motte — On the 14th day of May 1752 Henry Peronneau jun: & Anne Motte Spinster ꝑ Lic

Jones & Woolf — On the 24h day of May 1752 were Married William Jones & Sarah Woolf ꝑ Licence

You & Reed — On the Eleventh day of June 1752 were Married Charles You & Mary Reed ꝑ Licence

Jordon & Nelme — On the Ninth day of July 1752 were married Thomas Gordon and Ann Nelme, Widow ꝑ Licence ꝑ the Revd A. G.

Hinds & Brush — On the twenty Eighth day of October 1752 were Married Patrick Hinds and Sarah Brush ꝑ Licence ꝑ the Revd. A Garden

[208] Marriages

Buncker & Wills — On the sixtenth day of November 1752 were Married John Buncker & Catherine Wills ꝑ Licence

Lloyd & Boone — On the twenty third day of November 1752 were Married Capt. John Lloyd & Rebecca Boone ꝑ Licence

Coughlan & Fryley — On the thirtieth day of November 1752 were married Nathaniel Coughlan & Margaret Fryley ꝑ Licence

Rodgers & McKenzie — On the twelfth day of December 1752 were married Charles Rodgers & Isabel McKenzie ꝑ Licence

Pinckney & Brewton — On the second day of January 1753. were Married Charles Pinckney the Younger & Miss Frances Brewton ꝑ Licence ꝑ the Revd. Alexr Garden.

Lining & Ware — On the first day of March 1753 were Married Thomas Lining of Chas Town Cabinet-Maker & Mrs. Ann Ware ꝑ Licence

Marriages [209]

Ewins & Cox — On the sixth day of March 1753 George Ewins and Priscilla Cox were married ꝑ Lic by the Revd Mr A Garden

---

Sinclair & Stephens — On the 22d. day of March 1753 were married Daniel Sinclair of Charles Town Mariner & Mary Stephens (Daughter of Edward Stephens late of Glostershire & Catherine his Wife) by the Revd. Mr: A: Garden, ꝑ Licence.

Giles & Rennie — On the 23d day of March 1753. were Married John Giles and Jane Rennie ꝑ Lic by the Revd. Mr A Garden

---

Purdue & Gegerin — On the 12 Day of September 1758 John Perdue and Christiana Rosina Gegerin were Married ꝑr. Publication of Banns ꝑr. the Revd, Mr. Richard Clarke Rector

---

Treasvant & Timothy — On the 24h. day of April 1753 were Married Theodore Treasvant & Catherine Timothy ꝑ Lic ꝑ the Revd A. G.

Wragg & Rothmahler — On the first day of May 1753 were Married Samuel Wragg & Judith Rothmahler ꝑ Lic ꝑ the Revd A G

Rodgers & Cornish — On the 5th- day of May 1753. were Married Christopher Rodgers & Elizabeth Cornish ꝑ Lic ꝑ the Revd A. G.

---

vide fol. 149

[210] Burials Brought Back from Fo 315

1744			
Decemr	20	Then was Buried Sarah Pritchard	pd
	22	Then was Buried Thomas Lord	
	30	Then was Buried Anne Lecrafts	pd
	30	Then was Buried Joseph Howard	pd
Jany	4	Then was Buried John Cragg	pd
	5	Then was Buried Joseph Bartlett	
	6	Then was Buried Richard Wright	pd
	10	Then was Buried Elizabeth Clifft	pd
	15	Then was Buried a child found at Mr Jas Tomsons	
	21	Then was Buried James Weaver	
Feby	1	Then was Buried Richard Osgood	
	5	Then was Buried William Thomas mariner	pd
	7	Then was Buried Joseph Robinson	pd

11 Then was Buried Robert Marlin........ pd
15 Then was Buried Hodggis........ pd
21 Then was Henry Scuder Buried........ pd
March } 4 Then was Buried Mary Roper........ pd
8 Then was Buried William Grickson........ pd
14 Then was Buried Susannah Marguas........ pd
18 Then was Buried William Wamsley a Child........
22 Then was Buried Juliana Gorden........
1745 25 Then was Buried Elinor Joy........ pd
29 Then was Buried Benjamin Osborn........ pd
April 4 Then was Buried Mathew Green........
4 Then was Buried Retten........
5 Then was Buried Joseph Billings........
13 Then was Buried Samuel Whitup........
15 Then was Buried David Lewis........
19 Then was Buried William Whitmill........
20 Then was Buried Elizabeth Clapp........
21 Then was Buried John William Claypoole a Child........ pd
22 Then was Buried Johannah Rigney
19 Then was Buried John Pamber........
29 Then was Buried Zachariah Burton
30 Then was Buried Mary Rigney a Child ....
May 2 Then was Buried Isaac Tozier

Burials Continued [211]

1745
May 3 Then was Buried Ann Griffis a child........
4 Then was Buried Mary Randall a Child........
11 Then was Buried Mary Lesur a Child........
27 Then was Buried Charles Peale a Child........
June 4 Then was Buried John Mckilpin........
7 Then was James Prasha Buried mariner Pd
8 Then was Buried Benjamin Avery a Child
13 Then was Buried Robert Collis a Child no prayers
14 Then was Buried Catherine Anderson a Child no prayers
15 Then was Buried John Crappes Parish Charge........
15 Then was Buried Richard Cozens........
16 Then was Buried James Thomson........ pd
16 Then was Buried Mary Hammith a Child........
18 Then was Buried John Thomson a Child........
23 Then was Buried Abraham Radcliffe a Child........ pd
25 Then was Elizabeth Smith Buried a Child........
29 Then was Buried Thomas Wiare a Child........
29 Then was Buried Nicholas Carroule (P)
July 3 Then was Buried William Cooks (P)
9 Then was Buried William Harvey . a child........ pd
16 Then was Buried Lydia Lea a Child........

25 Then was Buried Samuel Stone mariner........................ pd
Aug[t]. 2 Then was Buried Elinor Smith........................ pd
9 Then was Buried Sarah Rand........................ pd
10 Then was Buried Cristinah Hunt........................ pd
11 Then was Buried Elizabeth Hall........................ pd
15 Then was Buried Arnout Johnstone a Child........................pd
15 Then was Buried Thomas Veazie mariner........................ pd
18 Then was Buried Eligah Tonkins a Child no prayers
20 Then was Buried Thomas Fidling a Child........................
21 Then was Buried William Guy........................
22 Then was Buried John Evens........................
24 Then was Buried Hannah Leaycroft a Child........................
24 Then was Buried Mary Claypole a child pd
25 Then was Elizabeth Lea a Child Buried........................
Sept[tr] 1 Then was Felix Voleur — Buried
[212] Burials Continued

1745
Sept[tr] 1 Then was Buried Rebeckah Lee a Child ————————pd
3 Then was Buried Bridget Trew
3 Then was Buried Mary Masson a Child........................
3 Then was Buried Jennet Avery........................
4 Then was Buried Elizabeth Lankister
5 Then was Buried James Porter........................
5 Then was Buried Anne Orchard........................
5 Then was Buried Humphrey Lyon........................
6 Then was Buried John Morrey a child........................
6 Then was Buried Abigal Iboore
7 Then was Buried Anne Huchson........................
7 Then was Buried John Huls........................
10 Then was Buried William Wallis........................ pd
10 Then was Buried George Dunning........................
11 Then was Buried Mary Hirries........................
11 Then was Buried Nicholas Wilson
11 Then was Buried Benjamin Alawayes
11 Then was Buried John Trew - a Boy
11 Then was Buried John........................
12 Then was Buried Andrew Broughton
13 Then was Buried Margaret Avery........................ pd
13 Then was Buried George Bolton
13 Then was Buried Mathew Bramfield........................
13 Then was Buried James Allan........................
14 Then was Buried Gabriel Banbury........................
14 Then was Buried Peter Atkinson........................
15 Then was Buried Samuel Ball........................
15 Then was Buried Michael Crander........................
15 Then was Buried Richard Buxton

15 Then was Buried Thomas Higgman
16 Then was Buried John Mackey
16 Then was Buried Mary Smith
17 Then was Buried Domanick Latham
18 Then was Buried John Yovitt a Child
18 Then was Buried Samuel Parsons a boy

Burials continued [213]

1745
Septr 19 Then was Buried, Hannah Potenger
19 Then was Buried, Thomas Low a Turner
20 Then was Buried, Ann Orchard a Girl
20 Then was Buried, William Lea a Child
20 Then was Buried, Henry Beekman a Child
20 Then was Buried, Thomas Tischurch
20 Then was Buried, John Bryan (Parish)
21 Then was Buried, Henry Hutchins
21 Then was Buried, William Moss. Taylor
22 Then was Buried, Elizabeth Mackenzie
23 Then was Buried, Thos: Hall a Child
25 Then was Buried, Mary Frederick
25 Then was Buried, William Palhampton
25 Then was Buried, Thomas Bint
26 Then was Buried, Elizabeth Fitchett
26 Then was Buried, William Lessley
26 Then was Buried, James Preston.
27 Then was Buried, Doctr: Patrick Talfier
27 Then was Buried, John Vaughan Bricklayer
28 Then was Buried, Ann Butler a Child
29 Then was Buried, Samuel Baley (Parish)
29 Then was Buried, Robert Davis, from Man of Warr
30 Then was Buried, Rhody Crokatt a Child
30 Then was Buried, Gospar Miller
Octobr. 1st. Then was Buried, Mary Peake a Child
2 Then was Buried, James Auber
2 Then was Buried, David Shehand (Parish)
6 Then was Buried, Joseph Deay ... Mariner
6 Then was Buried, George Cooke
6 Then was Buried, William Roan
7 Then was Buried, George Coker
8 Then was Buried, Beech Pall Heathcott
9 Then was Buried, Hannah Baptis. Parish
11 Then was Buried, Alexr: Monroe .... Parish
11 Then was Buried, Simon Seglor.
12 Then was Buried, Francis Goddard
13 Then was Buried, Alexander Smith Taylor
13 Then was Buried, Eleanor Coker a Child

14 Then was Buried, Mary Fletcher..

[214] Burials continued

1745

October 14 Then was Buried, Thomas Platers a Child..........................
16 Then was Buried, Jacob Fidling...
17 Then was Buried, Thomas Lawrence (Parish)..................
17 Then was Buried, John Priston. Mariner.......................
17 Then was Buried, John Thompson boy..............................
18 Then was Buried, Edw[d]: Kelly Mariner...............................
18 Then was Buried, John Davis . . ditto....................................
18 Then was Buried, Sam[l] Doam . . . ditto....................................
18 Then was Buried, Katherine Netham (Parish)...................
22 Then was Buried, William North a Child...........................
23 Then was Buried, Mary Smith...
24 Then was Buried, John M[c]acky . . } Marriners ....
25 Then was Buried, Timothy Samladge } Marriners
25 Then was Buried, Abraham Hasty } Marriners
26 Then was Buried, George Axx (man of warr)....................
26 Then was Buried, Charles Smith..
27 Then was Buried, Mary Bushill...
28 Then was Buried, Elizabeth Burnham..................................
31 Then was Buried, Michael Lynham } Mariners.....................
Novem[r] 1 Then was Buried, William Smith } Mariners
2 Then was Buried, John Newton Man of warr.........................
3 Then was Buried, John Fitchett...
7 Then was Buried, William Wamsley.......................................
8 Then was Buried, Mary Randel...
9 Then was Buried, John Houghton Sheppard a Child............
12 Then was Buried, Phileman Mackentosh (Parish)..............
17 Then was Buried, Margaret Blake..
24 Then was Buried, Martha Greenland.....................................
28 Then was Buried, Thomas Levey. Mariner.........................
30 Then was Buried, Elizabeth Ash...
Dec[r]. .... 1 Then was Buried, Sarah Trott..
1 Then was Buried, James Wilshear mariner.........................
3 Then was Buried, William Hammitt a Child........................
6 Then was Buried, Robert Cromball (Parish).......................
7 Then was Buried, Joseph Harvey a Child...........................
9 Then was Buried, Martha Weekley..
11 Then was Buried, Mathew Rice...
14 Then was Buried, Thomas Heyman late Register...............
14 Then was Buried, John Wood...
20 Then was Buried, John Row (Parish)...................................

1745 Burials continued [215]

Decem[r] 24 Then was Buried, Edward Wyatt (Parish).............................
30 Then was Buried, Mary Gorden..

30 Then was Buried, William Davis (Parish)
31 Then was Buried, Doct[r] Benjamin Hall
Jan[ry] 3[d] Then was Buried, Mary Dingwell
6 Then was Buried, George Pepper .... a Child
9 Then was Buried, Ashby Utting Esq[r];
9 Then was Buried, Margaret Partridge
12 Then was Buried, Richard Hunter (man of Warr)
12 Then was Buried, George Morgan (Mariner)
13 Then was Buried, William Bradley (Parish charge)
15 Then was Buried, John Watson (Mariner)
18 Then was Buried, Church (Parish Charge)
21 Then was Buried, Elizabeth Moore
Febry 4 Then was Buried, James Withers jun[r]
8 Then was Buried, William Smith
10 Then was Buried, John Allison Mariner
12 Then was Buried, Mary Gaultier in the French Church Ground
19th Then was Buried, Capt: John Pennefather
22[d] Then was Buried, Elizabeth Anderson a Child
23 Then was Buried, Thomas Rees, Mariner
Mar—.. 9 Then was Buried, Ann Wamsley... (Parish Charge)
13 Then was Elizabeth D' S[t] Julian Buried.
23 Then was Buried William Smith
1746 29 Then was Buried Magdalen Stears P
April 6 Then was Buried Mary Maine P
8 Then was Buried Sarah Stanyarne
15 Then was Buried John Townsend, Cooper
26 Then was Buried Talbot Brown
27 Then was Buried Francis Stockwell Marriner
30 Then was Buried Lydia Laurens
May.. 4 Then was Buried Robert Hume a Child
4 Then was Buried Barnet Ackerman a Marriner
8 Then was Buried Henry Laurens a Child
10 Then was Buried Sarah Kirk .. a Child
15 Then was Buried William Stephens (Parish)
16 Then was Buried Thomas Gailliard (Mariner)
17 Then was Buried John Kingston
21 Then was Buried Mary Crisp.

[216]
1746 Burials continued
May.... 24 Then was Buried, Rebeccah Vann. a Child
25. Then was Buried, Hipsibah Bullard Wife of Griffith Bullard
25. Then was Buried, Joseph Church Doct[r] of the Aldborough
25. Then was Buried, Elizabeth Sheppard a Child
27 Then was Buried John Ashton

..................30 Then was Buried Ann Higgins..

June 4.... Then was Buried Jane .... Pringle in the Presbyterian Gro[d]:

..................6 Then was Buried Edward Kandal a Soldier..............................

..................8 Then was Buried Francis Mongin Parish..................................

..................10 Then was Buried Redman Kating Parish..................................

..................12 Then was Buried Isabel Rhine wife of Patrick Rhine

..................16 Then was Buried Samuel Cheesman Cook of y[e] Aldborough

21 Then was Buried Ann Dexter on y[e] parish..............................

..................22 Then was Buried Elizabeth Howell at a private Burial place

..................25 Then was Buried Elisha Prioleau..

..................25 Then was Buried David Hailey a Soldier..................................

..................29 Then was Buried Mary S[t] John a Child...................................

July.... 2[d] Then was Buried Margaret Oheax Parish..................................

..................7 Then was Buried Nathaniel Izard a Child..................................

..................8 Then was Buried Sarah Smith..

..................14 Then was Buried Henry S[t] Martin a Child..............................

19 Then was Buried Doct[r]: Joseph Gaultier in the French Church Ground

19 Then was Buried Ann Harvey a Child.....................................

..................24 Then was Buried James Nightengale a Child..........................

..................26 Then was Buried George Forster (Parish Charge)............

..................28 Then was Buried Cap[t]. John James. ....

August 6 Then was Buried Francis Thompson..

22 Then was Burtied Francis Bremar..

27 Then was Buried William Smith..

Sept[r] 4 Then was Buried John Hudson—Parish Charge................

6 Then was Buried M[rs]: Elizab[th]: Shubrick............................

6 Then was Buried Mary Glitton..

7 Then was Buried Robert Sammond ....

13 Then was Buried Richard Acreman...

21 Then was Buried John Motherby a Soldier..............................

23 Then was Buried Mary Killpatrick...

28 Then was Buried Alex[r]: Murray..

28 Then was Buried David Williamson..

1746 Burials Continued [217]

Sept[r]. 30 Then was Buried Dorothy Jones..

Oct[r] 3 Then was Buried John Connor a Soldier..............................

4 Then was Buried Thomas Stephens from y[e] Workhouse..

5 Then was Buried John Amory. ....

6 Then was Buried M[rs] Sarah Miller (Parish Charge).........

7 Then was Buried Hugh Steward a Soldier..........................

13 Then was Buried Miss Mariane, Mazyck..................................

24 Then was Buried Deborah Burn..

27 Then was Buried Katherine Mitchell
27 Then was Buried Samuel Carne a Child
28 Then was Buried Joseph Rann a Child
29 Then was Buried Lewis Delegé
Nov[r] 6 Then was Buried Tobias Butler a Sailer
7 Then was Buried Ann Rothmaller
12 Then was Buried Duncan M[c]Pharlin a Soldier
14 Then was Buried Thomas Glover
14 Then was Buried Martin Lyon (Parish Charge)
17 Then was Buried Anthony Sackville
21 Then was Buried Frances Stone (Parish Charge)
22 . Then was Buried Daniel Griffen a Soldier
28 Then was Buried Mary Baker
30 Then was Buried William Clark a Child
Decem[r]: 4 Then was Buried Ashby Easton a Child
6 Then was Buried John Griffin a Child
11 Then was Buried John Cope, a Soldier
26 Then was Buried John Ax. a Sailer
27 Then was Buried Katherine Hope
29 Then was Buried John . . . Stephenson a Child
Jan[ry]. 3 Then was Buried John Modern
3 Then was Buried Daniel Litchfield Soldiers
7 Then was Buried Sarah Millar (Parish Charge)
8 Then was Buried Richard Curr.
15 Then was Buried Richard Grimstone
25 Then was Buried at the Parish Charge a person that was Drowned & his Name unknown
30 Then was Buried George Strong, from y[e] Workhouse
30 Then was Buried, Philip Punch . . . d[o]:
Febr[y]. 1 Then was Buried, William Greenland
6 Then was Buried, M[rs]: Schermerhorn
5 Then was Buried Alexander Holzendorf in the french Ground

[218] Burials Continued

1746

February 7[h] Then was Buried, Catherine Beekman
9 Then was Buried, Thomas Clark
8 Then was Buried, Sarah Goodman
10 Then was Buried, Col[l] Anthony White
16 Then was Buried, James Thompson a Child
17 Then was Buried Thomas Cook
24 Then was Buried, Sarah Colleden.
19 Then was Buried Edmond Hawkins
26 Then was Buried, Joseph D' S[t] Julien
20 Then was Buried Thomas Kirk a Child
27 Then was Buried, Elizabeth Vann a Child

March 5 Then was Buried, Ann Smith..
5 Then was Buried, William Elliot, a Sailor drowned..........
5 Then was Buried, Willm: Farr, from ye Workhouse..........
9 Then was Buried, Ann Grimke,..
14 Then was Buried, Hannah Robertson,................................
19 Then was Buried, John Redman,..
20 Then was Buried, Thomas Poor, Man of Warr......... ....

1747.

April 2 Then was Buried, Mary Harvey..
8 Then was Buried, Edwd. Tool. ....
8 Then was Buried, Mr: Dedicote (Parish)............................
15 Then was Buried, John Knight, Sailer..................................
16 Then was Buried Mrs Wade a Soldiers wife
17 Then was Buried, Hendrick Tyson Sailer............................
19 Then was Buried, David Thomas Roper a Child..................

May.... 5 Then was Buried, George White..
8 Then was Buried, Joseph Perriam......................................
10 Then was Buried John Scovil ——— Parish Charge
11n. Then was Buried, Lucretia Moultrie..................................
10 Then was Buried Susannah Jones
11h Then was Buried, Martha Weaver a Child........................
12 Then was Buried, James McClerkey (Man of Warr)........
13 Then was Buried, Joseph Barr . . . do..............................
15 Then was Buried, Ann Blacklidge a Child..........................
16 Then was Buried, John Payn, Sailer....................................
18 Then was Buried Morreau Sarrazen a Child......................
26 Then was Buried, Capt. Lewis Lormier (Messenger to his Majestys honble: Council) in the ffrench Church Ground
30 Then was Buried Name Unknown a Sailor Drowned
31 Then was Buried John Laurans,——— Sadler.

June 1st. Then was Buried The Revd: Mr: Robert Betham Assistant to the Rector of this Parish
3 Then was Buried Robert Fatlake a Sailor Boy
7th. Then was Buried William Saxby, Searcher of this Port

N B. The above Interlineations were occasioned by Mr Doble's Neglect of Entering them in his Accots.[1]

1747 Burials Continued [219]

June 16 Then was Buried Mary Smith Daugr. of Saml Smith
17 Then was Buried Mary Smith Daugr. of Bn Smith
25 Then was Buried Robt: Cartwright..
29 Then was Buried Mary Valens...

[1]Burial records for Cook, Hawkins, Kirk, Mrs. Wade, Scovil, Susannah Jones, and John Laurens are interlined.

29 Then was Buried George Lucas Pinckney..............................

July. 6 Then was Buried Peter Laurans..............................

7 Then was Buried John Davis, Parish Charge

7 Then was Buried George Avery, Child,..............................

9 Then was Buried Susannah Philips,..............................

10 Then was Buried Mark Anthony Besselleu a Child

11 Then was Buried Mary Saunders, Child..............................

12 Then was Buried Margaret Michie, Child..............................

16 Then was Buried William Fellow, a Soldier..............................

17 Then was Buried Thomas Proo. Child..............................

17 Then was Buried John Pearson, Sailor,..............................

17 Then was Buried Mary Gibson,..............................

19 Then was Buried Hannah Lee,..............................

19 Then was Buried John Hutchinson, Man of War

19 Then was Buried Cornelius Dorgan, from Workhouse

Omitted ye 12th Then was Buried Elizabeth Vanall..............................

Augt. 1st Then was Buried Ann Campbell Child on Parish

3 Then was Buried Mary Summer..............................

5 Then was Buried Mary Ann Davis..............................

6 Then was Buried Jane Anderson (a Child)..............................

10 Then was Buried Thomas Watson joyner..............................

11 Then was Buried Sarah Yerworth..............................

14 Then was Buried Frances Thorn..............................

15 Then was Buried Summers Lightwood Sailer..............................

15 Then was Buried Alexander Knox. Child..............................

15 Then was Buried John Bull..............................

17 Then was Buried Charles Easton a Child..............................

25 Then was Buried, William Holzendorf in the french Ground

[220] Burials

1747

Augt. 24 Then was Buried John Daniell, Shipwright...............................

27 Then was Buried Dr: William Grace..............................

29 Then was Buried Thomas Kennedy in the Scotch Meeting Ground

31 Then was Buried Thomas Howard Child..............................

Septr. 1st. Then was Buried Charlott Welshousen Child..............................

2d Then was Buried Hugh McColloch a Soldier..............................

3d Then was Buried Ann Smith, Child..............................

3d Then was Buried Elizabeth Teen, (Workhouse)..............................

6h Then was Buried William Collis, Child. ....

11 Then was Buried Barbara Carpenter...............................

15 Then was Buried Margaret Shaw, a Child,..............................

22 Then was Buried Dr William Watkins..............................

24 Then was Buried Mary Crawford..............................

27 Then was Buried a Sailer............

29 Then was Buried Hannah Allen
29 Then was Buried Mary Fryley a Child
29 Then was Buried Joseph Harrison a Sailer
30 Then was Buried Captain Richard Lyddell
Octr. 1st: Then was Buried Providence Grimke a Child
2d Then was Buried William Wiatt a Sailer
3 Then was Buried William Gear a Sailer
3d Then was Buried Mary Killpatrick.
10th: Then was Buried William Plimley Sailer
14th Then was Buried James Forlong.... do:
15th Then was Buried George Williams
15th Then was Buried John Bragg, Soldier
18th Then was Buried Henry Travers
18th Then was Buried Ann Dennis
21st Then was Buried Catherine Serre.
23d Then was Buried Nicholas Haynes.
25 Then was Buried Martha Acreman a Child
26 Then was Buried Elizabeth Barnes a Child
27th: Then was Buried Thomas Ferguson, Sailer
28 Then was Buried James Frew from Workhouse
Novr 4 Then was Buried Ann Lamb from Workhouse
5 Then was Buried John Paywell Sailer
6 Then was Buried Richard Evance, Soldier

1747. Burials [221]

Novemr 11th. Then was Buried Felix Burn
12 Then was Buried Richard Butler, Child
20. Then was Buried William Clifton a Sailer
22 Then was Buried Catherine Sheppard a Child
24 Then was Buried Elizabeth Barnes
29 Then was Buried John Meek
29 Then was Buried George Hall Richardson a Child
Decem 2 Then was Buried Mary Hogg.
8 Then was Buried Joseph Cook.
8 Then was Buried Robert Cleland in the Ground belongg. ——— to the Scotch Meeting
13 Then was Buried Elizabeth Harramond.
18 Then was Buried Samuel Howard.
28 Then was Buried Sarah Howard.
30 Then was Buried Sarah Whitaker
January 2d Then was Buried Abraham Mattyson.
2d Then was Buried Thomas Colson.
2d Then was Buried Elias Coffee in ye French Ground
3d Then was Buried William Hancock
4 Then was Buried Francis Delgrass
4 Then was Buried Isaac Bryan Sailer
6 Then was Buried John Thompson } Soldiers
9 Then was Buried Jeremiah Gray }

	15	Then was Buried Elizabeth Gilbert
	16	Then was Buried David Caw a Child
	27	Then was Buried James Lubbeck
	30	Then was Buried Capt. Adam BeauChamp
	30	Then was Buried Christopher Stophel a Sailer drowned
Februry	7	Then was Buried Robert Steil
	16	Then was Buried George Burnet
	17	Then was Buried Sarah Saxby
	25	Then was Buried James Clarke Child
March	16	Then was Buried Margaret Hughes
	18	Then was Buried Charles Shepheard
	22	Then was Buried Thomas Rivers a Child
	25	Then was Buried Daniel Dwight
1748		
April	18	Then was Buried Robert Chedreal Soldier
	23	Then was Buried John Leger a Child

[222] Burials

1748		
April	25	Then was Buried Benjamin Godin, Merchant
	26	Then was Buried Giles Fitchett
	26	Then was Buried William London Soldier
	28	Then was Buried William Lambert Soldier
May..	4	Then was Buried Alexander Murray
	4	Then was Buried Elizabeth Nelsson Child
	9	Then was Buried Richd Lindar a Sailer
	11	Then was Buried Henry Campbell
	14	Then was Buried William Powers Child
	14	Then was Buried Thomas Craven Sailer
	23	Then was Buried Chas. Killpatrick Parish
	26	Then was Buried William Lancaster Parish
	27	Then was Buried Richard Way.. Child
	28	Then was Buried Barnard Ferrel.. Parish
	30	Then was Buried Lewis Janvier
June.	8	Then was Buried Robert Upton a Child
	14	Then was Buried Edward Webb.
	15	Then was Buried Doctr Featherston Bailie
	16	Then was Buried Elizabeth Poole a Child
	16	Then was Buried Moses Griffen a Soldier
	16	Then was Buried Thomas Ventrus a Sailer
	18	Then was Buried John Courren a Soldier
	18	Then was Buried Rebecca Champneys a Child
	18	Then was Buried Mary Vouloux at the French Church
	24	Then was Buried Elizabeth Legere a Child
	30	Then was Buried John Green, Soldier,
July	4	Then was Buried Dennis Mathews Soldier,
	7	Then was Buried John Girgee, Sailer of the Fowey,

11 Then was Buried Ann Harvey a Child.
18 Then was Buried Mary Mackay-
27 Then was Buried Nicholas Skinner Parish
27 Then was Buried Thomas Mallacy Sailer
Aug[t]. 1 Then was Buried Henry Gibbes Esq[r]. One of His Majesty's Justices

1748 Burials [223]

Aug[t] 6 Then was Buried Forrester a Soldier
6 Then was Buried Susannah Pischard a Child
7 Then was Buried William Dick, Sailer of Aldbor[h]:
8 Then was Buried Thomas Trowel ——
11 Then was Buried Sarah Mackay. Parish
11 Then was Buried Mary D' Lorne ffrench Ground
17 Then was Buried Lewis Benham Sailer..
17 Then was Buried Samuel Hopton Child....................................
17 Then was Buried John Barnet (Parish)....................................
21 Then was Buried Robert Tarnel of the Arundel
21 Then was Buried Richard Boddicott..
23 Then was Buried Robert Marks Sailer......................................
24 Then was Buried Cap[t]. Arthur Gold..
25 Then was Buried Dorothy Gwyn..
26 Then was Buried Edward Roberts of y[e] Arundel
26 Then was Buried Edward Townsend }
26 Then was Buried Andrew Linby.... } Sailers..........................
27 Then was Buried John Torby............ }
27 Then was Buried Isaac Luther of y[e] Arundel
27 Then was Buried Robert Waller Merch[t]. ....
28 Then was Buried W[m]: Osborne Pilot..
30 Then was Buried Charles Brackenbury....................................
31 Then was Buried John Barton— }
Septem[r] 1st Then was Buried William Greenley } Arundel.........................
1 Then was Buried John Harris Sailer..
3 Then was Buried Mathew Chapman Arundel
4 Then was Buried Samuel Lacey..
5 Then was Buried William Hovel Hill..
6 Then was Buried Robert Vaun..
7 Then was Buried W[m]: Allen, Arundel...
7 Then was Buried Rachael Porcher..
7 Then was Buried Thomas Sherry Sailer....................................
8 Then was Buried Elizabeth Trowell. ....

[224] Burials

1748 Sept[r]. 8th. Then was buried George Lewis...
12 Then was buried Jane Rogun from Workhouse.......................
12 Then was buried Thomas Wood, Sailer...................................
12 Then was buried Jame Kirk...
13 Then was buried John Clark...

13 Then was buried Fryley a Child........................
13 Then was buried Capt Samuel Smithson........................
13 Then was buried William Hunt........................
16 Then was buried Simon Stead........................
16 Then was buried James Smith Sailer........................
16 Then was buried Elias Vellum Sailer........................
18 Then was buried John Terry in the ffrench Ground
19 Then was buried Hannah Commett........................
19 Then was buried Henry Hennewood........................
19 Then was buried John Griffin Parish........................
20 Then was buried William Martin Parish........................
20 Then was buried Capt John Lloyd Commander of his Majestys Ship Glascow........................
22 Then was buried Morris the Govrs. Man
23 Then was buried Johannes Willes Parish........................
23 Then was buried Luke Fitzgerald, Soldier........................
24 Then was buried Thomas Kirk junr........................
26 Then was buried Mary Smith........................
27 Then was buried Amelia Mazyck Child........................
27 Then was buried Ann McLean........................
29 Then was buried Daniel Reans Parish
October 1st Then was buried Elizabeth Desborough Parish
5 Then was buried Luke Stoutenbrough Child........................
10 Then was buried Stephen Blankshaw........................
12 Then was Buried Richd. Turner, Soldr undr Col Vander dussen
14 Then was buried Catherine Lewis........................
15 Then was Buried Adam Snider. Soldier........................
16 Then was Buried Sarah Lea, Child........................
16 Then was buried John Forbus Sailer........................
20 Then was Buried James Hilliard Sailer........................

1748 Burials [225]

October 26 Then was Buried Henry Petty Merchant........................
27 Then was Buried Abraham Crofton Soldr:........................
Novemr 4 Then was Buried Doctor James Archer. ....
11h Then was Buried Joseph Oram, Child........................
16 Then was Buried Mary Elfe........................
22 Then was Buried Hugh Anderson........................
22 Then was Buried Richard Linter........................
22 Then was Buried Danning Baks Sailer........................
28 Then was Buried James Voloux........................
28 Then was Buried John Mudd Sailer........................
Decemr. 4 Then was Buried John Wainwright, Child........................
17 Then was Buried John Harden, parish........................
24 Then was Buried Ann Wells........................
25 Then was Buried George a poor Man

that dyed on Shute's Bridge parish Charge
30 Then was Buried Alexander Henderson
January 4 Then was Buried Lewison Bonnotheau French Ground
10 Then was Buried Mary Riggall parish
11 Then was Buried John Brunett Child
11 Then was Buried Margaret Anderson Child
18 Then was Buried Thomas Smith Child
18 Then was Buried James Hand parish
24 Then was Buried William Cooley Child
27 Then was Buried Charlotte Izard Child
27 Then was Buried John Coleman, bred a Quaker & baptized one day before his Death
27 Then was Buried James Bushell, Boatswain of ye Foy
Febry- 2d Then was Buried Penelope Pratt
4 Then was Buried Rebecca Allen Parish
7 Then was Buried Robert Dunstan Pilot
9 Then was Buried Thomas Shubrick Child
9 Then was Buried Sarah Smith
10 Then was Buried Thomas Duncan
12 Then was Buried Sarah Allen Widow
15 Then was Buried Ruth County
18 Then was Buried Robert Pinckney Child
21 Then was Buried Charlotte Mary Timothy

[226] 1748/9 Burials

Febry—. 22 Then was Buried Maurice Gwyn
24 Then was Buried Mary Fitchett Child
28 Then was Buried Sarah Bremar Child
March 2 Then was Buried Rachael Harrison Parish
3 Then was Buried Tamer Trench
4 Then was Buried Catherine Shaw. Child
15 Then was Buried John Abbot. Child
16 Then was Buried Dennis McBride Parish
20 Then was Buried Capt Gilbert Albertson
1749 26 Then was Buried James Wrightman Otter Sloop.
29 Then was Buried Edward Boardman parish
30 Then was Buried Edward Fitzgerald Child
April 5 Then was Buried Mary Beekman Child
8 Then was Buried Jenkin Hughs
8. Then was Buried Martha Lemmon
10 Then was Buried Thomas Wheeler Soldier
23 Then was Buried Mary Bremar Child
23 Then was Buried Andrew Stiperata parish
23 Then was Buried Catherine Reyner parish
24 Then was Buried George McLean Child
24 Then was Buried George McDay, Sailer
25 Then was Buried Jane McLaughlan Roulain Child

May 1 Then was Buried William Smith Butcher
11 Then was Buried Sarah Smith, Child
13 Then was Buried William Smith, Child
14 Then was Buried Susannah Duresseau
15 Then was Buried Robert Waller, Child
16 Then was Buried Charles Avery, Child
16 Then was Buried Elizabeth Williamson
17 Then was Buried John Muncreef
24 Then was Buried Gabriel Bonnetheau, Child
25 Then was Buried William Farewell Soldier
June 1 Then was Buried Catherine Ball, parish

1749 Burials [227]

June 6 Then was Buried Nicholas Wastcoat Soldier
6 Then was Buried John Holmes, Sailer
8 Then was Buried Elizabeth Smith, Child,
9 Then was Buried Esther Powers, Child
11 Then was Buried John Powers, Child
16 Then was Buried Abraham Howard, Arundel
16 Then was Buried Thomas Triner Soldier Vand
16 Then was Buried Mary Poinsett, Child
18 Then was Buried Joseph Wilson, Soldier from Georgia
18 Then was Buried John Northwood
18 Then was Buried June Taylor
24 Then was Buried Joshua Hide—Sailer
28 Then was Buried Mary Greenswick—Child
July 4 Then was Buried William Appleby
4 Then was Buried John Hawkins
7 Then was Buried Susanna Lea
11 Then was Buried Nathaniel Phillips - - Arundel
15 Then was Buried John Frederick Chedro, Parish
23 Then was Buried a Sailor. Arundel
25 Then was Buried Eleanor Evans Soldiers Child
27 Then was Buried Elizebeth Harrison Soldiers Child
31 Then was Buried Thomas Henry Champneys (Child
August 1 Then was Buried George Walter Parish
4 Then was Buried Charles, Son of y[e] Relict of D[r] Repeault
5 Then was Buried George Adler Sailor
5 Then was Buried Ann Jones Child
7 Then was Buried Mary Mongin
10 Then was Buried Catherine Warden
16 Then was Buried Ann Hill
21 Then was Buried James Oldridge
22 Then was Buried Alice Graham
23 Then was Buried Mary Gibbs Parish
26 Then was Buried Margaret Holmes

[228] Burials

1749

August 27 Then was Buried Soldiers Child
28 Then was Buried Martha Coomer Child
29 Then was Buried Thomas Lawson Rye
30 Then was Buried Mary Avery

September 4 Then was Buried Rebecca Vaun Child
5 Then was Buried John Jones Sailor
6 Then was Buried Elizabeth Anderson
7 Then was Buried Amey McCorneck Soldiers Wife
13 Then was Buried William Scott
16 Then was Buried Joseph Foreman Parish
21 Then was Buried Mary Pinckney
24 Then was Buried Eleanor Miles—Soldiers Daughter
Colln Herren Co
28 Then was Buried Mary Hilliard
28 Then was Buried Joshua Dungworth Child
29 Then was Buried William Pearce Sailor drownded

October 3 Then was Buried Thomas Hosier Soldier
6 Then was Buried Anthony Brennen Sailor
7 Then was Buried John Carden Child
14 Then was Buried Ann Coleman Child
15 Then was Buried Eleanor Club Soldier's Child
16 Then was Buried John Gittens
Then was Buried Sarah Johnson from Bear Inn
22 Then was Buried Benjamin Michie
23 Then was Buried Jonathan Green
24 Then was Buried Francis Clark
25 Then was Buried Mary Orsborn
29 Then was Buried Paul Mazyck Child
29 Then was Buried John Yerworth
30 Then was Buried Mary Wildermott

Novr: 1st Then was Buried Sarah Johnson Child
2 Then was Buried Kenneth Michie
3 Then was Buried Mary Brian Parish
6 Then was Buried Augustus Beauchamp

Burials [229]

13 Then was Buried John Neufville[1]

Novr: 10 Then was Buried Mary Rider Soldiers Wife
22 Then was Buried James Hilliard
22 Then was Buried John Brown a Sailer
23 Then was Buried David Guttery Parish

Interline.

24 Then was Buried Mary Tyger........Child Parish....................
28 Then was Buried Stephen Leopard..
28 Then was Buried Jn[o] Michie........Child...................................
Decem[r]: 4 Then was Buried Eliz Gonoe...
5 Then was Buried Sarah Wish....Soldiers Child....................
7 Then was Buried George Moss........Parish................................
11 Then was Buried Thomas Thompson...................................
18 Then was Buried John Bourchier..
18 Then was Buried Antonia Reggia Spaniard—Parish........
27 Then was Buried Culchith Golightly....................................
28 Then was Buried Mary Drivers—Sold[rs]. Wife....................
31 Then was Buried Collins Graham........Parish..........................
31 Then was Buried Elener Hare........Child...............................
Jan[y]. 1 Then was Buried Nicholas Frank........Sailer Arrundel
2 Then was Buried Roger Holdfast.......ditto...............................
3 Then was Buried Ann Golding........Child.................................
8 Then was Buried William Harding—Soldier Col Horon's
21 Then was Buried M[rs] Lightwood..
22 Then was Buried Griffith Bullard..
24 Then was Buried Collings............Sailer......................................
26 Then was Buried Ann Bradshaw........Child...............................
31 Then was Buried Robert Stead...........Child..............................
Feb[y]. 6 Then was Buried M[rs] Garret Vanvelson..................................
12 Then was Buried Adrian Loyer..
23 Then was Buried John Bolton Sailer M[rs] Underwood
27 Then was Buried John Falconner...
1749/50
March 5 Then was Buried Unknown Person Drowned Parish............
7 Then was Buried Rachel Lee........Child.......................................
7 Then was Buried Mathew Hardy........Sailer...............................
10 Then was Buried John Atkins...
21 Then was Buried Nicholas Mattyson (Workhouse)
21 Then was Buried Eliz[th] D'Gray...
21 Then was Buried William Bezely...........Child...........................

[230] Burials

1749/50
March 21 Then was Buried Thomas Lupton........Child...........................
1750 31 Then was Buried Mathew Lownds............Sailer........................
April 5 Then was Buried M[rs] Sarah Goodman........Parish........................
11 Then was Buried Sailer..
18 Then was Buried William Grace . . Coro[s]: Inquest....................
19 Then was Buried Thomas Smith . . . Child....................................
24 Then was Buried James Dumbleton . . . Parish................................
May... 3 Then was Buried Elizabeth Woodbury..
5 Then was Buried Ruth Beekman..
12 Then was Buried Mary Boyd...

15 Then was Buried Elizabeth Broughton
16 Then was Buried James Cole
20 Then was Buried Mary Purdy............Child
29 Then was Buried Sarah Hilliard......Child
29 Then was Buried William Jefferys......Sailer
31 Then was Buried Joseph Ward
June.. 2 Then was Buried Michael Dalton Parish
3 Then was Buried Crokatt......Child
8 Then was Buried Margaret Hinds
13 Then was Buried William Moore......Child
17 Then was Buried William Hulker
22 Then was Buried George Salter.....Child
24 Then was Buried Isaac Humphreys
25 Then was Buried Francis Treasvant
26 Then was Buried Marmaduke Aish Sadler
26 Then was Buried Joseph Powers........Child
27 Then was Buried Joseph Lacey....Child
28 Then was Buried John Sinnet.....Parish
28 Then was Buried Mary Rupen.....d[o]
28 Then was Buried Benjamin Perry Merchant
29 Then was Buried Mary Wish
July.. 2 Then was Buried Henry Beekman Child
3 Then was Buried Butler Parish
6 Then was Buried James Fletcher............Parish

1750 Burials [231]

July.. 6 Then was Buried, Henry Hill........parish
6 Then was Buried Elizabeth Wilkinson
13 Then was Buried Francis Barrow
14 Then was Buried Peter Lavillette....Parish
19 Then was Buried Daniel Wilkinson..Parish
19 Then was Buried Thomas Summer, Man Warr
21 Then was Buried George Viney...Child
22 Then was Buried Margaret Fowler
27 Then was Buried Mary Summers
29 Then was Buried Elizabeth Tucker....Child
August 1 Then was Buried Thomas Logan.....Child
7 Then was Buried Deborah Mariner
13 Then was Buried Rebecca Wainwright..Child
15 Then was Buried Harriotte Motte....Child
16 Then was Buried Elizabeth Smith & the same day (Antoine Baron a Cooper.——)
18 Then was Buried Margaret Kinsey
19 Then was Buried Mary Esther Gaultier wife of D[r]. Gaultier
24 Then was Buried John Fitzgerald a Child
24 Then was Buried John Frances...Child
26 Then was Buried John Kinsey...Child

28 Then was Buried John Jones..Man Warr..............................
31 Then was Buried Mary Smith....Parish..............................
31 Then was Buried Thomas Young...Man Warr..............................
September 4 Then was Buried William Moisseau....Sailer..............................
5 Then was Buried Ann Owen who was Widow of Edw[d] Scull
5 Then was Buried Edward Keller..M W..............................
5 Then was Buried James Howell..Seaman..............................
12 Then was Buried Thomas Gadsden....Child..............................
13 Then was Buried Mary Eycott..............................
15 Then was Buried Charles Theodore Patchable ——————late Organist of this Parish..............................
23 Then was Buried Mary Richardson..............................
28 Then was Buried Lewis Almond........Parish..............................
October 1 Then was Buried Ann Kelly................Parish..............................
[232] 1750 Burials
October 8 Then was Buried Martha Butler....Child..............................
10 Then was Buried Ann Brewton..............................
12 Then was Buried Henry Butler..............................
13 Then was Buried Mary Gliddon..............................
21 Then was Buried James Badger....Child..............................
28 Then was Buried William Amey..............................
29 Then was Buried John Lindsey...Sailer..............................
29 Then was Buried John Smith..............................
30 Then was Buried James Hopkins ....
30 Then was Buried William Smith..............................
Novem[r]. 2 Then was Buried Ann Frazer..............................
4 Then was Buried John Ratcliff....Child..............................
10 Then was Buried Thomas Rumage Sailer..............................
13 Then was Buried Thomas Tosser Parish..............................
17 Then was Buried Mary Reece..............................
17 Then was Buried Henrietta Fisher..............................
19 Then was Buried Eneas Mackay . . . Parish..............................
20 Then was Buried Sarah Turner..............................
21 Then was Buried Foster Harrison..............................
22 Then was Buried Isabella Campbell—Parish..............................
25 Then was Buried Thomas Howard. Parish..............................
Decem[r] 1 Then was Buried Samuel Wragg Esq[r]; late of London
24 Then was Buried Thomas Atkins.
26 Then was Buried Hannah Smith
27 Then was Buried Doct[r] John Rutledge
Then was Buried Rob[t] Warren—Sailor
30 Then was Buried John Champneys Esq[r]—:
Jan[ry] 2[d] Then was Buried Eliz[a] Gregory
4 Then was Buried William Clouston Sailor
Then was Buried John Fitzgerald

8 Then was Buried Nathaniel Todd Parish
24 Then was Buried Thomas Juckes
28 Then was Buried Robt Perkins Child

1750 [233]

Janry 29 Then was Buried John Murphey Sailor
30 Then was Buried Saml Somersall do
Then was Buried Harvey Child
8 Then was Buried Richard Peak
13 Then was Buried Thos: Higgins Psh
15 Then was Buried Doctr: John Hayden
17 Then was Buried John Lea
19 Then was Buried Thos Welch
28 Then was Buried Richard Lampart
March 1st Then was Buried Joseph Wragg son of Joseph Wragg Esqr
Then was Buried Mary Swinney Psh
10 Then was Buried John Gallen Chd:
Then was Buried William Dubberly Psh
13 Then was Buried Jones do
22 Then was Buried Barthw: Graves...Sailor
1751 26 Then was Buried Eliza. Woodward
Then was Buried James Mitchell
28 Then was Buried Eleanor Laurence Chd
31 Then was Buried Esther Randall
April 3d Then was Buried Elizabeth Smith
4 Then was Buried Thomas Bonney
Then was Buried David Matthison
6 Then was Buried John Dunlap Chd
11 Then was Buried Elizabeth Benison
12 Then was Buried Sarah Wooldridge Psh
Then was Buried William Irving Chd Irving
14 Then was Buried Eliza: Smith
17 Then was Buried Mary Hinds Chd
19 Then was Buried John Martin Sailor
20 Then was Buried David Swinney Chd
21 Then was Buried Cathne: Caw
Then was Buried Mary Furnihough Chd
26 Then was Buried Ann Booth Chd
27 Then was Buried William Hoyland Chd
May... 2 Then was Buried William Hopton Child
do Then was Buried Thomas Summer Parish
11 Then was Buried Margaret Catherine Mary Timothy Child

[234] Burials

1751

14 Then was Buried Thomas Brann
15 Then was Buried John Coffe Chd:

20 Then was Buried Samuel Honeyhore d°:
26 Then was Buried Mary Swinney d°:
28 Then was Buried Wm. Carey Psh
29 Then was Buried John Caw Chd:
30 Then was Buried Sarah Champneys d°
31 Then was Buried Ann Sharp Psh
June 9th Then was Buried Saml. Smith Psh
d° Then was Buried Saml. & Ann Dunlop
10 Then was Buried Wm. Smith Chd
11 Then was Buried Joseph Mazyck, Child
14 Then was Buried John Eycott
15 Then was Buried Ann Nash
19 Then was Buried Benjamin Mc.Call Chd
20 Then was Buried Daniel Pichard d°
d° Then was Buried Elizabeth Colson
21 Then was Buried Simon Jenkins—Parish
d° Then was Buried Susannah Crockatt—Child
22 Then was Buried Joseph Wragg—Esqr.
26 Then was Buried William Lupton—Child
d° Then was Buried Ann Steward—Child
30 Then was Buried Elizabeth You
July— 2d Then was Buried Mary Cloud
6 Then was Buried Elizabeth Gunter—Child
13 Then was Buried Robert Chalmers—Child
18 Then was Buried Sarah Hosiar—Parish
24 Then was Buried John Guerard—Child
24 Then was Buried Andrew Broughton—Child
26 Then was Buried Chas: Stevenson—Child
26 Then was Buried Elizabeth Ball
27 Then was Buried Margaret Bostock—Child
28 Then was Buried Jane Thompson—Child
28 Then was Buried Rosannah Colt—Parish

1751 Burials [235]

August 1st Then was Buried Elizabeth. Sinclair—Parish
6 Then was Buried Ann Carvell—Parish
12 Then was Buried Mary Walker
16 Then was Buried Mary Hamilton
18 Then was Buried Greene—Parish
18 Then was Buried Francis Christina
21 Then was Buried Joseph. Hill—Parish
24 Then was Buried Elizabeth: Ann Henderson Child
25 Then was Buried Sarah Agnes Dungworth—Parish
27 Then was Buried William. Playtes—Parish
27 Then was Buried William Tarpy
28 Then was Buried Tackabener Clemantina McKinsey Parish

September 3 Then was Buried Mary Burgett.
5 Then was Buried Charlotte Martha Dungworth—**Parish**
15 Then was Buried Rebekah. Motte.—Child
23 Then was Buried John Coosaw
October 5 Then was Buried Daniel Gardner
8 Then was Buried Sarah True—Parish
13 Then was Buried Elizabeth Smith
22 Then was Buried Revd. Robert Stone
30 Then was Buried Elizabeth Moore Parish
November 1th Then was Buried Frederick Booth S
3 Then was Buried Samuel. Clase
6 Then was Buried Elenor Sandwell
8 Then was Buried Katherine Hartman—Child
8 Then was Buried Christopher Roche—Child
10 Then was Buried Alexander Goodby
17 Then was Buried John Mandeville
21 Then was Buried James Rodgers—Parish
28 Then was Buried John. Roberson
29 Then was Buried John Friley
December 4th Then was Buried Littleton Hill S
5 Then was Buried Perrigrine Moore
10 Then was Buried Wm. Bartoll
17 Then was Buried Peter Bremar—Child
[236] Burials
24 Then was Buried—Edward Hendley
1752 25 Then was Buried Elizabeth Remington, Child,
January 2 Then was Buried Gallagar. S
7 Then was Buried Susanna Kennan Child
12 Then was Buried Mary Godin
24 Then was Buried Marian Kennan Child
Feby— 1st Then was Buried Katherine Crofts
2 Then was Buried Thomas. Cox
4 Then was Buried James Whitwood Parish
8 Then was Buried Charles Bradford
11 Then was Buried Elizabeth Hendcock
14 Then was Buried William Griffith S
15 Then was Buried Peter Williams
17 Then was Buried Jeremiah Henesley
26 Then was Buried Cassandra Mengaqueen
March 2d Then was Buried James Davis. S
6 Then was Buried Elizabeth: Marlo—Child
7 Then was Buried Rebecca Elsinore
15 Then was Buried Ann Taylor
17 Then was Buried Mary Brown—Parish
22 Then was Buried Thos: Easton=Child
26 Then was Buried Susannah Stoutenburgh

29 Then was Buried John Godfrey
29 Then was Buried Charles Doughty—Child

April 1 Then was Buried Richard Tea. Man Warr
14 Then was Buried Stoutenburgh Child
15 Then was Buried Samuel Legare
22 Then was Buried John Reid
26 Then was Buried Charles Carroll, Perukemaker,
27 Then was Buried John Crofts
28 Then was Buried Susanah Wainwright—
29 Then was Buried Thomas Hull—

[237]

30 Then was Buried, Samuel. Prioleau,
30 Then was Buried George Sheed Child

May— 1 Then was Buried John Fleming, Parish—
5 Then was Buried Mary Lloyd.
9 Then was Buried Richard Allen Parish Child
12 Then was Buried Arno. William Whittel, Child,
Then was Buried Nathaniel Lattrep, Man Warr
14 Then was Buried Ann Elizabeth Laurens Child
15 Then was Buried Elizabeth Denby, Child—
16 Then was Buried Thomas Crew,
19 Then was Buried Philip Gadsden, Child
21 Then was Buried Mary Hearn,
26 Then was Buried Elias Bate Captn. of His Majestys Ship Mermaid
27 Then was Buried Ann Chalmers, Child
28 Then was Buried David Oliphant, Child
29 Then was Buried Charles Hume, Child
Then was Buried Jordan Roche, Esqr.

June 3d Then was Buried Sarah Nellson, Child
5 Then was Buried Sarah Radcliffe, Child
6 Then was Buried Thomas Fletcher,
6 Then was Buried Mary Radcliffe do.
7 Then was Buried Martha Chalmers do.
10 Then was Buried John Beekman do—
10 Then was Buried Mary Cook
12 Then was Buried Robert Withers, Child
13 Then was Buried Hammett, Child
18 Then was Buried Susanah Sommers, Child
21 Then was Buried John Owen, Taylor
24 Then was Buried Mary Kirkwood Child
Then was Buried Jas Thomas Sailor
29 Then was Buried John Taylor Child

[238] Burials

1752

July. 3. Then was Buried Jane Travize
5 Then was Buried William Yeomans Merchant
7 Then was Buried Thomas Goodale Child
8 Then was Buried William Fisk Man Warr
Then was Buried Henery Harvey Child
Then was Buried Ann Easten
9 Then was Buried William Steward Child
13 Then was Buried Samuel Wainwright Child
15 Then was Buried William Williamson
16 Then was Buried William Needler Sailer
16 Then was Buried
17 Then was Buried Elizabeth Senser
18 Then was Buried William Farroe
Then was Buried Susanah Thompson
19 Then was Buried Thomas Lynch
26 Then was Buried Sarah Lloyd Child
August 1 Then was Buried Edward Ladson Sailor
10 Then was Buried Loughton¬
21 Then was Buried John Firnihough Child
23 Then was Buried John Thompson Child
27 Then was Buried William Secen Sailor
30 Then was Buried James Græme Esqr. Chief Justice
Sep[t]. . 16 Then was Buried Elizabeth Gallagoe Child
Then was Buried Gascoin Child
Then was Buried Elizabeth White
Then was Buried
October. 3. Then was Buried Ann Thompson Child
6 Then was Buried Jane Evans Parish
11 Then was Buried William Smith:
17 Then was Buried Richard Baker
22 Then was Buried Ann Shaw Child
31 Then was Buried James Lupton

[239]

1752

Novem[r]. 4 Then was Buried
6 Then was Buried George Green Sailor
Then was Buried Mary Dart
15 Then was Buried Edward Gunther
17 Then was Buried John Sommers Child
18 Then was Buried John Ditten Sailor
23 Then was Buried William Murphy Parish
25 Then was Buried Benjamin Packrow—
Decem[r]. 5 Then was Buried Patrick Marrow Sailor
15 Then was Buried Mary Rippon

Then was Buried Ann Pearce Parish
17 Then was Buried Peter Miller Parish
18 Then was Buried Eleanor Simmons Parish
Then was Buried a Woman from ye- Barracks Parish
18 Then was Buried John Bonner Sailor
23 Then was Buried Drayton
25 Then was Buried William Wilberfoss
29 Then was Buried a Duch Woman from Mrs. Hardings Parish

1753
Janury 7 Then was Buried George Harvey Child
8 Then was Buried Thomas Suttle Sailor
10 Then was Buried Roberts—
12 Then was Buried William. Earl Sailor
15 Then was Buried George Hardin
21 Then was Buried a man from Mr Crottys on ye Parish
25 Then was Buried Thomas Marshal Sailor
26 Then was Buried White Parish
27 Then was Buried Ann Stone
Febry— 2 Then was Buried Edmond Larken Organist
6 Then was Buried William Morgan
13 Then was Buried Nathaniel Ambler
13 Then was Buried Mary Stone.
24 Then was Buried Capt. James Ramsay
26 Then was Buried Harman Frox Parish

[240] Burials

1753
March 14 Then was Buried William Gerrard.
18 Then was Buried Mary Cook
19 Then was Buried Hall Richardson, Parish
25 Then was Buried Capt. Wm: Whittal. do:
April 11 Then was Buried Ann Beekman . . .
21 Then was Buried Magdalene Parish
25 Then was Buried Trevor Lloyd.
29 Then was Buried Mary You.
May 6 Then was Buried Beekman Parish
16 Then was Buried John Gadsden
18 Then was Buried Henry Dickenson—
18 Then was Buried John Oliphant—
27 Then was Buried Race—
29 Then was Buried Sarah Walker
30 Then was Buried Charlotte Lewis
June 8 Then was Buried Edward Neufville.
11 Then was Buried Pickering
11 Then was Buried John Vincent
14 Then was Buried Mary Stevenson

20 Then was Buried Catherine Dalton
21 Then was Buried John Martin
23 Then was Buried Peter Guerard
24 Then was Buried Elizabeth Ball
30 Then was Buried William Smith
July 4 Then was Buried Damaras Carne
5 Then was Buried Dr: William Scott
9 Then was Buried Ann Stott, Parish
August 1st Then was Buried Beekman do—
5 Then was Buried Edward Lloyd
14 Then was Buried Mary Stammers
26 Then was Buried Davis, Parish—
Septr 2 Then was Buried Mary Haramond
3 Then was Buried George Anderson
9 Then was Buried John Smith
10 Then was Buried from the W: House

[241]

1753
Septr.... 14 Then was Buried John H
17 Then was Buried Sarah Buchanan Psh
23 Then was Buried Stone
25 Then was Buried Cockran P.sh
Octr. 1 Then was Buried James
2 Then was Buried Ann Nightingale
8 Then was Buried Sr Alexander Nisbett
10 Then was Buried from W House
12 Then was Buried Gaspar Strick
13 Then was Buried Burrows Psh
14 Then was Buried Margaret Rampton Psh
14 Then was Buried Martha Haines
17 Then was Buried Henry Beekman
20 Then was Buried Grashmore Psh
21 Then was Buried George Milligen Outerbridge
29 Then was Buried Lupton Twins of Alice
Nov: 1st Then was Buried Lupton Lupton's
3 Then was Buried Girl from W. House
9 Then was Buried boy............ditto
10 Then was Buried man............ditto
12 Then was Buried Cook

Burials. **[251[1]]**

1720—
May 10th: Then was buried Mortimer a Child, by ye Revd: Mr: Garden.
11 Then was buried Bridgwater a Ship Carpenter, by Do:.

---

[1] All pages between 241 and 251 are blank.

11 Then was buried Mrs:— Gray, by Do:.
24 Then was buried, John Burnham, a Child, by Do:.—
28 Then was buried, Jones, a Ship Carpenter, by Do:
June 3d: Then was buried, Richard Rowe, a Child, by Do:.
8 Then was buried, John Robinson, a Child, by Do:—
13 Then was buried, Mr: John Trott, by Do:.
22 Then was buried, Philip Pilpot, a Sailor, by Do:.
25 Then was buried a Surgeon, by Do:.
26 Then was buried, John Mc:Ginney, a Child, by Do:
28 Then was buried, Peter LeGrout, a Child, by Do:.
Do: Then was buried, John Harvey, a Child, by Do:.
29 Then was buried, Samuel Le Ron, als Lawrence, a Child, by Do:.
30 Then was buried, Wm: Anderson, belong: to ye: Man of War, by Do:.
July 1s Then was buried, Peter Johnson, Do:- Do:.-
9 Then was buried, Sarah Wilson, a Child, by Do:.
15 Then was buried, Sarah Holmes, a Child, by Do:.
23 Then was buried, Elis Moore, by Do:.
Do: Then was buried, Mary Newman, a poor-woman, by Do:.
Augt: 5th: Then was buried, John Everet, a Child, by Do:.
20th: Then was buried, John Berry, a Child, by Do:.
Do: Then was buried, James Hutson, by Do:.
23 Then was buried, Eliza: Hencock, by Do:.
24 Then was buried, Sarah Eves, by Do:.
Sepbr:.. 1st: Then was buried, Ellis Edmonds, by Do:.
23 Then was buried, Hugh Duffey, by Do:.
Octobr: 2d. Then was buried, John Simrell, by Do:.
5 Then was buried, John Lane, belonging to a Man a War, by Do:.
15 Then was buried, John Le Roun ,a Child, by Do:.
23 Then was buried, a poor=woman by Do:.
25 Then was buried, Nicholas Hamerser Cramer, by Do:.
30 Then was buried, Eliza: Burnham, a Child, by Do:.
Novbr: 8 Then was buried, Joseph Holbich, by Do:.
15 Then was buried, Dr: Cothorp, Surgeon, by Do:.
[252] 1720—
Novbr: 22 Then was buried, Francis Honnour, by the Revd Mr: Garden.
Xbr: 8 Then was buried, Mary Banton, a Child, by Do:.
13 Then was buried, John Bullock, by Do:.
Do Then was buried, Joshua Haslehurst, by Do:.
25 Then was buried, Nevil Kidwell, a Child, by Do:.
Janry:- 19 Then was buried, Joseph Wilson, a Saylor, by Do:.
21 Then was buried, Joseph Hutchinson, a Child, by Do:.
24 Then was buried, Anne Smith, a Servt: maid, by Do:.

20 Then was buried, Mrs-: Axtel, an Anabaptist.—
Febry-: 3d: Then was buried, Capt: Willoughby..
5 Then was buried John Fowles.
23 Then was buried, Blinkhorn.
March 8 Then was buried, Mrs: Hester Collins, a Child
15 Then was buried, William Spencer.
1721
April 15 Then was buried, Richd: Gladman.
21 Then was buried, Stephen Wyat.
May Then was buried, Duncan Mc:intosh.
20 Then was buried, John Oliver.
30 Then was buried, William Smith.
June 2 Then was buried, John Leversley. } Soldiers
5 Then was buried, John Pert. } Soldiers
11 Then was buried, William Morris } Soldiers
24 Then was buried, William Loughton, a Child.
25 Then was buried, Mary White a Child.
July Then was buried, Harvy a Child.
8 Then was buried, Daniel Green, a Child.
13 Then was buried, Mary Harvy, a Child.
Then was buried, Major Fairchild, a Child.
Then was buried, Eliza: Chambers, a Child.
16 Then was buried, Alexr: Robinson, a Child.
Then was buried, John Lancaster, a Child.
27 Then was buried, Thomas Moore.
Augt: 14 Then was buried, belonging to a Man of War.
23 Then was buried, Samuel Splatt, a Child.
24 Then was buried Moore, a Child.
Sepbr: 2 Then was buried, William Dick, a Child.
4 Then was buried, Lydia Larans.
12 Then was buried, Mrs: . . . . Pilson.
1721 [253]
Octobr: 1s: Then was buried, Richd: Symonds, by the Revd: Mr: Garden
8 Then was buried, Stevenson, a Child, ℘ Do.
11 Then was buried Richard Fairfield, ℘ Do:.
14 Then was buried, Mrs: Bellinger.
15 Then was buried a Sailor.
Novbr: 19 Then was buried, Christian Boyden, a Child
Janry: 4 Then was buried, Mr: Bradshaw.
26 Then was buried, Mr: Perkins.
28 Then was buried, Anne Fairchild.
March: 5 Then was buried, Bates.
1722
Apll: 4th: Then was buried, William Becket.

5 Then was buried, Thos: Allen, at his Plantation, in Christ Church Parish.
10 Then was buried, Mary Basnet Widow.
16 Then was buried, Edward Nichols.
20 Then was buried, Stephen Langley.
Do: Then was buried, Thomas Figsley, a Soldier.
22 Then was buried, Thomas Hedges, a Child.
May .8 Then was buried, Thomas Merryman, Enseign.
9 Then was buried, John Bass, a Saylor.
12 Then was buried, Eliza: Drayton.
14 Then was buried, Natha: Partridge.
15 Then was buried, Mary Dodd, a Child.
20 Then was buried, John Garrard.
21 Then was buried, a Sailor.
June 1s: Then was buried, Adams, a poor=woman.
10 Then was buried, Thomas Dennis, Son of Benja: Dennis.
13 Then was buried, Morrice Williams.
19 Then was buried, Jeremiah Cogswell,
21 Then was buried, Dod.
July 8 Then was buried, Anne Roderick.
15 Then was buried Christian Tunley.
21 Then was buried Thomas Gasden, a Child.
Then was buried, Joseph Holbich, Do:.
Augt: 2 Then was buried, Mary Ward.
Sepbr: 2 Then was buried, Robert Dews.
14 Then was buried, Thomas Crofts.
Then was buried, Nichs: Nary, a Child.
29 Then was buried, Martha Clifford. in ye French Church Yard.
[254] 1722
October 9th Then was buried ,Anne Izard, a Child, by ye Revd: Mr: Garden.
22 Then was buried, Conyers, poor.
24 Then was buried, Esther Lewis.
25 Then was buried, Mary Bainton.
30 Then was buried, John Heard, a Child.
Novbr: 18 Then was buried, Mrs: Mary LLoyd.
Decembr: 16 Then was buried Mrs: Hannah Williams.
30 Then was buried, Jeffry Burrows.
Janry: 10 Then was buried John Sturbridge, a sayler.
14 Then was buried Colo: William Rhett.
26 Then was buried Ralph Poile, a Sayler.
Then was buried Humphry Potter.
Then was buried John Knight a sayler, belongg: to a Man of Warr.
Febry: 2d: Then was buried William Williams a Negro.
28 Then was buried Mary Mariner a Child.

March: 19 Then was buried John Croskeys.
Febry: 28 Then died Anne Mariner a Child, & was buried ye: 1s: March 1722/3
March: 4 Then died Mary Friah & was buried ye: 3th: March 1722/3
17 Then died Geo: Martin & was buried ye: 18th: Do: Do:
18 Then Died John Crosskeys and was Buried the 19th: of March 1722/3
April 8 Then Died John Whitmarsh and was Buried the 9th- of April 1723.

1723

21 Then Died Jouneau, and was Buried the 22th. Ditto
27 Then Died Edward Croft a Child and was Buried the 28 Ditto
28 Then Died William Crook Aged 50 years and was Buried ye 29th: Ditto
May 18 Then died Nathaniel Simmonds Mate of the Ship Dolphin & was Buried the 19th. Day of May 1723.
June 16 At Night, was Drowned John Milles belonging to the Henrietta Yatch, and was Buried the 17th. of June 1723—
17 Then Died Mary Anne Walker the Daughter of Thomas and Anne Walker, and was Buried the same Day.
29 Then Died Thomas Walker, son of the said Thomas and Anne Walker, and was Buried the same Day.
July 8th. Then was Drowned John Rivers, Aged 50 years, and was Buried the 9th. Day of July 1723.
10 Then Died Marg'ret Moore, and was Buried the same Day.
August 3d Then Died Thomas Dyer Carpenter from Weymouth, and was Buried the 4th- of August
29 Then was Buried Captn. John L'roche in the French Church yard (By the Reverend Mr. Garden)

1723 [255]

Septemr. 7th. Then was Buried Sarah Lee a Child by the Revrend Mr- Garden
13 Then was Buried Abigail Conyer
14 Then was Burried Mrs. Susanah Prioleau
Octob. 6 Then was Buried Powell Hayward
20 Then was Buried Mary Foster a Child
Novemr: 4 Then was Buried Mr. James Smith
10 Then was Buried John Samms a Child
26 Then was Buried Mrs. Anne Hutchinson
Decemb: 25 Then was Buried James Mills, (belonging to the Blanford.)
30 Then was Buried Joseph Harrison
31 Then was Buried Mrs. Anne Martin
Februy. 2 Then was Buried James Wood
6 Then was Buried William Tattle a Melatto

12 Then was Buried John James a Sailor who was accidentally Drown'd the 15th. of January last past—

18 Then Died Radugal Dennis a Child, and was Buried ye 19th: Februry.

9 Then was Buried James Sadler.

March 29 Then was Buried Deborah Hancock a Child

1724 30 Then was Buried Mary Taylor a Child

May 8 Then was Buried John Abrams Mate of the Success Snow

June 4 Then was Buried Keinard De La Bere a Child—

July 2 Then was Buried William Foot Bricklayer

3 Then was Buried Johanna Hayes

5 Then was Buried Mrs. Elizabeth Palmer

Augut. 25 Then was Buried Thomas Walker—

Sept. 1st—Then was Buried Edward Davis

Octob. 15 Then was Buried Mrs. Mary Sadler

23 Then was buried Edward Paulin

26 Then was Buried Ann Mews a Child—

27 Then was Buried John Boucher Surgeon of ye Pearl

Novr. 1 Then was Buried Mary Packereau a Child—

5 Then was Buried George Martin a Child (in the French Church Yard by the Reverend Mr. Garden.)

15 Then was Buried William Aaron, marriner late belonging to the Ship Greyhound, at the Charge of the Parish—

21 Then was Buried Alexander Robinson by Mr. Murritt

26 Then was Buried Richard Card Bricklayer by Ditto

June 9 Then was Buried Mary Davis, by ye Revd. Mr. Garden

Decemr: 9 Then Dyed Joseph Monk and Was Buried in the New Church Yard, by the Revd. Mr. Garden Prayrs: in ye Church

15 Then Dyed John Up John a Child, and was Buried the 18th. of December by the Reverend Mr. Garden—

Janury: 24 Then Dyed Daniel Gale a Black Smith, and was Buried the 25th of January, by the Reverend Mr: Garden, Prayer's in the Church—

Februay: 4 Then was Buried, Mr. John Smith a Merchant, by the Reverend Mr: Garden, Prayers in the Church

[256] Burials

March 5th, Then was Buried the Honble: William Gibbon Esqr. Merchant, by the Reverend Mr. Alexander Garden, Prayers in the Church.

16 Then was Buried Joseph Morgan a Child, by the Reverend Mr. Garden-

22 Then Dyed Mrs.Elizabeth Gadsden, and was Buried the next Day, by the Reverend Mr. Alexr: Garden, Prayers in the Church—

23 Then Dyed Mrs. Margt: Hall, and was Buried the 25th. Ditto by the Reverend Mr: Garden

31 Then Dyed Mrs.   Breton, and was Buried the 1st. of April by the Reverend Mr- Garden, in the French Church yard—

1725

May 28 Then was Buried Mary Pellet a Child ,by Mr. Garden

June 7 Then was Buried Joseph Palmer a Child ꝑ Ditto

9 Then was Buried John Read a Sailor ꝑ Ditto

18 Then was Buried Samuel Smith Barber ꝑ Ditto

23 Then was Buried Robert Ker ꝑ Ditto

July 10 Then was Buried Benjamin Bullock ꝑ Ditto

22 Then was Buried John Cable ꝑ Ditto

Do. Then was Buried John White ꝑ Ditto

Augt: 16 Then was Buried William Lane Mate of ye Scarborough ꝑ Ditto

27 Then was Buried William Kennett ꝑ Ditto ,

28 Then was Buried Richard Mashett a Child ꝑ Ditto

30 Then was Buried John Greenland ꝑ Ditto Prayers in the Church

Septr: 4 Then was Buried Elizabeth Pope, ꝑ Ditto

5 Then was Buried Susannah Greenland ꝑ Ditto, Prayers in ye Church

20 Then was Buried James Ma'zick Du Pois D'Or, ꝑ Ditto, Ditto. .

23 Then was Buried Peter Kingwell Saylor ꝑ the Revd. Mr. Morritt

24 Then was Buried Margaret Knight ,without a minister

27 Then was Buried Elizabeth Godfrey, ꝑ the Revd. Mr. Garden

do. Then was Buried William Foster ꝑ ditto Prayers in the Church

28 Then was Buried John Thorp ꝑ Ditto

Octr: 1 Then was Buried Benjamin Monteux ꝑ Ditto Prayers in ye Church

do: Then was Buried Elizabeth Foster a Child ꝑ Ditto in the Old Church yard

do. Then was Buried William Bell a Saylor ꝑ Ditto

2d Then was Buried Elisha Prioleau a Child ꝑ Ditto

25 Then was Buried Charles Wainwright Carington a Lawyer ꝑ Do

26 Then was Buried William Burt a Saylor ꝑ Ditto

1725 [257]

Novr: 12 Then was Buried   Staples ꝑ the Reverend Mr. Garden

13 Then was Buried Hanah Danford ꝑ Ditto

19 Then was Buried Anne French a Child ꝑ Ditto

Decr. 10 Then was Buried Charles Mackleane ꝑ Ditto

16 Then was Buried John Cawood Esqr: ℘ Ditto Prayers in ye Church

19 Then was Buried Thomas Garrett, no minister

31 Then was Buried Jonathan Newton by the Parish, no minister

Jany: 22 Then was Buried Lancaster a Child ℘ Mr. Garden

Febry. 10 Then was Buried John Burnham ℘ Ditto, in his own Plantation

15 Then was Buried Jennet Drummond ℘ Ditto

20 Then was Buried John Barns Clerk of the Scarborough ℘ Ditto

March 6 Then was Buried Bullard a Child ℘ Ditto

1726

April 6 Then was Buried William Williams a Sailor ℘ Ditto

10 Then was Buried Priscilla Croft ℘ Ditto Prayers in ye- Church

24 Then was Buried Thomas Conyers in the French Church Yard by the Reverend Mr. A: Garden, Prayers in the New Church

May 27 Then was Buried James Thompson a Child ℘ Mr. Garden

June 2 Then was Buried, Francis Geÿer a Child ℘ Ditto

5 Then was Buried Sophia Lockyer a Child ℘ Ditto

July 31 Then was Buried John Burton a Child ℘ Ditto

Augt: 6 Then was Buried Nicholas Kidgel ℘ Ditto

11 Then was Buried Leslie a Mariner ℘ Ditto

26 Then was Buried John Harris a Mariner ℘ Ditto

25 Then was Buried Mary Bullock widow ℘ Ditto

30 Then was Buried John Cowie a Mariner ℘ Ditto

Octr: 1 Then was Buried James Williams

12 Then was Buried Mrs: Lancaster ℘ Ditto

30 Then was Buried William Byrem a Child ℘ Ditto

Novr. 24 Then was Buried Joseph Pierce ℘ ditto

27 Then was Buried Mary Timmans ℘ ditto

30 Then was Buried James Nicholson Seaman ℘ d

Decr. 1 Then was Buried Henry Houser, Prayers in ye Church d

3 Then was Buried William Harris ℘ ditto.

4 Then was Buried William Wood. ℘ ditto

12 Then was Buried Mrs: Katherine Winderas ℘ do.

[258] Burials

1726/7

Jany. 6 Then was Buried Mrs. Lydia Arnoll ℘ the Revd: Mr. Garden

11 Then was Buried Mrs. Talbert ℘ ditto

15 Then was Buried Mr. Albert Muller, Prayers in ye Church ℘ do.

25 Then was Buried Dorothy Fowler ℘ ditto
26 Then was Buried Esther Conyers in the French Church Yard ℘ the Rev^d^. M^r^. Garden

Febr^y^. 9 Then was Buried M^rs^. Elizabeth Barry ℘ d^o^. had prayers
15 Then was Buried Robert Sandwell, (Scarborough)
22 Then was Buried M^rs^. Mary Thomas had Prayers in the English Church & Buried in the French Church Yard
23 Then was Buried M^rs^. Jane Trott, had Prayers in the Church
28 Then was Buried M^rs^. Alice Hogg ℘ M^r^. Garden.

Marc. 11 Then was Buried Duncan M^c^.pherson, (Scarborough)

1727

April 1 Then was Buried Sophia Bampfield a Child.

May 9 Then was Buried Anne Splatt a Child.
13 Then was Buried Susanna Stevenson ditto.
16 Then was Buried Jonathan Burnham ditto
17 Then was buried Jane Finch—
22 Then was Buried John Sibley a Joyner
24 Then was Buried Jacob Pickering a Child
d^o^. Then was Buried M^rs^. Katherine Taveroon in the French Church Yard by M^r^. Garden
26 Then was Buried M^r^. John Haley ℘ ditto
29 Then was Buried William Walker

June 10 Then was Buried Benjamin Hope a Child
13 Then was Buried Clarke
28 Then was Buried M^rs^. Tootle widow

July 7 Then was Buried William Blakewey Esqr—
15 Then was Buried Robert Palmer a Boy.
23 Then was Buried Richard Scott
26 Then was Buried James Batterson

Augt. 3 Then was Buried Miles Croft a Child
11 Then was Buried M^rs^. Manigault
17 Then was Buried Mary Lea —

Burials— [259]

1726

April 29 Then was Buried Roger M^c^.lemorrow
May 1 Then was Buried John Fraser—
22 Then was Buried Eleana Barn's
} all 3 at ye Charge of ye Parish

1727

Augt. 20 Then was Buried Samuel Pickering Esqr.
27 Then was Buried William Smith a Child—

Sept. 2 Then was Buried M^r^. Richard Wigg
7 Then was Buried Samuel Pottle
13 Then was Buried Richard Bay a Seaman—
22 Then was Buried Charles Hope a Child
25 Then was Buried Mary Day

29 Then was Buried Sophia Haley
Oct. 1 Then was Buried George Howes at the Parish Charge
5 Then was Buried James Brown a Seaman
6 Then was Buried Margaret Stuart
9 Then was Buried Barnet Fagen a Seaman
do. Then was Buried Margaret Stuart's Child
19 Then was Buried William Tutton by Mr. Dyson
25 Then was Buried Cornelius Longhair by the Revd Mr. Garden
26 Then was Buried Captn. Hugh Hardy, Prayers in ye Church
27 Then was Buried John Bolton
28 Then was Buried Doctr. Thomas Lockyer
Novr: 4 Then was Buried Josiah Cornish a Ship Carpenter
7 Then was Buried Ferdinando Cayer by Mr. Ludlam
15 Then was Buried Edward Tayler a Seaman
Decr. 12 Then was Buried Mr. William Loughton ℘ Mr Garden
Jany 10 Then was Buried William Rhett a Child
19 Then was Buried Thomas Savery
15 Then was Buried John Harris
Febry 14 Then was Buried John & Thomas Wright, Twins-
Marc: 11 Then was Buried William Evans a Seaman
— do Then was Buried Thomas Denton a Taylor
do Then was Buried John Smith the Gunner.
April 12 Then was Buried Rachel Moore
14 Then was Buried Millicent Brewton
17 Then was Buried Mary Miller
24 Then was Buried William Chambers

[260] Burials———

1728

May 12 Then was Buried Mrs. Weekley by the Revd: Mr. Garden
13 Then was Buried Gregory Moore Haines a Boy.
do. Then was Buried Thomas Hepworth Esqr. Chief Justice
14 Then was Buried Hugh Haines a Boy.
do. Then was Buried Elizabeth Morgan a Child
22 Then was Buried John Willis
23 Then was Buried Mary Thomas
27 Then was Buried Martin Motte a Child
29 Then was Buried Jane Warden a Child
June 6 Then was Buried Mary Pinckney a Child
11 Then was Buried Thomas Cooper—
15 Then was Buried Phebe Smith
do. Then was Buried John Parsons a Boy
18 Then was Buried Hannah French
Augt 5 Then was Buried William Langley-

20 Then was Buried William Nichols
Sept. 4 Then was Buried Thomas Dickson a Seaman
5 Then was Buried John Duncan
14 Then was Buried Cyprian Southack
18 Then was Buried John Kirkland
do. Then was Buried Willm: Johnson & William Huxley
21 Then was Buried Alexander Clench—
22 Then was Buried Anne Lorey
23 Then was Buried Captn. Benjamin Rumzey
25 Then was Buried Eleana Taylor
do. Then was Buried Anne Rhodda
26 Then was Buried Anne Dundon
26 Then was Buried John Sharp
Octr. 6 Then was Buried Mr. Harris Boatswain of the Fox
11 Then was Buried John Jones
do. Then was Buried Elizabeth Dupree
12 Then was Buried Elizabeth Hutchinson
13 Then was Buried William Cutbread a seaman
17 Then was Buried Alexander Mc.kenzie a Boy
18 Then was Buried Mr. Richard Splatt, merchant
19 Then was Buried James Jodgson a seaman
23 Then was Buried Elizabeth Burridge
25 Then was Buried Margaret Smith a School-mistress.

1728 Burials— [261]

Octob. 31 Then was Buried Timothy Standford by the Revd. Mr. Garden
Novr. 9 Then was Buried Captn. Lovibond
13 Then was Buried Jacob Godin son of Mr. Benja: Godin Mercht.
19 Then was Buried William Beck
23 Then was Buried Charles Faldoe a Seaman
26 Then was Buried Susan Duvall
28 Then was Buried Sarah Partridge
Decr. 3 Then was Buried William Winderas, an old Mathematician.
5 Then was Buried Rebeka Dicks
6 Then was Buried John Smith the Pilot
11 Then was Buried John Cray the Barber
15 Then was Buried Margaret Willson
17 Then was Buried John Robinson
do. Then was Buried Jonathan Vincent a Seaman
do. Then was Buried William Purnell a Convict lately brought from Bristol by Captn. Mc.kenzie.
20 Then was Buried Thomas Delaney a Fencing Master.
26 Then was Buried Elizabeth Needham
Janry: 2 Then was Buried Graves

5 Then was Buried David Carmichael
7 Then was Buried Stephen Rhodda a Child
8 Then was Buried John Hope a Barber
14 Then was Buried Mrs. Susanna Poinsett
16 Then was Buried Dr John Arnott
18 Then was Buried Solomon White
20 Then was Buried Walter Keith
21 Then was Buried Thomas Clark
23 Then was Buried Capn. John Stollard
24 Then was Buried Mr. John Bee
24 Then was Buried Mrs. Margaret Willson
25 Then was Buried Mr. Thomas Satur
Febry. 9 Then was Buried William Sullavan
16 Then was Buried William Rhett Esqr. & Mary his Wife
17 Then was Buried Elizabeth Osborne a Child —
28 Then was buried Thomas Dunn.
March 2,, Then was buried Jacob Simmons.
9,, Then was buried Henrietta Johnston
11,, Then was buried John Harwood.—

[262] Burials.

1728/9
March 12 Then was Buried Richard Vickery.
17 Then was Buried Miles Mccentosh.

1729
April 15. Then was Buried Anne Needham.
16 Then was Buried Elizabeth Lea.
20 Then was Buried Martin Glazebrook.
May 15,, Then was Buried Mary Hankock.
17,, Then was Buried William Clifford.
19,, Then was Buried Margaret Arnold. &
,, Then was Buried John Hankock.
22,, Then was Buried Oswel Eves. &
Then was Buried James Jenkins.
24 Then was buried Henry Gignilliat
25 Then was Buried Samuel Grassett.
June 5 Then was Buried Childermus Croft
7,, Then was Buried Steven Stevenson &
Then was Buried Henry Gibbes.
8,, Then was Buried Joseph Harvey
11,, Then was Buried William Wilkie
15,, Then was Buried James Stanaway. &
Then was Buried Thomas Haines.
July 15,, Then was Buried Thomas Cutfield
21 Then was Buried Mary Johnson
22,, Then was Buried Steven Tauroon Augt 13th. Eliza-Gadsden 15—John Lambert

26,, Then was buried John Gardener. 29—Mary Cart

October 16,, Then was buried John Postel. & on ye 26th John Hutchinson

Septemr 24,, Then was buried William Robertson. 9.ber-5th- Mary Byrem

Decemr. 10,, Then was buried Mr Peter Manigault. Xber-18th-Richd. Bayly—

July 21,, Then was buried Mary Smith

Octor- 12,, Then was buried Matthew Newberry.

1730

April 11,, Then was buried George Sinclair.

June 12,, Then was buried Richard Saxbee.

25,, Then was buried William* Linthwaite

28,, Then was buried William Inglefield-

August 20,, Then was buried William Hepworth—

28,, Then was buried Anne Gignilliat

Septemr. 30,, Then was buried John Gray- ———

1729 Burials. [263]

March 17th. Then was buried William Edwards a Sailer

17. Then was buried James Brown. a sailer. belonging to the man of warr

1730

April 9,, Then was buried John Perry.

11,, . Then was buried George Sinclair.

May 10,, Then was buried Jane Wright

Then was buried Gideon Lea. a Sailer

16,, Then was buried Quick Sailer

21,, Then was buried Mebitabel Cooper —

26,, Then was buried William Augustin. a Sailer

28,, Then was buried Anne Ramsay.

June 21,, Then was buried Richard Saxby.

26,, Then was buried Wm- John Linthwaite

28,, Then was buried William Inglefield a Child

July,, 11,, Then was buried Elizabeth Waters.

23 Then was buried Elizabeth Sharp a Chd.

August 20 Then was buried William Hepworth.

22,, Then was buried William Morgan

28, Then was buried Anne Gignilliat Chd.

Septemr. 30,, Then was buried John Gray

Do. do Then was buried Anne Upton

Do :.,, Then was buried John Harvey Chd

Octor. 2,, Then was buried Martha Bastion

5,, Then was buried George King

---

*There is something inserted here that looks like "Jr."

* Then was buried Wyat a Ch[d].
22,, Then was buried William Kelly a Sailer
23,, Then was buried Benjamin Walker-
Novem[r] 7,, Then was buried Mary Batten
9,, Then was buried Richard Chape —
D[o]. ..,, Then was buried Francis Hope Ch[d].
14,, Then was buried Elizabeth Leopard Ch[d].
18,, Then was buried Catherine Le Brasseur
D[o] ..,, Then was buried. Thomas Jennings a Sailer
19,, Then was buried Manassey Courage
21,, Then was buried Mary Bee
22,, Then was buried Thomas Morgan
24,, Then was buried Frances Robyns
27,, Then was buried John Hill. a Ch[d]. } twins
Decber- 11,, Then was buried Farmer Hill. a Ch[d] }
Do 11 Then was buried Paul Viart.

[264]
Burials

1730
Decem[r] 13,, Then was buried John Hogg-
January 9,, Then was buried Elizabeth Jones.
11,, Then was buried William Fleck.
12,, Then was buried Arabella Wright
D[o]. d[o] Then was buried . . . Hedges.
22,, Then was buried John Cain a Sailer
D[o] 23., Then was buried John Shute.
Then was buried Thomas Townsend.
24,, Then was buried John Glasby.
27,, Then was buried Mary Wyatt.
March 6,, Then was buried John Wallis a Sailer
11,, Then was buried Mary Weaver. a Ch[d].
12,, Then was buried Benjamin Bates.
do Then was buried John Abbot. (P)
21., Then was buried Michael Walters ℘ Coron[rs] Inquest
23,, Then was buried Anne Husbands
1731 28,, Then was buried Humphry Salter
Then was buried Lucy — Brown.
April 11,, Then was buried Richard Scott. ch[d].
15,, Then was buried Hester Lawrence. a Ch[d].
May .8,, Then was buried Barnard Ollier. a Ch[d].
14,, Then was buried John Rice. a Ch[d]
Then was buried Anne Killpatrick a Ch[d].
18,, Then was buried Hezekiah Holton. a Ch[d].
,, Then was buried Eliz[a]. Morgan Vander dyson Serv[ts] Ch[d].

---

*Date of month broken out.

25,, Then was buried Anne Lindsey. (Parish)
June .2,, Then was buried John Mcgregory. (P)
6,, Then was buried. Mary Squire —
9,, Then was buried William Bates a Chd.
11., Then was buried Anne Rogers. (P)
12,. Then was buried James Smith a Sailor
13,, Then was buried Susanna Townsend a Chd
17., Then was buried Mary Delabere a Chd.
18,, Then was buried Anthony Poitevine
19., Then was buried John Stanhover
20,, Then was buried Thomas Monk. Walliss Apprentice
25,, Then was buried Joseph Hext a Chd.
do Then was buried Collins Gadsden
July 2 Then was buried Richard Turner
3 Then was buried Frances Bonnetheau

Burials [265]

1731
July ,, 5,, Then was buried James Owen. a Child.
6,, Then was buried Samuel Trott.
Do. . Then was buried William Smith a Child
14,, Then was buried Jonathan Collins
do,, Then was buried Thomas Sharp a Child
18,, Then was buried Richard Germier
21,, Then was buried Jonathan Hargrave.
25,, Then was buried William King. a Sailer
August. * Then was buried Samuel Williams a Sailer.
,, Then was buried Joseph Jolly. . . .
12,, Then was buried Elizabeth Ireland
13,, Then was buried Mary Grant. (P)
do,, Then was buried Edwd. Gover—a Sailer
20,, Then was buried Richard Long.—
22,, Then was buried Richard Miller
Septemr 17,, Then was buried Richard Rowe
do,, Then was buried James Lincoln
Octor,, 7,, Then was buried David Rays.
10,, Then was buried Gibbon Wright.
11,, Then was buried Francis Moratt a Chd.
21,, Then was buried Susanna Morat.
do,, Then was buried Nicholas Grill a Sailer
23,, Then was buried Margaret Havens.
30,, Then was buried John Lea. a Child
Novemr 2,, Then was buried Thomas Robyns—
22,. Then was buried Esther Montjoy.
26,, Then was buried Grace Scott.

---

*Date of month undecipherable.

Decem^{r} 2,, Then was buried George Ransford a Sailer
15,, Then was buried William Moore
28,, Then was buried Elizabeth Dennis—
Jan^{ry}. 3,, Then was buried Hill Croft.
14,, Then was buried John Gardner
17,, Then was buried George Keith (P)
Feb^{y}- 6,, Then was buried Gabriel Mayn
Feb^{y},, 15,, Then was buried Anne Hooper. (P)
16,, Then was buried Susanna Bacold
26,, Then was buried Edmond Bush (W)
March 5,, Then was buried Moses Bennet. a Ch^{d}
6,, Then was buried Eliz^{a}- Clench.
10,, Then was buried Mary Roule. (B.)
d^{o},, Then was buried Richard Evans (W)

[266] Burials

1731
March 12,, Then was buried Hannah Scott.
14,, Then was buried Robert Lorey
1732 28,, Then was buried Joseph Haines—
April 2,, Then was buried Samuel Martin
3,, Then was buried James Read a Child
4,, Then was buried Edward Richards.
5,, Then was buried Mariann Mazycke
26,, Then was buried William Hammerton
May ,, 6,, Then was buried Richard Seb. a Child.
19,, Then was buried Mary Bodicot, a Child
22,, Then was buried Katherine Moultrie a Child
26,, Then was buried William Wilkie
27,, Then was buried Joseph Lee.
June * ,, Then was buried Sarah Millens
11,, Then was buried John Ollier a Child. Oliver John
12,, Then was buried Mary Read
14,, Then was buried James Druman
19,, Then was buried John Madlor
,, Then was buried Captn- John Jordan
20,, Then was buried Thomas Evell
July †,, Then was buried George Thomas
,, Then was buried Anne Vanvelsy—
3,, Then was buried Madam Johnson. the Govern^{r}. wife
11,, Then was buried Anne Evell. & Elinor Ward
12,, Then was buried Daniel Brown
14,, Then was buried William Lawrence
,, Then was buried Sarah Pigfatt.

---

*Day of month broken out.

†Day of month undecipherable:

„ Then was buried George Nichols
„ Then was buried Martha Dakers.
15„ Then was buried David Robinson
„ Then was buried Mary Pengrave.
16 Then was buried Martha Jones
„ Then was buried Bridget Blake
18„ Then was buried Miles More
„ Then was buried Sarah Ward
Then was buried Elizabeth Pain
„ Then was buried Edward Bateman

1732 Burials [267.]

July 19„ Then was buried John Ingland
Then was buried Alexander Steward
21 Then was buried Claudius Lambert.
„Then was buried Marget Grant
Then was buried William Morgan
22„ Then was buried lemon Rillam
23„ Then was buried Joseph Higgins.
„ Then was buried Alexander French
„ Then was buried Thomas Macarty.
„ Then was buried John Cradock. P.
23„ Then was buried Robert Linton P.
„ Then was buried Martha Croxson
„ Then was buried John Lechanter.
„ Then was buried David Cumberland.
„ Then was buried William Norman.
23„ Then was buried Paul Hussy.
25„ Then was buried Peter Olliar
26„ Then was buried John Shaw.
„ Then was buried Sarah Torring
„ •Then was buried Mongo Welsh
„ Then was buried John Smith,
„ Then was buried Catherine Fisgarue
„ Then was buried Honora Murphy.
26„ Then was buried Edward Burlett.
„ Then was buried Charles Crofts P
Then was buried Thomas Bertram.
27„ Then was buried Thomas Freeman
Then was buried Elizabeth Doxsaint a Child
Then was buried Hester Lechanter. a Child
Then was buried George Rolfe
Then was buried Elinor Leacraft
Then was buried Mary Fisher.
28„ Then was buried William Pigfat.
„ Then was buried Rebekah Coke.
30 Then was buried Elizabeth Grasset P.

Then was buried William Davis.
Then was buried Rodea Holes.
31„ Then was buried John Arnott

[268] Burials

1732

July * Then was buried Richd Cafford
„ Then was buried John Holland. a Child.
August † Then was buried Mr. Wm. Johnson The Governrs. Son.
Then was buried Mary Daile
2„ Then was buried Mary Wetherly
3„ Then was buried Charles Cart
„ Then was buried Mary Daws
4„ Then was buried Mr Henry Hargrave
Then was buried Samuel Faulkner.
6„ Then was buried Samuel Eldridge
Then was buried Hugh Brown
Then was buried Jane Pink.
Then was buried David Davis.
8 Then was buried Jonathan Turner
9„ Then was buried Marget Burnham
„ Then was buried Richard Hocknall
10 Then was buried John Smith P
„ Then was buried John Curtley.
11„ Then was buried Richard Bridges. Charles Burnham
12„ Then was buried Daniel Benson
„ Then was buried Thomas Puxions
13„ Then was buried Charles Holyday.
„ Then was buried Nicholas Duke
14„ Then was buried Joseph Sutton
17„ Then was buried John Randells
October 13. Then was buried Mighells an infant the Son of Capn: John Gascoigne by Mary Ann his wife at the East end of the Church of St. Philips Charles town
August 18„ Then was buried John Page
21„ Then was buried Patience Field a Child
23„ Then was buried Thomas Crafts.
„ Then was buried Amy Trewin
24„ Then was buried John Dynes.
26„ Then was buried Charles Lockly.
Then was buried William Gunns.
28„ Then was buried William Huney
Then was buried Mary Welshuyssen
30„ Then was buried Martha Jeys.

---

*Day of month broken out.

†Day of month undecipherable.

„ Then was buried Charles Crisp.
31„ Then was buried Mary Hargrave. P.
Septemr. 4„ Then was buried Thomas Hargrave P.
1732 * [269]
Septemr † Then was buried George Cluellen
„ Then was buried Michael Maning
Then was buried John Amy a Child
„ Then was buried Mrs- Jean Bisset.
Then was buried Mary Arnol, a Child
Then was buried Christopher Lancaster a Child
„ Then was buried Henry Wools. a Child.
„ Then was buried Ephraim Paine
October „ Then was buried William Johnston a Child
„ Then was buried James Mackonaway
„ Then was buried Thomas Morryson
„ Then was buried Elizabeth Kenordet
„ Then was buried John Otley
„ Then was buried Howel Humphrys P.
„ Then was buried Andrew Mackentosh
„ Then was buried Alexander Gray.
Novemr. „ Then was buried John Coleman
Then was buried Mrs. Elizabeth Vanderdysen
Decemr. „ Then was buried Edmund Stead
Then was buried John Gettins
January „ Then was buried Habocock Sear
Then was buried Joseph Miller
„ Then was buried William Ramsey
„ Then was buried Anthony Harris
„ Then was buried Robert Lea
Then was buried Mrs. Gittens
Then was buried William Smith
„ Then was buried Catherine Randall
febry. Then was buried James Vandeson
March „ Then was buried Anne Walters.
„ Then was buried William Gibbes
„ Then was buried Jonathan Mayne
1733
April „ Then was buried Martin Mumpilion
7„ Then was buried Christopher Linkley
12„ Then was buried Mrs. Margaret Clap
12„ Then was buried Martha Wilkins
26„ Then was buried Sarah Turner
May 10„ Then was buried Thomas Sanders.

---

*The top of the page is broken off after the date.

†The dates of the months have been broken out of this page.

[270*]

1733

May 25 Then was buried Arthur Osmond a Child
27,, Then was buried Sarah Proctor a Child
June 2,, Then was buried Capt. Cornock
3,, Then was buried Nicholas Stone
,, Then was buried John Weaver a Child
4,, Then was buried Thomas Henning a Child
14,, Then was buried Anne Burshett
20,, Then was buried Thomas Page
29,, Then was buried Richard Sinclair
July 4,, Then was buried John Holling
,, Then was buried Thomas Sevel
9,, Then was buried Peter Murry
11,, Then was buried Andrew Batton, Adam
August 17,, Then was buried John Smith
18,, Then was buried Richard Biven
20,, Then was buried Joseph Bloodwerth.
May 14,, Then was buried Michael Stone
July 27, Then was buried William Anderson.
Septemr 11,, Then was buried Mary Whiteley
18,, Then was buried Mr John Lewis
22,, Then was buried Thomas Whitmarsh
27,, Then was buried John Rolfe.
29,, Then was buried Robert Stanton
30,, Then was buried Langford
Octor,,14,, Then was buried Daniel Dier
22,, Then was buried Sarah Peacock
25,, Then was buried Thomas Jenkins
27,, Then was buried Mary Corant
29,, Then was buried Richard Brown
30,, Then was buried Jane Mier
Novemr,, 30,, Then was buried Mary Dukes.
Decemr,, 3,, Then was buried Thomas Daniel
15,, Then was buried Mrs. Smalwood
27,, Then was buried Mrs Tomfield
,, Then was buried James Lusesis
28,, Then was buried Richard Owen
28,, Then was buried James Bishop
Janry 8,, Then was buried Dorothy Clark.
5,, Then was buried William Axon
Then was buried Isaac Moore

1733/4
Jany: 3d: Bur: Sarah Pouillette (a child)

---

* The headline has been broken from this page.

[271*]

1733—

Novem 24,, Then was buried John Harden
July 30,, Then was buried John Becit:
Jany 18,, Then was buried Sarah Farles
25 Then was buried Sarah Wigg, the wife of Mr Richard Wigg
30,, Then was buried Hannah Jerom
Then was buried Capt John King—died the 29h.
Febry 3,, Then was buried John Gosling
11,, Then was buried Robert Nisbett.
Janry- 1,, Then was buried Frederick Miers
Decemr 13,, Then was buried Mary Miers
Septemr. 15,, Then was buried Christopher Lancaster
July 1732 18,, Then was buried Mitie More
Augt. 1732 23,, Then was buried James Read

1734

March 28,, Then was buried William Scott
febry ,,Then was buried francis Gardner
April 14,, Then was buried Joseph Panton

1733

October 5,, Then was buried Eliza- Osmond.
6,, Then was buried Elizabeth Somerville
March 7,, Then was buried Thomas farless a Child
10,, Then was buried James Sanders.

1734

May 11, Then was buried Anne Puxam
23,, Then was buried. Margaret Burn
June 15,, Then was buried, Mrs. Mary Parris.
July 1,, Then was buried Lawrence Hendrix
4 Then was buried Anne Chatrell
15,, Then was buried Thomas Jenkins.
20,, Then was buried Mr- Thomas fairchild.
21,, Then was buried Mrs. Hill. ye wife of Mr Richard Hill-
Augt 1,, Then was buried Daniel Savy—a Child,
5,, Then was buried Elizabeth Smallwood.
25,, Then was buried Elizabeth Young.
Sepr. 17,, Then was buried St Roger Lownes.
19,, Then was buried Owen a Child.
21,, Then was buried. Benjamin Newbal
24,, Then was buried Mrs. Sarah Baker ye wife of Mr John Baker
25,, Then was buried Samuel Swann
29,, Then was buried Thomas Weaver a Child

---

*Headline of page broken off.

31†,, Then was buried James Lawrense —
Sepr. 1,, Then was buried Susanna Hall a Child
6,, Then was buried Joseph Kidd - - -
17,, Then was buried Paul Gonson

[272*]

1734

Septem^{r} 28,, Then was buried William Howell.
October 3,, Then was buried Thomas Blundell.
6,, Then was buried Mr John Franklyn.
8,, Then was buried Gabriel Taylor.
8,, Then was buried Alexander Smithers.
13,, Then was buried Calvin Anderson
13 Then was buried Samuel Tossell.
20,, Then was buried Blake Lee.
21,, Then was buried Edmund Smith.
27,, Then was buried Elizabeth flasher.
30,, Then was buried Cap^{n}. . Gordon.
Novem^{r}. 8,, Then was buried Penelope Williams.
11,, Then was buried Benjamin Dennis

21,, Then was buried . . . Gaddens*
Decem^{r}.,, 1,, Then was buried John Fowler.
2,, Then was buried Daniel Furbush.
7,, Then was buried John M^{c}.Nary.
Jan^{ry} 12,, Then was buried Samuel Roberts.
29,, Then was buried Capt. Edward Macenzy—
febr^{y} 1,, Then was buried Anne Shutes-
2,, Then was buried Richard Smith
7,, Then was buried Samuel Pickering
15,, Then was buried Cap^{n}. Thomas Dawes.
23,, Then was buried John Powell
March 2,, Then was buried Mathew Larkin
7,, Then was buried Susanna Wills.
feb^{ry} 26,, Then was buried Deborah Reade
Jan^{ry}- 4,, Then was buried M^{rs}. Elizabeth Bamfield.

1734

March 28,, Then was buried Sarah Tomson
feb^{ry},, 14,, Then was buried Mary Sadler
D^{o} 4,, Then was buried Benjamin Clark-
Nov^{r}- 24,, Then was buried Richard Shaw
ber 10,, Then was buried M^{rs}. . . Tomson

1734 Burials [273]

Novem^{r} 21st Then was Buried Sarah Gitten by the Rev^{d}.: M^{r}: Garden

---

†30th meant no doubt.

* Headline of page broken off.

*All on this page below this line is crossed out.

Novemr 22d Then was buried Abraham Mason
Novemr 24th Then was Buried Robert Shaw
Decemr 1st: Then was Buried James Fowler
Decemr 2d Then was Buried Daniel Forbes (Georgia)
Decemr 6th Then was Buried John Nery Child
Decemr 8th Then was Buried William Hatton
Decemr 29th Then was Buried Mary Loyd
Jany 4th Then was Buried Elizabeth Bamfield
Jany 12th Then was Buried Samuel Nathaniel Roberts' Child
Jany 19th Then was Buried Edward Mc:Kever
Febry 1st Then was Buried Ann Thulesse
Febry 2d Then was Buried Richard Smith
Febry 5th Then was Buried Benjamin Clarke
Febry 7th Then was Buried Samuel Pickering
Febry 14th Then was Buried Mary Sadler
Febry 15th Then was Buried Phillip Daws
Febry 23d Then was Buried John Powell-
Febry 26h Then was Buried Deborah Honr: Read
Mar: 2d Then was Buried Martha Larkin
Mar 4th Then was Buried Susanah Wills
Mar 4th Then was Buried John Lowry
Mar 10th Then was Buried (a Sailer) Bur: by Mr: Fullerton
Mar: 28th Then was Buried William Dr Gibson—
Mar 28 Then was Buried Sarah Simpson-
[274] Burials

1735

March 30 Then was Buried John Stivenson by the Revd: Mr. Garden
April 19th Then was Buried Elizabeth Read (Child)
May 5th Then was Buried His Excellence Robert Johnson Esqr. Govr:
May 6th Then was Buried Elizabeth Stone (child)
May 9th Then was Buried Grace Hall (child)
May 10th Then was Buried John Wilson
May 10th Then was Buried James Jaffery (W.) —
May 15th Then was Buried Mary Tarbett
May 22d Then was Buried Panton
May 12th Then was Buried Elizabeth Hambleton (Child)
June 2d Then was Buried Edward Weekly
June 3d Then was Buried Elizabeth Morgan Dr: M:
June 7th Then was Buried Francis Brasseur (Child)
June 11th Then was Buried Elizabeth Mellish Brasseur
June 11th Then was Buried Crosthwaite (child)
June 12th Then was Buried Walter Wallace
June 13th Then was Buried David Loyd (Child)
June 15th Then was Buried Catherine Smith (Child)
June 24th Then was Buried James Brown

July 1st Then was Buried Alexander Turner
July 1st Then was Buried Martha Sharp (Child)
July 5th Then was Buried John Freeman (Child)
July 6th Then was Buried Richard Harward
July 7th Then was Buried Ann Bennet (Child)
July 16th Then was Buried Mary Godfrey (Child)

Burials [275]

1735

July 16th Then was Buried Richard Cowley (Sailor) ℘ the Revd: Mr Garden
July 18th Then was Buried Samuel Yoke
July 18th Then was Buried Catherine Naes
July 23d Then was Buried John Wanger
July 24th Then was Buried James Sparks (W)
July 24th Then was Buried Patrick Burn (P)
July 31 Then was Buried William Lancaster
Augst: 2d Then was Buried Sarah Palmer
Augst: 3d Then was Buried Josep Fox
Augst: 3d Then was Buried Ann Smalman
August 4 Then was Buried Lucy Shepherd (Child)
Augst 8th Then was Buried Joseph Roberts
Augst: 9th Then was Buried Elizabeth Eagle
Augst : 12th Then was Buried Paul Lewis Timothy (Child)
Augst: 16th Then was Buried Ann Burget
Augst: 17th Then was Buried John Lowns
Augst: * Then was Buried (P)
Augst: Then was Buried William Mc:Kenzie (Child)
Augst: Then was Buried Jane Grasset
Augst: Then was Buried John Gittens (Child)
Septr Then was Buried William Brodfoot
Septr: Then was Buried Bartholomew Shepherd
Septr Then was Buried Martha Harison
Septr Then was Buried Elizabeth Yeomans—

[276] Burials

1735

Septr 26th Then was Buried Peter Parry ℘ the Revd: Mr Garden
Sept 26th Then was Buried Peter Prew
Octor 6th Then was Buried James Parrot
Octòr: 7th Then was Buried John Savie (child)
Octor: 12th Then was Buried Mary Delamere
Octor 13th Then was Buried John Baswick
Octor: 16th Then was Buried Samuel Brown
Octor 22d Then was Buried Sarah Bancroft

---

*Rest of dates broken from page.

Octor 22th Then was Buried Thomas Ashurst (P)
Octor 24th Then was Buried Thomas Goodal
Octor 24th Then was Buried (P)
Octor 25th Then was Buried Jacob Forster (Child)
Octor 28th Then was Buried George Cutler
Octor 30th Then was Buried William Carr
Novr 3d Then was Buried Anne Stephens.. (Child)
Novr 4th Then was Buried a Palatine
Novr: 10th Then was Buried Richard Pilkinson
Novr: 10th Then was Buried Mary Currant (Child)
Novr: 14th Then was Buried John Fontaine (Child)
Novr: 15th Then was Buried William Perryman
Novr: 16th Then was Buried John Clark—
Novr: 19th Then was Buried Allen Curry
Novr 25th Then was Buried Lawrence McKay
Novr 29th Then was Buried John Holland (W)
Novr: 30th Then was Buried Hugh Dally (S)
Decr: 1st Then was Buried Richard Compton
Decr 4th Then was Buried Roland Savey (a Soldier)
Decr: 6th Then was Buried Mary Thomas- (P)

1735
Decr: 6th Then was Buried Jane Wilson ℘ Revd: Mr: Garden
Decr: 8th Then was Buried Edward Wills
Decr: 8th Then was Buried a Woman Servant to Dr Barker
Decr: 11th Then was Buried Mary Magdalene Poideore
Decr:† Then was Buried Francis Miller
Decr: Then was Buried Thomas Fisher
Decr: Then was Buried Rebekah Croft (Child)
Decr: Then was Buried Catherine Wolford (Child)
Januy: 8th Then was Buried Samuel Suff (S)
Jany 12th Then was Buried Martin Glaizbrook
Januy 18th Then was Buried Mary Holyday (Child)
Jany 18th Then was Buried William Gray
Febry 3d Then was Buried Eleonor Evans
Febry 14th Then was Buried Catherina Ryal (Child)
Febry 16th Then was Buried Frances Amy
Febry 24th Then was Buried James Langley
Febry 29th Then was Buried John Moore
March 7th Then was Buried Elizabeth Gummes (Child)
Mar: 12th Then was Buried Alexander Parris

1736
April 27th Then was Buried Carwithen
May 7th Then was Buried James Barnes
May Then was Buried Joseph Townshend

†Four dates of month destroyed.

May 20th Then was Buried Lucy Holiday (Child)
May 25th Then was Buried Bullen Loyd (Child)
June Then was Buried John Reynolds
June 4th Then was Buried William Goar
June 8th Then was Buried Thomas Robinson
[278] Burials
June 6th Then was Buried Ralph Sharlecke (S)
June 16th Then was Buried Thomas Brown (Child)
June 20th Then was Buried Margaret Craige
June 21st Then was Buried Cartwright (Child)
June 26th Then was Buried Robert Shepherd (Child)
July 9th Then was Buried Daniel L
July 9th Then was Buried Henry Garard
July 10th Then was Buried John Storey
July 11th Then was Buried Jane Price (Child)
July 13th Then was Buried Richard Goodwin
July 15th Then was Buried Sarah Thorpe
July 19th Then was Buried John Croft
July 19th Then was Buried Richard Brickles (Child)
July 21st Then was Buried Alexander Osborn
July 22d Then was Buried Robert Hall (Chil)
July 22d Then was Buried Benedick Aish
July 23d Then was Buried Henry Nolan
July 24th Then was Buried Richard Wilson (W)
July 25th Then was Buried Edward Walker
Augst: 5 Then was Buried Constant Baker
8 Then was Buried Augustus Osbound—
9 Then was Buried William Goldie Dr: of ye Men of Warr
10 Then was Buried William Watson
22 Then was Buried Thomas Jaxx—
22 Then was Buried William Rasbe-
23 Then was Buried Isaac Smith.... ℘ Parish
24 Then was Buried Charles Hart Esqr:
27 Then was Buried John Baker Mercht:
Burials [279]

1736
Augst 13st Then was Buried Catherina Hext
Septr 4 Then was Buried Rowland Waughan Esqr:—
10 Then was Buried John Dudley
13 Then was Buried Samuel Puxem (Child)
15 Then was Buried Stephen Tweeles ℘ Parish
15 Then was Buried Marianne Mazick in ye French Church Yard-
15 Then was Buried Thomas Fordyce (Child)—
16 Then was Buried Daniel Legrove - ℘ Parish
17 Then was Buried John Sexton - - ℘ Parish

19 Then was Buried Patrick Owen - - ꝑ Parish
22 Then was Buried John Brickles (a Child)
24 Then was Buried Richard Fisher ꝑ Parish
25 Then was Buried Mary Hill - - ꝑ Parish
26 Then was Buried Elias Horry in the French Church-yard—
28 Then was Buried James Crockatt (a Child)
Octor: 4 Then was Buried Thomas Ellis (a Child) ꝑ ye Parish
4 Then was Buried William Watson a Sailor—
5th Then was Buried William Akins—
6 Then was Buried William Tick — — ꝑ Parish
10 Then was Buried Sarah Weaver—
11 Then was Buried Nicholas Sheppard Carpenter of ye Men of Warr
11 Then was Buried Luck Mulkey—ꝑ Parish
13 Then was Buried Mariamne Mazick at ye French Church yard-
14 Then was Buried Patty Bridget ꝑ Parish
17 Then was Buried Thomas Dale (a Child)
17 Then was Buried William Nichols of ye Men of Warr—
18 Then was Buried William Baker Mercht:—
22 Then was Buried Mary Garden (a Child)
22 Then was Buried Nathaniel Grey of ye Men of Warr—
26 Then was Buried Peter Bees a Sailor—
Novr:— 6th Then was Buried Margaret Parr ꝑ Parish
11 Then was Buried Robert Watts - - ꝑ Parish
16 Then was Buried Agnes Whitteside ———
25 Then was Buried William Mear of ye Men of Warr ——

[280] Burials

1736
Novemr 25th Then was Buried Ursille Ridley (a Child)
Decr: — 2 Then was Buried Ralph Biggs - - ꝑ Parish
4 Then was Buried Thomas Quertier a Sailor
5 Then was Buried Francis Le Brasseur
7 Then was Buried Elizabeth Jeyes (a Child)
19 Then was Buried Joseph Ball ꝑ Parish
19 Then was Buried Benjamin Tanner
21 Then was Buried James Lane
23 Then was Buried Barnabe Owen (a Child)
27 Then was Buried Peter Jacobs- ꝑ Parish
28 Then was Buried Mary Bryan
30 Then was Buried Daniel Butler
Jany 4 Then was Buried James Yong (a Child)
7 Then was Buried James Lane ꝑ Parish a Servant to Coll Blake
10 Then was Buried Charles Walliss-

13 Then was Buried William Lynn
14 Then was Buried Isaac Chardon Caried by Watter to Stono—
15 Then was Buried Thomas Ryal (a Child)
ffebry 1 Then was Buried Mary Panton, Penton
5 Then was Buried Thomas Harbing—
9 Then was Buried John Mott of ye Men of Warr
20 Then was Buried Susannah James—
25 Then was Buried Elizabeth Watson
26 Then was Buried Mary Oborn
28 Then was Buried Elizabeth Pinckney (a Child)
28 Then was Buried William Lane
March 6 Then was Buried Jeane Johnston ℘ Parish
7 Then was Buried James Savage
10 Then was Buried Christopher Woorster ℘ Parish
13 Then was Buried Hester Tabart (a Child)
14 Then was Buried Capn Robert Pollixsen —
14 Then was Buried Richard Mathews (a Child)

1737
March 25 Then was Buried Jeane Martin (a Child)
27 Then was Buried Rebeca Brown (a Child)
April 6 Then was Buried John Gibbs a Yong Man

1737
April 7 Then was Buried Sarah de St: Julien by Commissary Garden
18 Then was Buried Henry Cooke - - - - - do:—
21 Then was Buried Ann Croft (a Child) - - - - do
21 Then was Buried John Howard (a Child) by Mr. Orr—
26 { Then was Buried Elizabeth Seimour
Then was Buried Mary Wigg (a Child } by Comissary Garden —
26 Then was Buried Prudence Mary Bonin (a Child- by ditto
27 Then was Buried Peter Dalles (a Child) by Mr Orr—
May 8 Then was Buried James Brown (a Child) by Comissary Garden
8 Then was Buried John Colcock a Child- by Ditto
13 Then was Buried Robert Pringle a Child— by Mr Orr—
24 Then was Buried Hellena Dennissin a servt: to Mr Jacob Woolford
25 Then was Buried Mary Dale and her Child Mary Dale both together } in one Coffin
26 Then was Buried Rebeca Roche (a Child)
29 Then was Buried Christopher Lang ℘ Parish
June 9 Then was Buried Ann Dalrymple —
9 Then was Buried Sarah Scott (a Child) —
13 Then was Buried Elizabeth Cox ℘ Parish
14 Then was Buried John Wicaridge

17 Then was Buried John Laroche (a Child)
17 Then was Buried John Griffith ℘ Parish
18 Then was Buried William Simpson (a Child)
21 Then was Buried John Brook a Sailor -
25 Then was Buried Peter Verger (a Child) ℘ Parish
26 Then was Buried Elizabeth Kipp (a Child) —
28 Then was Buried John Turner Doctor —
28 Then was Buried Thomas Hollins —
28 Then was Buried Johnston ℘ Parish
29 Then was Buried John Smith (a Child)
July 2 Then was Buried Martha Garden Wife of Comisary Garden
5 Then was Buried John Baldwin
6 Then was Buried John Cherry
6 Then was Buried William Dixsey —
6 Then was Buried Anthony Graham

[282] 1737 Burials 1737—

1737
July 10 Then was Buried Charles John Basnett (a Child)
12 Then was Buried Elizabeth Masson (a Child)
12 Then was Buried Antonia Pauli (a Child)
13 Then was Buried Jeane Beauchamp
13 Then was Buried Elizabeth Corbet - -
16 Then was Buried Eleonora Panton
16 Then was Buried Abram Austin of ye Men of Warr
17 Then was Buried Margaret Cooper (a Child)
17 Then was Buried Anne Blundel (a Child)—
19 Then was Buried Gabriel Bernard Esqr:
19 Then was Buried Anne Harden
20 Then was Buried Samuel Carr, a servt: to Mr Wigging Indian Trader
21 Then was Buried Margaret Koss, at Servt: to Secretary Hammerton
21 Then was Buried Anne Orom (a Child)
21 Then was Buried Elizabeth Burford (a Child)
22 Then was Buried Honora Barker
28 Then was Buried Robert Beswicke (a Child)
August 2d Then was Buried Jacob Godin (a Child)
3 Then was Buried Mary Beale
4 Then was Buried William Warmsley (a sailor)
7 Then was Buried Mary Watkins (a child)
8 Then was Buried Daniel Green Esqr.
11 Then was Buried Martha Blytman (a Child)
14 Then was Buried Charity Fickling
16 Then was Buried Richard Brickles
20th Then was Buried William Adams (a Child)
21st Then was Buried Thomas Hutchinson

21 Then was Buried Samuel Shaw of ye Men of Warr

23 Then was Buried James Scott-

25 Then was Buried Mary Davies (a Child) —

28 Then was Buried Mary Parson (a Child)

30th Then was Buried Mary Butterworth (a Child)—

Burials [283]

1737

Augst: 31st Then was Buried Mary Harvey - - - by the Revd Mr Garden

31 Then was Buried Mary Linter

31st Then was Buried Henry Robinson

Septr 4th Then was Buried Robert Dudley ℘r Parish

5 Then was Buried James Acking

8 Then was Buried Milisent Herbert

12 Then was Buried Sarah Christy a (child)

12 Then was Buried Joshua Mariner

20 Then was Buried Thomas Crawford ℘r Parish

21 Then was Buried Sarah Sommerfield

23 Then was Buried Anthony Busbes, (Drowned)

26 Then was Buried William Avery a (Child)—

27 Then was Buried Hester Peraira a (Child)

30th Then was Buried William Leander

Octobr 3 Then was Buried Robert Heume Esqr:

7 Then was Buried John Marshal of ye Men of Warr

10th Then was Buried Elizabeth Hamilton

12 Then was Buried William Meckenzie a (Child)

13 Then was Buried John Holliday — — — a (child)

23 Then was Buried William Saxby Senr: Esqr:

24 Then was Buried Edward Horn= Forest (out of Prison)

28 Then was Buried Robert Newington of ye men of Warr

30th Then was Buried - - William Carr —

Novr: 4th Then was Buried—John Hext of ye men of Warr

9 Then was Buried Lieut: Thomas Wood—

16 Then was Buried Sarah Evans a (child)

17 Then was Buried Edward Thomas of ye men of Warr

22 Then was Buried—Elizabeth Haydon

23 Then was Buried Nicholas Freeborn of ye men of Warr

28 Then was Buried Thomas Baker

29th Then was Buried Joseph Pestal (a Child)

Decr 2d ·Then was Buried Henry Lagsdell of ye men of Warr

[284] Burials

1737

Decr: 2d Then was Buried William Sadler ℘r Parish

4 Then was Buried—Elizabeth Collis a (child)

11 Then was Buried Anne Massingham

12 Then was Buried Richard Laurence ℘ Parish

16 Then was Buried—Anne Wright
19th Then was Buried Bonnet Wilsford
20th Then was Buried Nathaniel Johnson Esqr: in the Church
20th Then was Buried George Ridley ꝑ Parish
21 Then was Buried Patrick Kerry ꝑ Parish
22d Then was Buried Thomas Cload
31st Then was Buried Nelson Pettley ꝑ Parish
31st Then was Buried Mary Harley
31 Then was Buried Capn John McNiel
Jany 23d Then was Buried Martin Roud —
27 Then was Buried Mary Harramond a (chd)
ffebry 9th Then was Buried Gilson Clapp-
20th Then was Buried Mary Bonnain
Mar: 6 Then was Buried Thomas Reece - ꝑ Parish
9 Then was Buried John Hall of ye Rose (W)
21 Then was Buried Miles Godmore
24 Then was Buried Martha Harward
26 Then was Buried Mary Pemell
28 Then was Buried Mary Walter ꝑr Parish
28 Then was Buried- Dennis Molloy of ye Sea Horse (W)
29th Then was Buried John Bennett
1738 30th Then was Buried John Couillette a (chd)
April 17th Then was Buried Hannah Lusk
24 Then was Buried Elizabeth Linter
May 3d Then was Buried William Griffis a Sailor
4 Then was Buried Josiah Stanbery
5 Then was Buried Barbara Goodman

Burials [285]

1738
May 7th Then was Buried Elizabeth Lea a (Child)
24th Then was Buried John Watson
24th Then was Buried Henry Lorey - - } both of ye Rose (W)
24th Then was Buried William Emans }
30th Then was Buried Thomas Hollings a (Child) of ye Small Pox 1st:
June 3d Then was Buried Hannah Laurens
5th Then was Buried Juan Pintos Fernandes a Sailor
8th Then was Buried Joseph Griffith a (child)- - - -S P: 2d
11th Then was Buried Elizabeth Pinckney a (chd) - - S P: 3
13th Then was Buried Elizabeth Lyon - - - - S P: 4
15th Then was Buried Elizabeth Fairchild - - - - S P: 5-
15th Then was Buried James Brown a Sailor
15th Then was Buried Margeret Lewis a Child
15th Then was Buried Benedicta Aish a Child
15th Then was Buried Parnell Astwood - - - - S P: 6
15th Then was Buried William Farmer of ye Rose (W)

16th Then was Buried Peter Coutua - - - - - S P: 7
17th Then was Buried Robert Harris a Child - - - S P: 8
17th Then was Buried Mary Walker - - - - - S P: 9
20th Then was Buried Maurice Welsh-
20th Then was Buried Henrietta Kingyon
20th Then was Buried Richard Goodale a Child
23 Then was Buried- William Astwood a Child - - S P: 10
24 Then was Buried Mary Anne Prioleau a Child - - S P: 11-
25th Then was Buried Thomas Goodman - - - - S P: 12
26th Then was Buried Hannah Gale - - - -
27th Then was Buried Peter Mazick a Child - - S P: 13
27th Then was Buried Sophia Hall a Child
28th Then was Buried George Valantin Smith - - S P: 14
28th Then was Buried Charles Craven - - - S P: 15:

[286] Burials

1738

June 30th Then was Buried Lawrence Rhode of ye Seaford (W)
30th Then was Buried Sarah Sharpe....- - - - S P: 16
July 1st. Then was Buried Henry Reeny of ye Rose (W)
2d Then was Buried Joseph Seale ꝑ Parish
2d Then was Buried Anne Goodby a Child - - - S P: 17
3d Then was Buried Peter Prioleau - - - - - S P: 18
3d Then was Buried Sarah Perry-
4th Then was Buried Aimé Guex ꝑ Parish
5th Then was Buried Edward Turpinson } of ye Seaford (W)
5th Then was Buried John Ogley — — } of ye Seaford (W)
5th Then was Buried Martha Lambson - - - - S P: 19
6th Then was Buried David Skinner - - - - S P: 20
7th Then was Buried Mary Roche a Child - - S P: 21
7th Then was Buried Anne Broughton - - - S P: 22
8th Then was Buried Thomas Kilpatrick a Child - - S P: 23
9th Then was Buried Lewis Timothy a Child - - - - S P:24
12th Then was Buried William Lea - - - S P: 25
12th Then was Buried Grace Leavitop a servt to Capn Fenchard
13th Then was Buried John Young ꝑ Parish - -....S P: 26
do Then was Buried John . . . ꝑ Parish
14th Then was Buried Elizabeth Broughton a Child - - S P: 27
do Then was Buried Elizabeth Cottle - - - - S P: 28
15th Then was Buried William Sterland - - - S P: 29
do Then was Buried Thomas Kingyon ꝑ Parish - - S P: 30
16th Then was Buried Mary Thompson - - - S. P: 31
do Then was Buried Charlotte Harway a Child - S P: 32
17th Then was Buried Francis Green - - - - S P: 33
do Then was Buried George Higging - - - S P: 34
do Then was Buried Deborah Stanhover - - S P: 35
18th Then was Buried Cathrina Sarrazin a Child - - S P: 36

Burials [287]

1738

July 18th Then was Buried John Miller a Child) - - - S P: 37
do Then was Buried Thomas Hayes a Child - - - S P: 38
do Then was Buried Susannah Smith - - - - S P: 39
20th Then was Buried Elizabeth Bees a Child - - - S P: 40
21st Then was Buried Mary Anne Grasset a Child - - - S P: 41
do Then was Buried Mary Godmore a Child - - - S P: 42
22d Then was Buried Anne Hopkins a Child - - - S P: 43
do Then was Buried Sarah Hall a Child - - - S P: 44
23d Then was Buried John Lampard a Child - - -
24th Then was Buried Mary Ester Young a Child - - S P: 45
do Then was Buried James Hewett a Chd: ꝑ Parish
do Then was Buried Judith Grimshaw died in the street ꝑ Parish
do Then was Buried John Morgan - - - S P: 46
do Then was Buried Vertue a Negro Woman - - S P: 47
25th Then was Buried Mary McKfashion a Child - - S P: 48
do Then was Buried John Harris - - - - S P: 49
do Then was Buried Abraham Porteway a Boy - - S P: 50
26th Then was Buried Jeane Chairs
do Then was Buried William Jeanes a Boy - - - S P: 51
do Then was Buried Mary Millure & her Child - - S P: 52
do..Mary Millure - - - - S P: 53
27th Then was Buried Charlotte Le Brasseur a Child - S P: 54
do Then was Buried John Dunn a Child - - - S P: 55
do Then was Buried Susannah Elizabeth Leger - - - S P: 56
do Then was Buried Walter Halford of Fenix (W)
28th Then was Buried Anne Caillou ꝑ Parish - - S P: 57
do Then was Buried Christopher Smith - - - S P: 58
29th Then was Buried William Fryar - - - S P: 59
do Then was Buried Sarah Coates a Child - - S P: 60
do Then was Buried Richard Floyd ꝑ Parish - - - S P: 61

[288] Burials

1738

July 30th Then was Buried Mary Harris - - - - S P: 62
do Then was Buried - Philip Caillou a Chd) ꝑ Parish - - S P: 63
do Then was Buried Thomas Harris - - - - S P: 64
do Then was Buried—Jonas Millure a Child - - - S P: 65
31st Then was Buried Susannah Booth - - - - S P: 66
do Then was Buried Mary Anne Floyd ꝑ Parish - - S P: 67
do Then was Buried Robert Collis a Child - - - S P: 68
do Then was Buried John Vane a Child - - - S P: 69
Augst: 1st Then was Buried Thomas Steyshee of ye Seaford (W)
do Then was Buried Mary Martin a Child - - S P: 70

d° Then was Buried Elias Lea a Boy - - - S P: 71
2d Then was Buried Charles Keevener - - - S P: 72
5th Then was Buried Anne Monrow a Child - - S P: 73
d° Then was Buried Rachel Smith a Child - - - S P: 74
6th Then was Buried George Fowler - - - - S P: 75
d° Then was Buried Elizabeth Stone - - - S P: 76
d° Then was Buried Lydia Lea - - - - S P: 77
d° Then was Buried William Field a Child - - S P: 78
7th Then was Buried Anne Price a Child
8th Then was Buried William Dunn a Child - - S P: 79
d° Then was Buried Francis Miller a Child - - S P: 80
9th Then was Buried Anthony Writting a Boy - - S P: 81
d° Then was Buried Rowland Stadhams - - - S P: 82
d° Then was Buried William Abbot - - - - - S P: 83
d° Then was Buried Mary Duggles
10th Then was Buried Hannah White - - - - S P: 84
d° Then was Buried Anne Bonneteau a Child S P: 85
d° Then was Buried Elizabeth Sulivant ℘ Parish - - S P: 86
11th Then was Buried Margaret Magdelaina Cooper
14th Then was Buried George Beamish a Child - - - S P: 87

Burials [289]

1738
Augst: 14th Then was Buried William Campbel a Child - - - S P: 88
15th Then was Buried Fleet Stanborough - - - S P: 89
16th Then was Buried Sarah Minors - - - - -- S P: 90
d° Then was Buried Anne Martin a Child - - - S P: 91
d° Then was Buried Sarah Gale - - - - S P: 92
d° Then was Buried Hannah Rivers - - - - S P: 93
17th Then was Buried Francis Hyde - - -- S P: 94
18th Then was Buried Michael Buttler of ye Fenix (W)
19th Then was Buried Mary Harris a Child - - - S P: 95
20th Then was Buried Elizabeth Ginbee ℘ Parish - - S P: 96
d° Then was Buried Michel Millure - - - - - S P: 97
21st Then was Buried Anne Bayle a Child - - - S P: 98
22d Then was Buried Richard Boddicote a Child - - S P: 99
d° Then was Buried Catherina Cray - - - - - S P: 100:
24th Then was Buried James Tucker - - - - S P: 101
d° Then was Buried Anne Gallaway ℘ Parish - - S P: 102:
25th Then was Buried John Jennings ℘ Parish - - -
d° Then was Buried Anne Ginbee ℘ Parish - - - S P: 103
d° Then was Buried John Minors - - - - S P: 104
d° Then was Buried Josiah Smith a Boy
26th Then was Buried Patrick Stephens of ye Seaford (W)
28th Then was Buried John Cleland a Child - - - S P: 105
30th Then was Buried Anne Duggles a Child - - S P: 106

31st Then was Buried William Saxby a Child - - - S P: 107
Septr 3^{d} Then was Buried Margaret Basset ℘ Parish - - S P: 108
4th Then was Buried Rebeccah Thompson - - - S P: 109
d^{o} Then was Buried Childermus Croft a Child - - S P: 110
7th Then was Buried John Farrington
10th Then was Buried Elizabeth Smith a Child - S P: 111
11th Then was Buried Hubbert Stanborough - - - S P: 112

[290] Burials

1738
Septr 11th Then was Buried Eleonor Mills
12th Then was Buried Mary Anne Scott a Child - - S P: 113
13 Then was Buried William Smith a Child - - S P: 114
14th Then was Buried Robert Lesley
d^{o} Then was Buried Henry Mewse a Boy - - - S P: 115
17th Then was Buried Thomas Jones a Boy - - - S P: 116
d^{o} Then was Buried Mary Harris Fogartie - - - S P: 117
18th Then was Buried William McKenzie
19th Then was Buried Elster Todd
24th Then was Buried John Bason of the Seaford (W)
d^{o} Then was Buried John Parris
26th Then was Buried Elizabeth Ginbee a Child ℘ Parish
28th Then was Buried John Taylor of the Fenix (W)
d^{o} Then was Buried Martha Fox a Child
Octo^{r}: 2^{d} Then was Buried Elizabeth Orom a child
4th Then was Buried Mary Parree —
5th Then was Buried Lydia Thompson a Child
d^{o} Then was Buried Hannah Conyard ℘ Parish
d^{o} Then was Buried Samuel Hill of ye Seaford (W)
8th Then was Buried William Hamett ℘ Parish
d^{o} Then was Buried Peter Laroche—
9th Then was Buried Ruth Axson
d^{o} Then was Buried Sarah Leay
d^{o} Then was Buried Charles Wheeler
10th Then was Buried Thomas Bull of the Seaford (W)
13th Then was Buried John Bretton
d^{o} Then was Buried Moses Wilson Col:
d^{o} Then was Buried John Panton ℘ Parish
16th Then was Buried William Drougherty ℘ Parish
d^{o} Then was Buried Pennelloppe Raynold

Burials [291]

1738
Octob^{r} 18th Then was Buried Nathaniel Gilles
20th Then was Buried Benjamin Blundel a Child
28th Then was Buried Mary Susannah Mazick..............................
30^{t}: Then was Buried Samuel Gleser..............................
d^{o}: Then was Buried William Hamett ....

do: Then was Buried John Davies a Child
31st: Then was Buried Elizabeth Croxson
Novr: 9t, Then was Buried James Freeman a Child
11t: Then was Buried Richard Tidmarsh
15t: Then was Buried Charlotte Gorand ꝑ Parish
21t: Then was Buried Thomas Gredley of ye: Fenix (W)
Decr: 6t: Then was Buried Thomas Cooper a Child
23d: Then was Buried John Gill a Sailor of ye: Seaford
30t: Then was Buried Lewis Timothy
Jany 9t: Then was Buried Alexander Goodbee
17t: Then was Buried Jeremiah Seals ꝑr: Parish
18t: Then was Buried Deborah Patty
25t: Then was Buried Tisdale drown'd ꝑ Parish
ffabry: 17t: Then was Buried Philip Norton of ye: Fenix (droun'd) W)
27t: Then was Buried Henry Coe a Carpentr of ye Shark
Mar: 1t: Then was Buried Stephen Bond of ye Seaford (W)
8t: Then was Buried Peter Horry
13th Then was Buried Daniel Fidling
do: Then was Buried William Williamson
24th. Then was Buried Anne Randon
1739 25th. Then was Buried George Buckston a Salor
27th: Then was Buried William Gardner a Child

[292]

Burials

1739

April 11th. Then was Buried Jesse Badenhop
13th: Then was Buried William Frances a boy Sailor
17th: Then was Buried John Taunton a Sailor
20th: Then was Buried Joseph Clark a Sailor
29th: Then was Buried William Linthwaitte
May 4th: Then was Buried William Woodrope a Child
do. Then was Buried Patience Lambson a Child
5th: Then was Buried John Moore
do: Then was Buried William Fox a Child
11th: Then was Buried Francisco Calvia a Spaniard ꝑ Parish
20 Then was Buried Mary Withers a Child
21 Then was Buried Mary Salter
June 2 Then was Buried Herman Shuneman ꝑ Parish
5 Then was Buried Mary Croddy a Child
10 Then was Buried William Orr a Child
12 Then was Buried Darkes Coe
22d Then was Buried Thomas Clark
22 Then was Buried Robert Watkin a Sailor
23 Then was Buried William Goddard
do Then was Buried Darkes Coe a Child
28 Then was Buried Thomas Brown
29 Then was Buried Sarah Yarworth

30 Then was Buried William Coe a Child
July 2 Then was Buried Maryann Sarrazin a Child
8 Then was Buried David Harrison a Sailor
18 Then was Buried William Hutchinson
25 Then was Buried George Moultrie a Child
26 Then was Buried John Parris a Boy
28 Then was Buried Phebe Kent

Burials [293]

1739
August 2d Then was Buried Alexander Monrow a Child
3 Then was Buried John Dunn
6 Then was Buried Thomas Crosthwaite a Child
7 Then was Buried Anne Floyd
9 Then was Buried Thomas Johns
11 Then was Buried Robert Thompson a Boy
15 Then was Buried Anne Coit
16 Then was Buried Elizabeth Sampson, by the Parish
17 Then was Buried Maryann Turner a Child
do Then was Buried Samuel Jones
18 Then was Buried Edward Stephens
21 Then was Buried Margaret Ash
22 Then was Buried Sarah Sharpe a Child
22 Then was Buried Jean Carlton, a Child ꝑ Parish
25 Then was Buried John Barry
26 Then was Buried Martha Osmond a Child
26 Then was Buried Henry Castanier
26 Then was Buried Halland Delamare
27 Then was Buried Denis Read ꝑ Parish
27 Then was Buried Martha Godin a Child
29 Then was Buried Robert Thompson ꝑ Parish
31 Then was Buried Ralph Rodda
31 Then was Buried John Cooper a Sailor
Septr. 1 Then was Buried John Hayn's ꝑ Parish
1 Then was Buried Richard Andrews, Mariner
1 Then was Buried John Moore ꝑ Parish
2 Then was Buried Alexander Petty a Saylor
2 Then was Buried Henry Harris, a Saylor
2 Then was Buried Walter Jones a Saylor

[294]

1739
Septemr. 2 Then was Buried Thomas Griffith a Sailor
3 Then was Buried Walter Welch a Sailor
3 Then was Buried Elizabeth Mayern, a Servant
4 Then was Buried Mary Brown
4 Then was Buried Elinor Garland ꝑ Parish
5 Then was Buried Thomas Mallone ꝑ Parish

5 Then was Buried John Ross a Sailor
5 Then was Buried Arthur Strahan
5 Then was Buried Mary Martin
6 Then was Buried Samuel Biggs ℘ Parish
7 Then was Buried Gould Young a Sailor
7 Then was Buried Robert Richardson a Sailor
7 Then was Buried Edmond Holland ℘ Parish
8 Then was Buried James Winter
9 Then was Buried Richard Channon Boatsw^{n}. of the Hawk
9 Then was Buried Francis Glen ℘ Parish
9 Then was Buried Henry Mewse ℘ Parish
9 Then was Buried Mary Ward
10 Then was Buried John Herbert
10 Then was Buried Elizabeth Shepherd
11 Then was Buried Samuel Holmes
11 Then was Buried John Donn, Boatsw^{n} of the Seaforth
11 Then was Buried George Bridge
12 Then was Buried George Mells from the Work house
12 Then was Buried William Dean a Child from ditto
12 Then was Buried John Johnson
12 Then was Buried William Wilsford a shoemaker
12 Then was Buried Peter Dalles
13 Then was Buried John Desborough per Parish
13 Then was Buried John Worley, Butcher

[295]

1739
Septr. 13 Then was Buried Anne Vickeridge a Child
14 Then was Buried John Johns
14 Then was Buried Patty Moore
14 Then was Buried Nicholas Smith
14 Then was Buried Elizabeth Griffen
15 Then was Buried Robert Butt
15 Then was Buried Robert Stewart
15 Then was Buried Anne Prioleau
15 Then was Buried John Rine a Sailor
15 Then was Buried Thomas Hide
15 Then was Buried Sarah Hide
15 Then was Buried Benjamin Delaconseilere
15 Then was Buried William Phillips a Boy
15 Then was Buried Edward Neal
16 Then was Buried John Hill
16 Then was Buried Elinor Peter
16 Then was Buried Mary Robertson
16 Then was Buried Edward David
17 Then was Buried Joseph Sancock
18 Then was Buried Thomas Batsant

18 Then was Buried James Jones
18 Then was Buried Dodson Desborough
18 Then was Buried Edward Desborough
19 Then was Buried Charles Johnson
19 Then was Buried John Overand
19 Then was Buried Lewis Polston
22 Then was Buried Isaac Amiand

[296]

1739

Septem^r. 22 Then was Buried Samuel Vernot a Sailor
22 Then was Buried Charles Timothy a Child
22 Then was Buried Thomas Hext
22 Then was Buried Abel Harris a Sailor
22 Then was Buried David Horgist
22 Then was Buried Rose Lorash
23 Then was Buried Mary Berkley
23 Then was Buried Mary Bristol
23 Then was Buried Francis Bush
23 Then was Buried William Crofts
23 Then was Buried Francis Barbott
23 Then was Buried Elizabeth Walker
23 Then was Buried Robert Denison
23 Then was Buried John Linter
23 Then was Buried George Ferguson
24 Then was Buried Alexander Robertson
24 Then was Buried Elinor Shaw
24 Then was Buried Edward Slater
24 Then was Buried Samuel Barnett
25 Then was Buried William Harvey
25 Then was Buried John Bromer
25 Then was Buried Roger Gordon a Boy
25 Then was Buried Mary Walker
25 Then was Buried Thomas Proctor
25 Then was Buried Rachael Yours
27 Then was Buried John Whockup

[297]

1739

Septr. 28 Then was Buried Thomas Henning a Child
28 Then was Buried Isaac Abraham a Sailor
29 Then was Buried Sharlot Legear
30 Then was Buried George Morre a Sailor

Octob^r 1 Then was Buried John Johnson
1 Then was Buried William Broadwater
1 Then was Buried Susannah Brush
1 Then was Buried Jane Storey
2 Then was Buried Sarah Turner

2 Then was Buried Stephen Proctor
2 Then was Buried Mary Griffes
4 Then was Buried Edward Seamer
4 Then was Buried Susannah Stevenson
4 Then was Buried Jacob Covert
6 Then was Buried Richard Rowe
6 Then was Buried John Carney
7 Then was Buried Nicholas Radash
8 Then was Buried Daniel Green
8 Then was Buried John Billard
9 Then was Buried Joseph Timothy a Child
9 Then was Buried Isabeau Guichard in ye French Church Yard
10 Then was Buried Nathaniel Briggs
11 Then was Buried Michael Burn
13 Then was Buried Anne Lindsay
13 Then was Buried Benjamin Briggs a Child
14 Then was Buried Elizabeth Briggs

[298] Burials continued

1739

Octobr. 14 Then was Buried Anne Stevenson a Child
14 Then was Buried James Janery
14 Then was Buried Silant Beswicke
15 Then was Buried John Knight
15 Then was Buried Elizabeth Lord a Child
18 Then was Buried Gilbert Higginson
18 Then was Buried Bishop Roberts
20 Then was Buried Anne Dean
31 Then was Buried Robert Wells
31 Then was Buried Richard a Sailor
31 Then was Buried Margaret Fitzgerrald
Novemr. 1 Then was Buried Alexander Hase a Sailor
4 Then was Buried Mary Mingres
4 Then was Buried Christopher Tappy
7 Then was Buried John Adderly
16 Then was Buried John Sofield a Sailor
17 Then was Buried Stephen Proctor a Child
24 Then was Buried Sarah Smith
Janury. 4 Then was Buried Anne King
5 Then was Buried John Baker
6 Then was Buried Mary Read
12 Then was Buried Thomas Hogg a Child—
19 Then was Buried Judith Dubourdieu
23 Then was Buried Nicholas Trott
27 Then was Buried Daniel Carial
29 Then was Buried John Salter

Febry. 3 Then was Buried Elizabeth Wyaka
4 Then was Buried Lewis Jones

1739 Burials continued [299]

Februy 11 Then was Buried Andrew Barber a Child
16 Then was Buried Thomas Bennett—
18 Then was Buried Mary Kerr—
21 Then was Buried John Davis a Child
22 Then was Buried Paul Davis a Sailor
25 Then was Buried John William's a Child
29 Then was Buried Mary Janvier
29 Then was Buried Thomas Hamilton Scott
March 1 Then was Buried Captn. Thomas Parker
2 Then was Buried Elizabeth Green
18 Then was Buried Elinor Brown a Child
20 Then was Buried Rice Price a Child.
25 Then was Buried Owen Young a Sailor
1740
28 Then was Buried Thomas Wood a Child
April 2 Then was Buried Thomas Pincknell
3 Then was Buried Mary Coleman a Child
4 Then was Buried Roger Gough a Soldier
6 Then was Buried John Young a Child
8 Then was Buried Jeremiah Taylor
22 Then was Buried James Anderson a Child
May 2 Then was Buried Mary Lessley
8 Then was Buried Thomas Cawood
11 Then was Buried Francis Lord from the Workhouse
14 Then was Buried William Mews by the Parish
14 Then was Buried Daniel Cartwright
16 Then was Buried Charles Read a Boy
April 29 Then was Buried Anicy Thornton, by the Parish
29 Then was Buried Mary Wood a Child—

[300] Burials continued

1740
May 18 Then was Buried James Radford who was Shott—
20 Then was Buried Anne Scott the Wife of John Scott the Merchant
26 Then was Buried John Brown a Sailor who was kill'd
29 Then was Buried Peter Bullger
29 Then was Buried John Brand—
June 1 Then was Buried Jane Lake
3 Then was Buried Thomas Harramond a Child
5 Then was Buried Thomas Read a Child of Captn. Reads.
9 Then was Buried Martha Rumsey—
20 Then was Buried John Robinson at his Plantation ℘ Mr Orr

30 Then was Buried Waley Sheppard son of Charles Sheppard and Anne his Wife.—
July 14 Then was Buried John Coit—
20 Then was Buried Adam Siven
25 Then was Buried Thomas Fry—
27 Then was Buried Catherine Murphy ꝑ Parish
Augut: 10 Then was Buried James Watsone a Child
11 Then was Buried William Janes a Child.
15 Then was Buried David Dalbiac
24 Then was Buried Morris Amorett
27 Then was Buried James Warnock from ye Work house ꝑ Parish
28 Then was Buried Thomas Price
30 Then was Buried Edward Cheeks from Mr. Osmond
31 Then was Buried Abraham Leseur
Septr. 1 Then was Buried James Gordon
do. Then was Buried Mary Hext
5 Then was Buried William Marvin Mr. of the Anchona
8 Then was Buried John Baker
9 Then was Buried William Robertson Mate
do. Then was Buried William Sellick-

Burials continued [301*]

Septemr 13 Then was Buried John Weaver Mariner
do Then was Buried a Man from the Workhouse
14 Then was Buried Peter Eady
do. Then was Buried Robert Beaty from the Workhouse
15 Then was Buried George Blake of the Tartar
16 Then was Buried Tabitha Mc.Daniel by the Parish
do. Then was Buried Ann Willson
17 Then was Buried John Dunbarr
19 Then was Buried John Bagwell, mariner
21 Then was Buried William Ward, mariner
do. Then was Buried John Miller
22 Then was Buried Captn. William Wightman
do. Then was Buried Captn: Andrew Inglis
do: Then was Buried Simon Smith ꝑ Parish
23 Then was Buried Henry Servant to Captn: Allen
25 Then was Buried Thomas Morritt
Then was Buried John Woolf, Mariner of Captn. Fanshaw's Ship
Then was Buried William Hall Clerk of Capt. Townsend's Ship

---

*In the rebinding of the book leaf 301-302 was put in backwards, so that page 302 faces 300, and 301 faces 303.

26 Then was Buried James Beaven Mariner from Guiney
26 Then was Buried Sarah Gandy
27 Then was Buried William Eakins Mariner
do. Then was Buried Merey Murphy
30 Then was Buried David Coulton mariner.
Octobr. 2 Then was Buried John Burgis mariner from ye Ship Tartar
3 Then was Buried John Greame from the Workhouse ℘ Parish
do. Then was Buried Jermiah Coozin from the Tarter Pink
do. Then was Buried Jonathan Hardy, from the same Ship
do. Then was Buried Susanah Fownds Widow—

[302] Burials continued

1740
Octobr. 4 Then was Buried Andrew Mc.Clean, ℘ the Parish
do. Then was Buried Ann Wren a Child
5 Then was Buried Christopher Redwood
5 Then was Buried Captn: James Craige
7 Then was Buried John Feinton
7 Then was Buried John Gould Mariner
8 Then was Buried John Keene
8 Then was Buried Peter Vroome Gunner of the Privateer
8 Then was Buried John Clark
8 Then was Buried Robert Haselby from on board of the Tartar.
9 Then was Buried Benedict Bliss, belonging to Captn: Hall
10 Then was Buried James Fenegin belonging to Captn: Langdon
10 Then was Buried Henry Pillow, belonging to the Tartar
12 Then was Buried John Cooke Serjeant from Georgia
12 Then was Buried John Enmar Drummer from ditto
13 Then was Buried Patience Lullams
15 Then was Buried Giles Whittle Captn.. Coffins Cook
16 Then was Buried James Weaver
17 Then was Buried Sarah Winlass
20 Then was Buried, Susannah Bowling
21 Then was Buried, David Hoye of Captn. Langdon's Company
25 Then was Buried, Samuel Coast Mariner
28 Then was Buried, Henry Harrison
28 Then was Buried, Captn. Daniel Downe
29 Then was Buried, John Harty Mariner a Privateer
30 Then was Buried, Henry Scott, a Child

Burials continued— [303]

1740

October 30 Then was Buried Prudence Miller at the charge of the Parish

31 Then was Buried Philip Ball mariner belonging to the Tartar Pink

Novembr. 1 Then was Buried Patrick Conyers at the charge of the Parish

5 Then was Buried John Ridley a Ship Carpenter

7 Then was Buried Jonathan Long from the Work house

15 Then was Buried Sweet Kerby, a mariner belonging to the Ship Tartar

Then was Buried an unknown Person who was drowned.

Decembr: 1 Then was Buried John Mills mariner belonging to the Ship Phœnix

4 Then was Buried Joshua Miller a Boy at the charge of the Parish

4 Then was Buried William Pollard Silver Smith

17 Then was Buried Edward Gardner mariner

19 Then was Buried Joseph Spencer a Planter

19 Then was Buried Edward Bullard a Child

22 Then was Buried Joanna Dewick a Child

23 Then was Buried John Wallace Esqr. Justice of the Peace

Januy. 3 Then was Buried William Nicholas a young Pilot

10 Then was Buried Robert Hall Esqr. Provost Marshal

10 Then was Buried Anne Michie a Child

15 Then was Buried Joseph Chambers

29 Then was Buried George Waterhouse at the charge of the Parish

Februy: 6 Then was Buried Elizabeth Garnes from the Workhouse

8 Then was Buried Nathaniel Croft a Child

14 Then was Buried Anne Williamson Widow

18 Then was Buried Anne Roche a Child

24 Then was Buried Elizabeth Bounoe

25 Then was Buried a drowned man unknown

[304] Burials continued

1740

March 3 Then was Buried a Spaniard

13 Then was Buried Mary Welchyson

16 Then was Buried John Leger a Boy in the French Church yard

20 Then was Buried Philip Trelaney mariner belonging to the Ship Rose

1741. 28 Then was Buried John Evans Carpenter of the Dilligence, (drowned)

29 Then was Buried Elizabeth Russ

29 Then was Buried John Johnson, mariner

April 6 Then was Buried Sophia Anderson a Child

8 Then was Buried Anthony Ivery mariner belonging to the Ship Rose

8 Then was Buried William Williams a Child

12 Then was Buried Mary Sander from the Workhouse on the Parish

14 Then was Buried Anne Rybolt

15 Then was Buried William Atkins mariner belonging to the Ship Rose

17 Then was Buried Anne Rybolt a Child

20 Then was Buried Richard Ashton mariner belonging to the Ship Rose

25 Then was Buried Captn. Joseph Prew

27 Then was Buried John Hackafield mariner parish

29 Then was Buried Thomas Brace mariner belonging to the Ship Phœnix

May 1 Then was Buried Gabriel Escott merchant

4 Then was Buried William Morrison at the Charge of the Parish —

6 Then was Buried Richard Clifford

13 Then was Buried William Hare a Child

17 Then was Buried Robert Russ a Child

17 Then was Buried John Thompson a Child

22 Then was Buried Elias Hancock

23 Then was Buried Thomas Haddock a Child

24 Then was Buried Anne Bonethau

25 Then was Buried Peter Lawrence

June 1 Then was Buried William Wallis, merchant

3 Then was Buried James Tarrant, Carpenter—

Burials continued [305]

1741

June 11 Then was Buried Mary Harramond

June 14 Then was Buried Richard Lampon

June 15 Then was Buried Mary Davis a Child on the Parish Charge.

16 Then was Buried Mary Basdon

20 Then was Buried Williams Yeomans a Child

21 Then was Buried Benjamin Smith a Child

21 Then was Buried Elinor Newton

24 Then was Buried Mary Rice a Child

26 Then was Buried Henry Gallo, at the Charge of the Parish for [undecipherable word]

28 Then was Buried William Miller a Child

July 1 Then was Buried Nathaniel Clifford a Child

4 Then was Buried Eleanor Gadsden

d^o^ Then was Buried Captn. John Garnett
5 Then was Buried Elizabeth Teresa Trueman a Child
7 Then was Buried Anne Welch a Child
10 Then was Buried John Owens a Child
12 Then was Buried Mary Stone a Child
19 Then was Buried Martha Osmond a Child
20 Then was Buried Thomas Leman a Pettyauger man
23 Then was Buried Robert Laws a Child
26 Then was Buried Susannah Brewton
Augut. 4 Then was Buried Lawrence Couliette
6 Then was Buried Richard Howard a Child
8 Then was Buried Cosmus Robert Gordon
10 Then was Buried Jane BeauChamp
11 Then was Buried Catherine Anderson
do. Then was Buried Thomas Heathy a Child
17 Then was Buried Thomas Gadsden Esqr.
18 Then was Buried Neall German mariner
29 Then was Buried Jane Robinson a Child
30 Then was Buried Margret Menson in ye French Church Yard

[306] Burials continued

1741

Augut. 29 Then was Buried Robert Bradley
29 Then was Buried Robert Motte a Child
Septr. 6 Then was Buried John Brand Jeys a Child
21 Then was Buried Deborah Hall
Octob. 2 Then was Buried Thomas Crosswell Mate
6 Then was Buried William Harvey a Child
13 Then was Buried Jane Beau Champ a Child
15 Then was Buried John Deane mate of the Phenix
22 Then was Buried William Lesene.
23 Then was Buried George Adams a Sadler
Novr. 5 Then was Buried Michael Rice on the Parish
8 Then was Buried John Fox ditto
9 Then was Buried Elinor Snelling
17 Then was Buried Edward Owens mariner
18 Then was Buried Isaac King Clark
19 Then was Buried Joyce Ford
29 Then was Buried Mary Wright
Decemr 12 Then was Buried John Barham
14 Then was Buried Peter Picott
26 Then was Buried Thomas Innis
Janury. 3 Then was Buried Anne Henning
10 Then was Buried Catherine Perkins
do. Then was Buried Thomas Viney, he was carried into ye Church

15 Then was Buried Thomas Andrews, a sailor of the Burlington

d°. Then was Buried William Smith Planter, he was carried into the Church

16 Then was Buried an unknown Man, who appeared to be a mariner that had been drowned.

18 Then was Buried Henry the Son of Mr. Tho: Corbett

21 Then was Buried Thomas Gingell mariner of Capt Stevenson

21 Then was Buried George Bowman mariner of the Phenix

27 Then was Buried Mary Ann Jurdon

Februy 3 Then was Buried John Evance from the Workhouse

13 Then was Buried Thomas Sutton mariner of the Ship Rye

Burials continued [307]

1741

2 Then was Buried William Barns mariner murtherd himself.

Februy 18 Then was Buried Edward Hext, his Corps was carried into the Church

21 Then was Buried Alexander Robertson

24 Then was Buried Richard Webb, at the charge of the Parish

26 Then was Buried John Crocker Purser of a man of Warr

March 5 Then was Buried James Gibbons mariner of the Rose Man of Warr

7 Then was Buried Richard Davison mariner of the Hawk Snow

11 Then was Buried David Mc.Call a Child

17 Then was Buried Elizabeth Fraisland from the Workhouse

23 Then was Buried Martha Horry, her Corps was carried into the Church

23 Then was Buried Joseph Fidler

1742 25 Then was Buried Edward Hall a Child

April 3 Then was Buried Esther Laurens

4 Then was Buried John Robinson Pettyauger Man

13 Then was Buried William Maiden, Mariner

15 Then was Buried Nathaniel Cox, from the Workhouse

16 Then was Buried Edward Major, drowned, the Parish Charge

17 Then was Buried Mary Harvey a Child

28 Then was Buried James Randall of the Hawk Sloop

May 6 Then was Buried Elizabeth Owens a Child, at the Parish Charge

9 Then was Buried John Hext, the Corps carried into the Church

12 Then was Buried Peter Jeys, the Corps carried into the Church

13 Then was Buried William Thomas Williamson a Child
19 Then was Buried William Dixon
29 Then was Buried John, the illegitimate Son of Captn. Edward Lightwood
June 5 Then was Buried John Scott about Five Years of Age
5 Then was Buried Mary Farrow a Child
6 Then was Buried Hanah Passwater a Child
8 Then was Buried Matthew Shrubb
10 Then was Buried William Harris a Child
13 Then was Buried Captn. William Henry Bruce
17 Then was Buried Charity Prue [undecipherable word]
18 Then was Buried Robert Harvey a Child
[The entry on the last line has been almost totally destroyed.]

[308] Burials continued

June 25 Then was Buried Elizabeth Davis from the Workhouse
30 Then was Buried Captn Stephen Hammatt
30 Then was Buried William Davers Mate of the Flamborough
July 2 Then was Buried George Daniel a Child
6 Then was Buried Robert Leston Shipwright
7 Then was Buried Elizabeth Smith, her Corps carried into the Church
11 Then was Buried Rachael Sears
15 Then was Buried Rebecca Roche a Child
15 Then was Buried Captn. John Sikes
18 Then was Buried Philip Edwards
18 Then was Buried Thomas Fairchild
Augut: 11 Then was Buried Walter Rowland
15 Then was Buried Captn: Mansfield Tucker
15 Then was Buried John Dewicke a Child
18 Then was Buried Hannah Beekman a Child
26 Then was Buried George Ellsmore from the Workhouse
30 Then was Buried Andrew Charnock from the Workhouse
30 Then was Buried Anne Godin, her Corps carried into the Church
31 Then was Buried George Wattson Mariner
Septr. 1 Then was Buried Thomas Liston from the Workhouse
7 Then was Buried Mary Quincy
7 Then was Buried Mary Brairer a Child
7 Then was Buried Cooper Dicker Son of Benjamin Whitaker Esqr. (a Child)
13 Then was Buried Jeane Fallowfield a Child
18 Then was Buried Miles Brandon a Taylor—
23 Then was Buried Daniel Magrah Mariner of the Flambor [rest broken off]
23 Then was Buried [broken out] ul Douxsaint in the French Church Yard

Burials continued [309]

1742

Septemr. 23 Then was Buried Harry Selvin, Mercht: Corps carried into the Church
24 Then was Buried Catherine Keys
25 Then was Buried James Jordan Mate of Captn. Blowers
26 Then was Buried George Bampfield, his Corps carried into the Church
27 Then was Buried John Innis a Mariner belonging to Capt. Gregory
'30 Then was Buried Robert Cross Marine belonging to the Flamborough

Octobr. 5 Then was Buried Benjamin Stein on the Parish account
10 Then was Buried Amos Breed a Ship Carpenter
10 Then was Buried William Thomas, a Ship Carpenter
10 Then was Buried John Carney, of the Swift
11 Then was Buried John Mamour, from ye Workhouse
15 Then was Buried Richard Ford Mate of Captn. Walker
15 Then was Buried Mary Craige belonging to the Royal Regiment.
16 Then was Buried John Taylor Mariner belonging to Capt. Gregory
16 Then was Buried Mary Elizabeth Dingwell, a Child-
18 Then was Buried Robert Nelson, a Lieut. in the Royal Regim [rest broken off]
19 Then was Buried William White a Boy belonging to Captn: Wimble
19 Then was Buried Hannah Conner, a Servant maid to Col Fenwicke
24 Then was Buried Rebecca Ruck a Child—
28 Then was Buried Thomas Lloyd
28 Then was Buried William Mc.donnel a Soldier of ye Royal Regim [rest broken off]
31 Then was Buried Anne English at the Parish Charge

Novemr: 1 Then was Buried Richard Dauling Mariner of the Ship Rose
4 Then was Buried William Nickeson-
7 Then was Buried Bridget Matthyson
8 Then was Buried George Smith a Marine Soldier
8 Then was Buried Mary Ann Cook a Child

[310] Burials continued

1742

Novemr. 18 Then was Buried Margaret Grey from the Workhouse

---

18 Then was Buried Robert Morrison a Pettyauger Man
24 Then was Buried Sarah Levaly, at the charge of the Parish

24 Then was Buried Anne Clemens
Decem^r. 1 Then was Buried Mary Obryan
1 Then was Buried Patrick Magee Quarter Master of the Spy Man of Warr.
3 Then was Buried John Leay Carpenter
Janu^ry: 9 Then was Buried Catherine Leseur
17 Then was Buried Kennede Obrien
18 Then was Buried Lodovic M^c.goun
21 Then was Buried David Fitzgerald who was drowned accidentally
24 Then was Buried Samuel Smith a Child
28 Then was Buried Anne Dale
Febr^y. 3 Then was Buried Edward Gale, a Cooper
8 Then was Buried Stephen Hartley a Child—
11 Then was Buried Rebecca Mehoney, a Girl of 13 years
22 Then was Buried Henry Gignilliat in the French Church yard
24 Then was Buried Charles Sheppard a Child
28 Then was Buried Elizabeth Valence
March 1 Then was Buried Benjamin Smith a Child
10 Then was Buried Christopher Allisett at the charge of the Parish
25 Then was Buried Mary Leay Widow
1743 26 Then was Buried Hanah Norton a Child
27 Then was Buried Mary Perry a Child
April 6 Then was Buried James S^t: John Esqr. Surveyor General
16 Then was Buried Esther Campbell a Child
16 Then was Buried Francis Brandrett, Serj'ant of ye American Regiment
22 Then was Buried Jane Townsend a Child
24 Then was Buried Joseph Dingwell a Child
26 Then was Buried John Warwick
30 Then was Buried John Hands from the Workhouse
May 2 Then was Buried John Bryan, from the Workhouse.
20 Then was Buried Margaret Remington a Child
21 Then was Buried, Julia Craston
22 Then was Buried Anne Craston a Child
22 Then was Buried Theophilus Yeomans a Child.—
25 Then was Buried Elizabeth Roper
27 Then was Buried Samuel Tilly mariner belonging to the Prince William.

Burials continued [311]

1743
May 30 Then was Buried Alexander Moultrie a Child.
June 4 Then was Buried Sarah Sharp
4 Then was Buried James Grant, Mariner of the Ship North Cape

6 Then was Buried Edward Dean a Child
13 Then was Buried Elizabeth Osmond a Child
15 Then was Buried Isaac Amiand Croft.
18 Then was Buried William Sterling.
27 Then was Buried Alexander Mazÿck a Child
July 1 Then was Buried Thomas Hoare Pilot.
3 Then was Buried Mary Jones from the Work-house
9 Then was Buried Mary Hext, (5 years of Age).
19 Then was Buried William Bower, a Carpenter of Captn: Campbell's Vessel
22 Then was Buried Anne Menson a Child
28 Then was Buried William Valence
Augt. 11 Then was Buried Joseph Rand a Child.
12 Then was Buried Edward Palmer, master of a Vessel.
19 Then was Buried Captn. William Paul
22 Then was Buried Elinor Elliott a Child
22 Then was Buried Elizabeth Daniell a Child
26 Then was Buried Thomas Beale, a Butcher
26 Then was Buried James Watsone a Child
27 Then was Buried John, the Supposed Son of Edward Lightwood
28 Then was Buried Daniel Cannon, a Carpenter.
30 Then was Buried Harriot, the Supposed Daughter of Edward Lightwood
30 Then was Buried William Crossthwaite, a Child—
31 Then was Buried Edward Addison........at the Parish Charge
Septr. 5 Then was Buried Thomas Louch, a Butcher
14 Then was Buried John Morgan from the Workhouse
16 Then was Buried Charles Ripault
18 Then was Buried William Christie a Child
20 Then was Buried Paul Mazyck a Child
22 Then was Buried Andrew Dupuy
25 Then was Buried Captn: Richardson on the Parish Charge
29 Then was Buried Christopher Osmond a Child
29 Then was Buried James Addison on the Parish Account
30 Then was Buried Ambrose Peake mariner drowned
Octob. 1 Then was Buried Kate Fleminings
3 Then was Buried Mary Addison on the Parish Account

[312] Burials continued—

1743
October 7th. Then was Buried James Stevenson a Boy
8 Then was Buried Margret Mc.Cleland on the charge of the Parish
17 Then was Buried Captn. Jennings
17 Then was Buried Mary Cockfield, at the Parish Charge

19 Then was Buried Samuel Bowman a Child
19 Then was Buried Alexander Read a Boy
20 Then was Buried John Clark at the Parish Charge
24 Then was Buried John Richingham of the Rye Man of War
Novembr. 3 Then was Buried John Eaton of the same Ship
3 Then was Buried James Rochford
4 Then was Buried John Durant of the Rye Man of War
13 Then was Buried Mary Smith
15 Then was Buried Hannah Taplin a Girle
15 Then was Buried Smith a Child
15 Then was Buried Clement Galloway a boy from the Work House
17 Then was Buried Captn. John Murray
18 Then was Buried William Hayler of the Ship Flam-. borough
21 Then was Buried Henry Fletcher
21 Then was Buried Captn. William Bowler
23 Then was Buried Peter Allan a Boy
27 Then was Buried Joseph Tucker
Decemb: 5 Then was Buried Elizabeth Carr
12 Then was Buried George Colleton
16 Then was Buried Elizabeth Willson a Child
18 Then was Buried Abraham Cook a Child—
22 Then was Buried James Bell, mariner
22 Then was Buried John Jennings at the Charge of the Parish
Janury 3 Then was Buried William Brothers of the Rye Man of Warr.
5 Then was Buried William Levant, Mariner.
12 Then was Buried Robert Morris of the Rye Man of Warr.
14 Then was Buried John Legaree a Child
24 Then was Buried Burnham a Child
26 Then was Buried Elizabeth Pinckney—
Feby 5 Then was Buried an unknown Person who had been drowned.

Burials continued [313]

1743
Februy 6 Then was Buried David Artherlony
9 Then was Buried Rebecca Flavell
19 Then was Buried Margaret Wilson at the Charge of the Parish
March 3 Then was Buried John Turner Mariner drowned
6 Then was Buried Giles Lyme Mariner of the 40 Gun Ship.
7 Then was Buried William Hardiman a Marine
12 Then was Buried Rachel* Wood.—

---

*Mary is written over Rachel.

1744 25 Then was Buried Thomas Marriner Drowned
26 at the Charge of the Parish
2 Then was Buried Peter Johnson Mariner ....
29 Then was Buried Capt Joseph Pomroy..............................
April 5 Then was Buried Elizabeth Amory a Child ....
6 Then was Buried Mary Guy The Wife of William Junr.—
6 Then was Buried Thomas Hescot at the charge of the Parish
13 Then was Buried Capt Peter Simmons..............................
22 Then was Buried Jane Davis at the Parish Charge—
27 Then was Buried William Webster at the Parish Charge
May 12 Then was Buried Dominick Power Mariner a Boy..............................
13 Then was Buried William Demzey Mariner Drowned..............................
14 Then was Buried David Stiles a Child..............................
21 Then was Buried Nathaniel Greenland..............................
23 Then was Buried James Paris a Child..............................
24 Then was Buried John Commins Mariner..............................
26 Then was Buried Thomas Atwell..............................
28 Then was Buried Mary Allen..............................
31 Then was Buried Peter Shaw..............................
June 1 Then was Buried Elizabeth Perkins a Child..............................
2 Then was Buried Ann Shepherd..............................
4 Then was Martha Wright a Child Buried..............................
4 Then was Buried Stoutenbourgh a Child..............................
7 Then was Buried John Smith a child..............................
7 Then was Buried Mary Smith a Child..............................
12 Then was Buried William Bissett..............................
12 Then was Buried George Oliver..............................
13 Then was Buried Elizabeth Haddock..............................
15 Then was Buried William Slide..............................
27 Then was Buried Amey Motte a Child

[314] Burials continued

* 1 Then was Buried Richard Roberson a child..............................pd
7 Then was Buried John Bennett..............................pd
13 Then was Buried Samuel Brown..............................pd
15 Then was Buried James Lowder..............................
16 Then was Buried Jane Dixson..............................
31 Then was Buried Robert Hay..............................pd
3 Then was Buried Martha Hamelton a child
4 Then was Buried Thomas Roche a child..............................pd
10 Then was Buried Elizabeth Farrow a child..............................pd
12 Then was Buried Goodworth..............................pd
13 Then was Buried Mary Houghton a Child..............................pd
19 Then was Buried John Vaune a Child..............................pd
20 Then was Buried Millour....a Child

---

*All months broken from this page.

24 Then was Buried Cobas Vessells Sail Maker................................pd
27 Then was Buried Jacob Woolford................................pd
28 Then was Buried Andrew Fisseck................................pd
28 Then was Buried Richd Millar................................
2 Then was Buried William Johnston................................pd
10 Then was Buried Frances Foster................................pd
23 Then was Buried John Givin................................pd
23 Then was Buried Elioner Gardinor................................
24 Then was Buried Mary Jane Mongen................................pd
24 Then was Buried Thomas Beale Mariner................................pd
29 Then was Buried Daniel Parker Marriner................................pd
30 Then was Buried Richard Newland Marriner................................pd
† † Then was Buried Marke Davis................................pd
Then was Buried Vallentine Hardy................................
Then was Buried John Jones................................pd
Then was Buried Philip Penyard................................pd
Then was Buried Moses Heasle Semor a Child................................pd
Then was Buried James Hambleton Parish Charge
Then was Buried Martha Hext a Child................................pd
Then was Buried Edward Scull ....pd
Then was Buried Emanuel Smith................................pd
Then was Buried John Johnston................................pd
Then was Buried Anne Browney a Child................................
Then was Buried John Houghton................................pd
Then was Buried Elizabeth Holliday................................pd
Then was Buried Sarah Blake a Child................................pd
Then was Buried James Car................................
Then was Buried Elizabeth Lawrance a Child................................pd
Then was Buried Joyall Poinsett at ye French Church
Then was Buried Sarah Lecraft a Child

Carrd Back to Fo 210

Then was Buried Phillip Harman‡

---

†From here down both months and days are broken off.

‡Appears to be Harman—very dim.

INDEX.

1 Abbots indexed as Abbotts.

2 Bate is possibly recorded here in one or two instances for Bates.

1 In some cases it is recorded Byrum.

1 Some names indexed under Clark are obably Clarke

[1] Some of the names indexed under Cook are doubtless Cooke.

[1]Davis and Davies are both in the record, but are so mixed that all are indexed Davis.

---

[1]See also Faulkner and Fawkner.
[2] See also Finnekin.

1 The Greens and Greenes have all been indexed under Green, because the officials have not always observed the difference in spelling.

[1]See also Hide

*The Leas and Lees are so confused on the register that all are indexed under Lea.

[1]Mackey, McKay, McKee, and all other forms of the name indexed under Mackay.

[1]See also Melekin and Melligan.

[1]Muncrief, Muncreef, Moncreef and all similar names indexed as Moncrief.

[1]This name is spelled about six different ways on the register. The correct spelling could only be determined by finding an autograph of one of the family.

[1]Also given Rybold, Rybolt and Reybout.

[1]See also Seamer and Seymour.

[1]Several spellings used, but all indexed as above to be uniform.

[1] The distinction between Simons and Simmons is not often made in the register.